Good Grief

Exploring Feelings, Loss and Death with Over Elevens and Adults

A Holistic Approach

2nd edition

Barbara Ward and Associates

Jessica Kingsley Publishers
London and Bristol, Pennsylvania

First published by Barbara Ward in 1987 (ISBN 0-9512-882-2)
First published by Jessica Kingslry Publishers in 1993
Jessica Kingsley Publishers Ltd
116 Pentonville Road
London N1 9JB, England
and
325 Chestnut Street
Philadelphia, PA 19106, USA

www.jkp.com

Second edition 1996
Second impression 1998
Third impression 2002

Copyright © 1993 Barbara Ward and Associates, except where specifically attributed to another source
Foreword copyright © 1993 Professor Michael Marland CBE MA FRSA

Companion Volume:

Good Grief: Exploring Feelings, Loss and Death with Under Elevens 2nd edition
ISBN 1 85302 324 8 272p

Also available:

- a one day training course to accompany the pack
  - consulting/ counselling

Futher details from:

Barbara Ward, 3 Wheelwright Court, Walkhampton, Yelverton, Devon PL20 6LA

Library of Congress Cataloguing in Publication Data
Available from the Library of Congress on request

British Library Cataloguing in Publication Data
Available from the British Library on request

ISBN 1 85302 340 X

Printed and Bound in Great Britain by
Athenaeum Press, Gateshead, Tyne and Wear

CONTENTS

Section 1 – Introduction and Background

Section 2 – Activities

Section 3 – Appendices

DEDICATION

To all those who suffer loss
To educators who use this book
To my friends, colleagues and families for their patience,
support and encouragement
To Grimstone Community and our Residential Training Centre, for giving me the space
to make this extensive revision possible.

Barbara Ward

Acknowledgements

My thanks go to the wonderful team of contributors for their input, support and encouragement, and the people/organisations mentioned in the contributors and attributions. This pack could not have been written without them.

I also wish to thank the London Borough of Hillingdon Education Department for allowing me to do the original pilot work in their schools; also the following members for their expertise and encouragement: Jenny Chadwick, Principal Officer; Trisha Grimshaw, Assistant Borough Librarian; Richard Wales, formerly Humanities Advisor; Graham Wilson, formerly Senior Advisor, now an HMI.

Also Margaret Hayworth of The Compassionate Friends, Dora Black, Richard Lansdown, Pat Scowen of Cruse, Gillian Pugh *et al.* of the National Children's Bureau, Norman Keir, formerly Chairman of the Samaritans, Bill Rice, formerly director of TACADE, Denise Brady of St. Christopher's Hospice, Bill Yule of the Institute of Psychiatry and Michael Marland for agreeing to write the Foreword. Diana Whitmore of the Psychosynthesis and Education Trust, without those training this pack would not have been possible. Peter Stoker for his contribution to the first edition.

I am also indebted to Relate Bookshop, and all the magazines, newspapers and book publishers who have allowed me to quote excerpts.

Last and not least my Associates, without whom 'Good Grief' would not exist: Sally Crosher, my personal assistant for her endless patience and for 'keeping me on track'. Lyn Kimm for her personal contributions and also for being my 'sounding board'. Robbie, our 'Girl Friday' for the first edition.

FOREWORD

Rooted in the centre of a strong school curriculum is the requirement of Section 1 of The Education Reform Act 1988 that a school's curriculum 'promotes the spiritual, moral, cultural, mental, and physical development of students' and 'prepares such students for the opportunities, responsibilities and experiences of adult life'. Whatever the contents of 'the national curriculum' components of the school curriculum, these are over-riding. Clearly, they demand the inclusion of emotional preparation, and this must include enabling young people to understand loss and bereavement.

The 'content' of a school's curriculum consists not only of the facts – but also includes attitudes, concepts, and skills. This admirable teaching and learning material will immensely help schools in their planning of this aspect of their curriculum.

Many of our students will have experienced bereavement themselves or know of it through their friends. Only a few, though, will have had the opportunity to consider their feelings and how to develop their love for the lost person whilst developing their emotions and understanding of the life they are experiencing. Even fewer will have had preparation for the grief of bereavement. Schools from the earliest ages have a key, though of course not a sole, role to play. This has to be planned as an integral part of the curriculum and pastoral care of a school. Despite the obviously distressing nature of the topic, it requires the same form of intellectually sound curriculum planning as any other aspect. The material to help pupils consider their feelings and those of others needs skilful planning; and the mode of discussion needs sensitive leadership.

This publication will be found marvellously helpful, and I commend it to everyone working with young people.

Michael Marland CBE MA FRSA
Headteacher, North Westminster Community School; General Editor, Longman Tutorial Resources and Heinemann School Management; Honorary Professor of Education, Warwick University

STATISTICS FOR BRITAIN

In Britain there are   3,200,000 widows

750,000 widowers

approximately 180,000 children under 16 who have lost a mother or a father through death

1 woman in 7 is a widow

1 man in 8 is a widower

1 woman in 2 over age 65 is a widow

1 man in 6 over age 65 is a widower

Every day approximately 500 wives become widows and 120 husbands become widowers

Of the bereaved children under 16 approximately 120,000 are widows' children and 60,000 are widowers' children

(OPCS 1984)

'The divorce rate was 74,000 in 1971 – 146,000 in 1981 and 151,000 in 1987. Official estimates indicate that if divorce rates prevailing in the mid 1980s were to continue, then 37 per cent of marriages are likely to end in divorce.

Death still terminates the majority of marriages.

1 in 5 children will experience a parental divorce by the age of 16.'

Family Change, Future Policy
Kathleen Kiernan and Malcolm Wicks
Family Policy Studies Centre, 1990

It's the last and greatest taboo of the Western World – our fear of death and dying...we are afraid of death, we deny it, we are even ashamed of it.

'Death is one of the greatest taboos. It doesn't square with our worship of youth'. But the truth, after all, is that we are all terminally ill. Once we recognize that, we can enjoy the life we have left.

Elizabeth Kubler Ross, 1982

ORGANISATIONS

The Compassionate Friends is an international organisation of bereaved parents, offering friendship and understanding to other bereaved parents, through local regions or national membership.

Cruse is an organisation which offers, through local branches or national membership, a service to the bereaved; for example, counselling, someone to share things with, information on practical matters, opportunities for contact with others.

National Association of Bereavement Services. This is an umbrella organisation for Bereavement Societies throughout the UK. They provide support and information and a newsletter. There are also working parties on various aspects of bereavement and an annual conference.

National Children's Bureau is an organisation specialising in research into the care and well-being of children in the family/school and society in the areas of health, education, child welfare and legal aspects.

Psychosynthesis and Education Trust. Psychosynthesis is based on a psychology which offers a broad perspective of human life, with special focus on human potential. The Trust trains people in counselling and psychotherapy.

Research Trust for Metabolic Diseases was founded to offer financial support to help scientists and emotional support to help families with members experiencing metabolic disease. **RTMDC** now has an international reputation.

The **Samaritans** is an international organisation with over 185 branches in the UK and Ireland and 23 branches abroad. Their primary aim is to be available at any hour of the day or night to befriend those passing through personal crises and in imminent danger of taking their own lives. They also are available in a 'low key' way to support both victims and helpers at disasters.

Schools Outreach is a registered charity that facilitates the placement and support of fully-trained, high calibre, gifted persons who will enhance the lives of schoolchildren by being based long-term in a school and its local community.

HOW TO USE THIS BOOK

This book aims to help students to
- Understand and accept that loss and bereavement are natural parts of life and that there is a sequence to life: a time to be born, a time to grow, a time to flourish and a time to die.
- Recognize that there are various cultural, religious and personal attitudes towards death and dying.
- Understand the benefits of the grieving process and how this can occur in all types of loss, not just death.
- Identify and be able to make use of the available sources of help, information and support for people suffering through loss and death.
- Become aware of the practical arrangements necessary at the time of death.

Occasions when questions may be asked
- When a student loses someone who is close to them.
- When a member of staff or fellow student dies.
- Following media coverage of the death of a famous person.
- Following natural disaster, rail or air crash.
- After personal experience of a fatal accident, serious illness or disaster.

Section 1

Introduction and Background

Introducing The Teaching Programme

"GOOD GRIEF" has been designed to provide a framework for exploring the sensitive issues around Feelings, Loss and Death.

It is based on our wide experience of teaching the subject both in the world of education and the other caring professions.

Who is it suitable for?

This Pack has been designed principally for young people of different abilities in Secondary and further education. However, because of the basic philosophy and active learning methods, it is also suitable to be used in a wide variety of other teaching and pastoral situations.

Schools and Further Education

A variety of different approaches are suggested as the boundaries of different subjects are constantly changing. It is possible for Loss and Death to be covered in any or all of the following subjects - Personal, Social and Health Education, or PSD (see below), English, Social Studies or Humanities, as well as Religious Studies where Loss and Death are an important part of the G.C.S.E. examination.

The National Curriculum

All schools are now required by law to provide a broad and balanced curriculum which promotes the spiritual, moral, cultural, mental and physical development of pupils and prepares them for the opportunities, responsibilities and experiences of adult life (Section 1, Education Reform Act, 1988). Promoting pupils' personal and social development (PSD) means supporting them as they develop from dependent children into independent young people with a wide range of adult roles. At the heart of PSD is the promotion of personal qualities, skills, attitudes and values which enable individuals to think and act for themselves, to manage relationships with others, to understand moral issues and to accept social responsibilities.

The cross-curricular elements described by the National Curriculum Council make a significant contribution to PSD and the teaching of Loss and Death, as does the guidance laid down in NCC's Curriculum Guidance (3) "The Whole Curriculum". In addition NCC Curriculum (5) "Health Education", which I was asked to contribute to, has Feelings, Loss/Change, and Death included in every key stage. The subject is also included in all key stages of Religious Education. The 1994 N.C. Guidance allows each school to develop their own P.S.D. and R.E. Policy and from that to prepare "Programmes of Study" for practical guidance in the classroom.

Equal Opportunities - Race, Gender and Special Education Needs*
The activities in this pack have been designed to incorporate Equal Opportunities.

*Special Education Needs (SEN)

See Article "Teamwork for Children with Special Educational Needs" which shows how one school set about creating a climate for SEN which encourages all students to focus on the positive and maximises opportunities for young people with disability.

Youth and Community

The active learning methods of the Pack lend themselves ideally to the informal setting of Youth Work.

Health & Social Studies

As part of the basic training for nurses, midwives, district nurses, health visitors and social workers.

General In-service Training

Training Officers might also find parts of this Pack useful.

Who should teach it?

Educators need to have come to terms with losses in their own lives and not to have experienced major loss recently. They too should have a good support network and be used to teaching sensitive areas.

Training

Ideally all educators should have a short training to explore their own experiences of loss, look at the issues raised in this Pack and to learn appropriate listening skills.
Please write to Barbara Ward & Associates for details of the one day training she has developed to complement the Pack.

NCC Curriculum Guidance 5 Health Education

REFERENCES TO FEELINGS, LOSS AND DEATH

Key Stage 1

Family Life Education
* Know that there are different types of family and be able to describe the roles of individuals within the family;
* know about rituals associated with birth, marriage and death and be able to talk about emotions involved;
* understand the idea of growing from young to old;

Psychological Aspects of Health Education
* begin to recognise the range of human emotions and ways to deal with these;

Key Stage 2

Family Life Education
* know about the needs of the old/ill and understand what happens with death;
* know about helping agencies which can support families and individuals in different circumstances.

Psychological Aspects of Health Education
* understand that individual responses to events will vary and respect other people's emotions and feelings;

Key Stage 3

Family Life Education
* recognise the changing nature of relationships within the family, eg children gaining independence, new members of the family group, death.

Psychological Aspects of Health Education

* know how labelling and stereotyping can have a negative effect on mental health;
* understand the emotional changes which take place during puberty; understand differences in maturation and have a positive self-image.

Key Stage 4

Family Life Education
* be aware of problems which can occur in family life, eg domestic violence, abuse, bereavement, substance use, unemployment, illness; be aware of the effects of such problems; recognise that some individuals have special needs;
* understand that the roles of different members of the family may alter over time;
* know how to use the helping agencies, eg clinics, hospitals, dentists.

Psychological Aspects of Health Education
* be able to understand and manage changes in relationships;
* recognise the causes and effects of stress; be able to identify ways of reducing/ managing preventing stress; know how to ask for and give support.

CREATING THE CLIMATE

"If children were allowed to externalise pain, anger and guilt, they would love to go to school."
Elizabeth Kübler-Ross

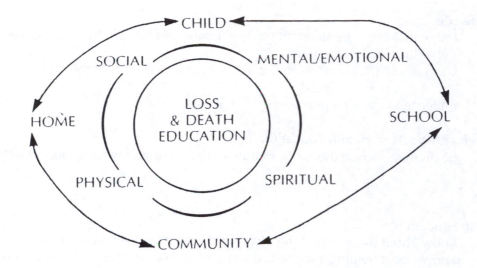

The ethos of the school/college will be at least as important as any formal context of teaching. A happy, caring institution is obviously the first priority. A major contribution can be made by its physical environment, aesthetic appeal and provision for different cultures, interests and needs.

However the greatest impact on any young person is their home. Therefore the most crucial factor will be the quality of relationships both within the school or college and with the parents and the community at large.

At times of loss and death, the staff need to be alert to the needs of the family and the support that is needed. Opportunities need to be given for students and their families to talk when ready, but also respect their right not to talk if that is their choice.

Once the climate has been created the hidden curriculum groundwork of this subject has been achieved.

PARENTS

It is essential that parents are aware of and experience the school as a caring institution and one in which they have faith, so they can share any losses or deaths that should affect their children. The formation of a Home/School Association parent meetings, day-to-day involvement and regular availability of the staff and headteacher assist greatly in making the relationships constructive and valuable. If the school's policy on Loss & Death Education can be developed together with parents, so much the better, at the very least the policy needs to be made explicit to parents and be part of a wider "The School as a Health Promoting Community Policy".

SUGGESTED POLICY

When new children start school ask their parents to inform you of any major losses such as death or divorce. The appropriate teacher/s then need to tell the children they know about their loss and are available to talk. Tell parents you want to work together. Ask them to keep the school informed of any major changes that could affect their children.

Include loss and death education in the curriculum, which should include self-esteem, so there is always a point of reference. This should incorporate training for staff and a policy for dealing with individual or group loss or death.

Make sure all the teaching and non-teaching staff are aware of the loss or bereavement, so that the child is not hurt by some chance remark.

Explain to the child's class or group what has happened before the child returns to the school. Remind them that tears are okay, as they are a natural and normal response when we are sad. Involve a friend or friends in the class as extra support.

Talk to the bereaved child/children and family before they return to school so that the families' needs and patterns of grieving and coping can be understood. (Some children prefer not to talk about the loss in school as they want somewhere to escape from the grief at home and want to be treated as normally as possible). Support is about providing opportunities, but recognising all people will not want to take them up.

Where appropriate acknowledge the death/s by having a memorial service.

Have suitable books available in the class or library for the child to read.

There may be times when the child, if upset, needs to go somewhere quiet on his/her own or with someone else.

For young children and those who have special needs, have a 'cuddle corner' in the classroom. It could have a large soft armchair or bean bags and soft toys and/or blanket or duvet.

Encourage support systems see 'Who helps me' page 153 - 157. This helps young people to realise that everyone has similar feelings and prevents alienation, one of the main effects of loss.

Notice any change in behaviour. Quiet children may become noisy or vice-versa. Aggression, moodiness, anxiety, lack of concentration and minor illnesses can be quite common in the first few weeks. Depression or suicide attempts are also possible with older children.

Watch for specific school problems, e.g. falling behind in school work, cruelty from other children, need for more attention and security. Recent research has shown that children that are bullied have often experienced loss or death.

Be aware of professional/voluntary agencies in the area which can support you or the parents, or to which the child can be referred, if necessary. They can also help you set up a group for bereaved children, where necessary. (See also Dora Black's book in "Educator's Book List" and the videos in "Additional Resources".

Finally, use all examples possible to show that loss and death are a normal and natural part of life. This can include discussing "soaps" and media happenings.

GOVERNORS

The 1986 Education Act encouraged the more positive involvement of governors in their schools, giving them extra representation and responsibilities.

DIRECTORS OF EDUCATION

Directors of Education like to be notified immediately of a death in school so they can write to the family concerned.

EDUCATIONAL PSYCHOLOGISTS

The involvement of Educational Psychologists with bereavement and loss might include . . .working directly with young people who have experienced loss. . . . advising the educators concerned on a likely response to the loss and the help they can give. This would include emphasising the importance of the stability and routine of school life at a time of disruption and unhappiness at home . . . . providing more general information to educators or other interested groups - e.g. an educational psychologist may lead a staff discussion on the impact of family break-up on young people.

When intensive help is needed for a child or the family, the psychologist might recommend approaching the local Child Guidance Service.

Access to an Educational Psychologist is usually open - anyone can contact the local School Psychological Service for advice - but teachers would normally do so through their Headteachers.

EDUCATIONAL WELFARE OFFICERS, SCHOOL NURSES, SOCIAL WORKERS & FAMILY COUNSELLORS

E.W.O's, School Nurses, Social Workers and Family Counsellors can provide valuable links between the school, parents and the community.

TEACHING APPROACHES

**"Tell them and they hear
Show them and they see
Do it and they understand."**

How people learn, why people behave as they do, whether and how or even if they want to change, are complex notions. Evidence suggests that a variety of approaches make for the most effective teaching of Personal, Social and Health Education, of which Loss and Death Education are a part.

Unless this Course is just to be a paper exercise it is essential to use active learning methods as incorporated in the activities. (Also to include it as part of a coherent PSHE or PDP Programme, based on the spiral curriculum and the cross-curricular philosophy of the National Curriculum in the case of schools.

Role Play

This needs very careful handling and should only be used in this subject if the Educators are experienced and confident in the use of this method. The importance of careful introduction and debriefing cannot be emphasized too much.

Quizzes

These can be used in the written form or read out, depending upon the age and ability of the students and the time available. In order for them to be beneficial as an education tool, a sense of fun needs to be instilled and reassurance given that they are not a test.

The exploration of knowledge and beliefs, the development of self-esteem and group support, are vital components when teaching about feelings, loss and death. The giving of information alone has been shown to be largely ineffective.

THE 'TEACHING APPROACH' NEEDS:

1) To recognize that there will be students in every group who will have experienced the loss or death of someone close to them, e.g. parental divorce/separation or death of a grandparent and that attitudes may vary from group to group and student to student, even within the same age range.

2) To treat bereavement as a natural and normal part of life, that although painful at the time, most people will come through with no problems.

3) To take cues from the group on the depth they want to go to, (Bereaved students may want to go further than the other members of the group or vice-versa).

4) To watch for signs of students who may need support, e.g. gigglers are often the most scared.

5) To reassure, where necessary, that tears are natural and normal. Stress that you or other members of the staff are available on a confidential basis for them to talk to at any time should the need arise.

6)   In order to fulfil this, to tell other teaching, and non-teaching, staff that the lessons are taking place, and be given the appropriate reading from Section 1.

7)   To create an atmosphere of trust where students feel free to share their feelings. It is often most helpful to sit their in a circle where everyone can have eye contact, this can be either in small groups or the whole class.

GROUNDING THE ACTIVITIES

Students should be encouraged to share and discuss these experiences. It usually helps to 'ground' the experience, see section on Evaluation.

It may be necessary to form smaller groups to give everyone the opportunity to share, and it may be easier to start by sharing with just two people rather than a larger group.

It is important that students are not forced to share something if they really do not want to. In this case, where possible, an opportunity needs to be given to share with an adult outside the class. Often students can be surprised to find that others have had similar experiences and/or difficulties. The realisation can not only be liberating but also prevents long term feelings of alienation, especially in situations like the loss of a parent, through separation/divorce or death, or other forms of loss.

Both positive and negative experiences need to be shared, with emphasis placed on the positive alternative. Often other students who have experienced similar situations are best at this.

THE USE OF VISITORS

The purpose of having a visitor, rather than a speaker, is to place responsibility, both for the visitor and for the questions asked, with the students. A visitor can respond to the needs of a group, whereas a speaker presumes the need/s.

SUGGESTIONS FOR USING A VISITOR

-    Decide with the students who to invite, for example a representative from a voluntary organisation.

-    The students are then asked to write to the suggested name/s inviting them to come at a special time and place, and to explain what the framework of the session will be. Alternatively the proposed visitor could be telephoned.

QUESTIONS/NEEDS FOR THE GROUP TO DECIDE

-    Who will meet the visitor and where.
-    How to greet them.

-    Will any refreshments be needed.
-    Who will be the time keeper.

-    How will the visitor be introduced to the group.
-    How will the group introduce itself to the visitor.

- How will the session be ended.
- Who will see the visitor out and thank them.

- Who will write to say thank you to the visitor.

ASKING QUESTIONS

Depending on the age of the students it is useful first to brain storm ideas. The group will then need to decide, who will ask the first question, who will go next etc.

Time needs to be given for the visitor to ask questions.

EVALUATION

Encourage the students to evaluate the session by asking all or some of the following questions, depending on age and ability:

- What did we learn/find out
- Were we well organised

- Was the visit enjoyable
- Did the visitor seem comfortable

- Are there any questions still unanswered
- Was there anything we could change before another visit?

EVALUATION

Evaluation is the way we tell whether we have met our objectives, and whether our approach, activities and students involvement have been effective.

Always debrief at the end of each activity by asking the students to discuss their feelings. This will enable you to assess the effectiveness of the activity both from your own and their point of view.

Learning relies on sharing and exploring the students experiences, attitudes, and values.

Evaluation needs to assess the process of these sessions, not just the content, that is: how did the students feel during these activities; what caused their feelings and reactions; what did they think; also what did they learn and how can they apply that leaning to their lives.

The following are typical "processing" questions:
- How did you feel during the activity?
- How are you feeling at this moment/now?
- What did you think during the activity?
- What are you thinking now?
- Did you changes anything you were doing? Give examples.
- Will you change anything you do in the future as a result of the activity? Give examples.

Other approaches could include:

A)   **Asking the students:**
-   What they enjoyed most/least about a session
-   How are they feeling e.g. I'm feeling sad/happy/etc at the moment, is anyone else
    feeling the same?

B)   **How are we feeling now:**
-   Ask the students to draw a circle ad divide it into four section and then write a word
    or draw something in each section to show how they are feeling.

The checklist below can be used to indicate how well the objectives for each session have been met. There may well be some changes in the students behaviour during the course of a session, although it is probable that significant changes will take longer. It is important therefore to look at the situation again in the weeks and months that follow.

Try to involve the students in monitoring their own progress. By doing this they will have a deeper insight into their own behaviour, and the educator can show them that their opinion is valued.

CHECKLIST
Refer to this checklist during the weeks that follow the session. It can be used to monitor changes in the class as a whole, or for individuals. The following questions can be answered with:

a)   **"Occasionally"**   –   "QC"

b)   **"Quite often"**   –   "QT"

c)   **"Nearly all the time"**   –   "NY"

For example **"Do the students"** :

	OC	QT	NY
explain their needs and express their own feelings openly when appropriate?	–	–	–
treat each other with consideration?	–	–	–
show an understanding of other people's needs and feelings	–	–	–
help anyone who has special needs or who is disabled if appropriate?	–	–	–
show sensitivity for and acceptance of cultural differences in others?	–	–	–
seek ways of helping others where appropriate?	–	–	–

N.B. Add any other statement of your own.

WHY TEACH ABOUT LOSS AND DEATH?   1.2

Background to Pack

"Pain can be physical, emotional or spiritual - whichever aspect it starts with, it will always spread to the others, so the earlier we start dealing with the pain of loss and death the less likely it is to affect the other aspects."

> Laura Mitchell
> International Stress &
> Tension Control - Annual
> Conference 1987.

"Because of the changes in lifespan and the fact that many deaths now occur in old age, many people are caught unprepared, not knowing how to behave or the practical procedure to follow. Mourning is treated as if it were a weakness, a self-indulgence, a reprehensive had habit, instead of a psychological necessity."

> Gorer, 1965.

The recognition of the effects on health and changing patterns in bereavement led to Loss and Death Education becoming an important part of the School Curriculum in the U.S.A. in the 1970s.

When I first introduced this pack in 1987, there was no recognized scheme for teaching the subject in Great Britain, despite the fact that Loss and Death was included in the content area of many Personal, Social and Health Education and Religious Studies courses.

Happily I was invited to contribute ideas for Loss & Death Education to the working party for the National Curriculum Guidance (5) Health Education (see fig.) and the subject is now included at every key stage. In addition, a series of fatal accidents on school trips and disasters such as Hillsborough and the sinking of the "Jupiter" have highlighted the need for educators to prepare their students to face death and bereavement. Loss also can be a major factor in bullying.

Many different types of loss can be the cause of grief and mourning. Death of or separation from a loved one is the most obvious and painful sort of loss.

In our experience in the field of education, we have encountered many young people who are unable to learn because of losses not recognised and worked through. This experience showed us that the changes young people experienced had the same potential for loss as death, but went largely unnoticed, with no recognition that the grieving process was necessary (see 'Understanding Loss'). All these losses require us giving up a familiar state or way of life for a new one. This is the basis of all grief.

If we don't mourn losses at the time they happen, major problems, e.g. severe depression, can be triggered off when later losses occur. Rutter 1970's found that psychiatric disorders were greatly increased where children had lost a parent by death. Bowlby in his work on "Loss" proposed that there is a specific connection between prolonged deprivation in the early years and the development of an affectionless psychopathic character extremely difficult to treat and given to persistent delinquent conduct. Toffler in his book "Future Shock" says many young people are in this state due to the rapid changes that are happening on all levels in modern society. Another reason for approaching the subject through loss is that 1 in 5 children will be affected by divorce.

Wallenstein & Kelly (1980 in their study of the effect of parental separation on children found the following:-

'Teacher observation indicated that approximately 2/3 of all youngsters showed some notable changes in school, subsequent to parents' separation. While youngsters differed both in the manner and intensity in which their distress was expressed, responses affecting academic achievement were most common. For more than half the students teachers reported a high level of anxiety. Most often this was described to us as new and unaccustomed restlessness. Children who used to sit and do their work now roamed about the room constantly, and in the process began to interrupt classroom activities'.

In addition, the importance of the help schools could give at this time was emphasised as follows:-

'It was clear that school was useful precisely because it provided structure in a child's life at a time when the major structure of his life, the family, was crumbling. Going to school daily, being required to perform certain tasks in and out of school, having routine social contacts, all these 'structural' supports potentially assist a child in his adaptation to divorce. It was clear that many children were supported by school in this basic way, regardless of the quality of their academic and social functioning within the classroom'.

It is generally accepted that the ability we have to deal with any crisis depends on our preparation for it. We prepare people for birth and marriage, but when it comes to death we like to feel we are immortal. All the other 'losses' we encounter in life, from the moment we leave our mother's womb, can be seen as 'little deaths' and how we deal with each one will affect how we deal with our own death and that of others close to us. Sudden tragedy, e.g. a car accident, may happen at any time in a school or community, with fellow pupils completely unprepared to handle the death of a friend, teacher or loved one. In addition, with unemployment figures around three million, many young people will be faced with the loss of the right to work when leaving school or further education.

In some Special Schools, this need particularly applies where it is more normal for one of the pupils to die. (See article in Sec (1).)

Delphine Fredlund, U.S.A., believes that children are interested in death at an early age, but soon learn from adults "that you don't talk about it". In a study with parents she found they felt very inadequate in handling this aspect of their children's development and, though they agreed it was primarily their responsibility, said over and over again "Churches and schools must help".

"In answer to the question "Can children really understand death", Grollman (1977) maintains that a child growing up today is "all too aware of the reality of death, i.e. a pet is killed, a funeral procession passes by, a grandfather dies, a leader is assassinated. TV nightly bombards us with death in many forms in glorious colour".

Thanatologists generally agree that death education for children, when developmentally appropriate, helps reduce fears and anxieties about death and dying.

It has been said that those who get the most out of life are those who are at ease with the fact they must die. Preparing for loss and bereavement then is part of the preparation for living.

> *"Man was made for joy and woe*
> *And when this we rightly know*
> *Thro' the world we safely go"*

> 'Auguries of Innocence' William Blake.

The benefits of accepting the words of the poem could perhaps help young people to think of their losses or 'little deaths' as opportunities for new beginnings.

Teachers may believe that children need to be protected from the facts of death: yet an over view of child development suggests that the discovery of loss begins during infancy. Perhaps it is the teachers own fears and attitudes which prevent them from mentioning the subject.

In one of our pilot schemes, a fifteen year old girl cried in class. Her father had died two years ago and this was the first time anyone in the school had mentioned it.

American research and our experiences of teaching loss and death showed that the majority of educators felt inadequately prepared to teach the subject and that information and guidance was needed. Hence the reason for our producing this Pack in association with CRUSE

If we believe that education is about prevention and developing potential, and not just academic success, we need to help students recognize loss and death as an inevitable part of all existence. They can then use these situations as opportunities for growth - hence the title of our teaching Pack "GOOD GRIEF".

The benefit of this could be far reaching in cutting down the dependence on, and, therefore the cost of our drugs, the overcrowding of our mental hospitals and the senseless violence and vandalism, resulting from the inability of many people to cope with the losses and changes in their life.

The need for education for loss was highlighted in the following extract from May 14th 1982 Times Educational Supplement:-

> "Task Force Children under Stress, by David Lister and Sarah Bayliss -
>
> The growing Falklands crisis had led to an increase in tension in schools in the Portsmouth and Gosport areas over the past week.
>
> Many pupils come from naval families and have fathers in the South Atlantic Task Force. Heads say that these pupils are finding it almost impossible to concentrate on preparation for examinations..........................
>
> One Head Teacher, Mr. Michael Pipes, said this week that there had been a sharp deterioration in the quality of work since the crisis worsened.
>
> "A particular concern is those boys who are approaching exams". He said "Their minds are clearly elsewhere and their concentration has been shattered. They are not being at all disruptive but they are walking around like zombies"."

These findings have been echoed in recent disasters (see Professor Yule's article in Sec (1)).

What are the rewards for teaching this sensitive subject?
At the end of a session, using the label game in "Living with Loss" a boy said to his teacher "This is the best lesson I have ever had".

GOOD GRIEF is, therefore, intended to help to allow young people to face the topic openly, to encourage them to share in an exploration of a human experience which must touch all of us at some time.

References

Gorer, Geoffrey. 'Death, Grief and Mourning in Contemporary Britain', Cresset, 1965.

Fredlund D.J. Children and Death from the School Setting Viewpoint. The Journal of School Health 1977.

Grollman D. 'The Journal of School Health' 1977.

Toffler A. 'Future Shock' 1971.

UNDERSTANDING LOSS   1.3

**"There is no growth without pain and conflict
and no loss that cannot lead to gain"**   **Lily Pincus 1961**

Loss touches all of us throughout life, yet its existence is generally not recognized except in extreme cases such as death and divorce.

Every time people make a change in their life, they take on a new role or let go of an old one, they lose something. The potential for loss is rarely considered part of changing school or teacher. Generally the capacity to adapt is recognized.

The loss event is likely to become and remain a source of stree rather than a potential for growth unless the loss aspect is recognized, acknowlwdged and grieving encouraged.

Bereavement can be described as 'the loss of something that is precious'. The word is most often used in the context of a person, but it may include, for example, the loss of an inanimate object or the ending of relationship, or a change in a particular situation.

No child can live very long without encountering loss. By the time a young person is ready to leave school they will have experienced most of the following:

Growing up. This process may also be seen as a loss of accustomed forms of support and attention as well as the gain of autonomy.

Going to school, which means temporary separation from parents as well as the gain of education, playmates etc.

Changing Play Group/Nursery School to Primary School to Secondary/Middle School to College means a periodic loss of familiar surroundings and people as well as gains of new experiences, e,g. teacher, playmates.

In addition there will be other losses, some predictable, some unpredictable affecting either the child themself, family or friends. These could include:

New siblings to adjust to, which can cause a loss of parental attention.

Death of a sibling. This can result in preoccupied parents with resulting feelings of isolation as well as the loss of someone close to you.

Parents changing jobs which can mean the move to another area and giving up their friends, schools and familiar environment.

Mothers returning to paid employment - sometimes resulting in the loss of someone to greet and listen to them on returning from school.

Bereavement as grandparents grow older and die.

Loss of parent through separation/divorce or death. In 1994 there were 160,684 under 16's affected by divorce. 4 out of 10 marriages now end in divorce. Over a third of marriages are re-marriages (where either or both parents have been divorced before). This can mean adjustment to a new step-parent too. It is now possible to go for up to 50 years without experiencing the death of anyone near to us, so that when death does touch us closely it is difficult to know how to react or what to do.

Family or friends moving away or ending or changing relationships. Change of Country/Culture.

CHILDREN IN CARE.   In 1994 there were 76,000 children in care in Britain, with approximately 38,000 in foster homes. Sonia Jackson of Bristol University outlined the factors contributing to the 'high risk of educational failure'. These included disrupted schooling, low expectations, low self-esteem and lack of continuity - all compounded 'by the low priority given to education by social workers who bear the main responsibility for the welfare and progress of children in care'.

SPECIAL NEEDS. During the school years about 20% of all children will at sometime experience being identified as having special educational needs (DFE 1994). Many difficulties (physical, sensory, emotional, behaviour or learning) are not identified at birth, but come to light during the early years at home or school. These can include minor difficulties such as discovering diabetes, wearing glasses or a hearing aid or more serious physical or learning ones. These difficulties can result in loss of status, self esteem, friends, participation in activities, achievements, and sometimes loss of family. The degree of loss will depend on the childs perception and the reaction of those around them.

Unemployment.   An increasing number will have experienced their parent's and elder sibling's unemployment and may in fact face unemployment on leaving school. Many 16-18 year olds will find the government training scheme the only opening for them.

Homelessness.   A growing problem facing young people in Great Britain. Shelter say there are 8,500 sleeping rough every night. In the first half of 1994 there were 64,120 households accepted by local authorities as being homeless.

Hospital Stay.   This can mean temporary loss of familiar surroundings.

Child sexual Abuse.   Defined as 'any sexual exploitation between an adult, whether by coercion or consent'. 10% of children are thought to have experienced some form of sexual abuse. This can result in a variety of losses on different levels including loss of innocence and self-esteem.

Serious illness e.g. cancer, heart disease and AIDS.   In 1994 in the United Kingdom there were 551 under 14's in schools who were HIV positive and up to July 1994 there were 175 under 14's with AIDS, 89 of whom have died. AIDS (Acquired Immune Deficiency Syndrome) is a condition which develops when the body's defences are severely damaged. As a result, people are more likely to get illness which the body would normally be able to fight off easily. At the moment there is no cure for AIDS. Some drugs are used to prolong life for people with AIDS. This disease may result in harassment, rejection and isolation as well as death.

Drug Misuse is a world-wide problem which is causing particular concern with/for children and young people. Drug misuse and abuse can occour with legal drugs as well as illegal ones. Legal drugs include alcohol, tobacco tranquillizers and coffee.

Drug abuse can result in loss of that which makes us a person, our personality. With the loss of personality is the restriction on our freedom of choice; our life is restricted, our horizons narrowed. Other losses may include loved ones, career, happiness, health and life itself. In addition giving up drugs may involve loss of a way of life and the contacts that go with it.

Some of the following losses mentioned by Peter Speck in his book 'Loss and Grief in Medicine' may mean young people having to deal with the grieving process of family or friends:

1) A miscarriage or stillbirth can often make a woman feel that she is a failure as a woman.

2) A couple who cannot conceive may feel a loss of status and purpose.

3) When a baby is born with a defect the parents may grieve for the normal child they have lost.

4) The most commonly experienced loss resulting from a hysterectomy is the knowledge that a woman can no longer conceive and bear children and that her reproductive life is over.

5) If the body image is disrupted by amputation, or other surgery, it can lead to a grief-like reaction which requires a period of mourning before resulting trauma is resolved and a new, acceptable, body image is formed. The acceptance of this by others is important.

6) The initial reaction to loss of vision may render the person immobile, expressionless and depressed. The person may be preoccupied with the total dependancy they feel and the loss of individual freedom.

7) To be designated 'disabled' can be an important change in status which seems to emphasize the loss of capability and self-esteem for many. The loss of a sense of future and of security can lead to a sense of hopelessness.

8) 'Redundancy Neurosis' affects mainly young or middle-aged people who cannot find employment. Their feelings of loss of status, self-respect and earning power have lead to depressive illness.

The way young people deal with any of these losses or 'little deaths' will affect the way they deal with the ultimate one of their own death or someone close to them. The intensity of the grief reaction will depend on how they have experienced the other losses, their personal characteristics, their religious and cultural background and the support available.

TEAMWORK
for Children with Special Educational Needs

Peter Williams
Head of Shavington High School

I am the head of a comprehensive school and as such I am usually preoccupied with the things that secondary heads are preoccupied with, examination results, behaviour of my pupils, balanced curriculum and so on. How do we handle those pupils who have come into our school recently with special needs?

In the last decade we have had a number of education acts. The one that gives me most pleasure, is the 1981 Act.

It was an Act of its time. It responded to the sensitivity of our nation particularly in education. It started for the first time looking at children's real needs in an educational context by looking at their handicap and trying to categorise it on the basis of some medical diagnosis. I'm delighted by that, both as a teacher and because I have a personal interest, which I will tell you about later. This Act gave me a chance to introduce into my school, some absolutely wonderful children, whom I was convinced my colleagues and I could help. Mostly, though, I was convinced that they would enlighten and enrich the school by their very presence there. I shall describe four children. They are quite different. They are just 4 in 900, 3 of them were in my school and one of them is my nephew.

I'll start with John. He came to school three years ago with spina bifida. Then we hadn't got any facilities at all for the physically handicapped. Most of the school is on the ground floor, there is just the mathematics suite and science lab upstairs, but there are a couple of little awkward steps. I was convinced that within a matter of days the physical resources were going to be easy to fix. I asked the caretaker to make a ramp to go over a couple of steps which he made very willingly. I don't know if it would satisfy all the health and safety requirements as it doesn't have handles, but it gets John up and down these stairs very effectively.

John had a few problems with his spina bifida. We had to re-timetable him primarily downstairs for lessons. So for just one or two lessons John will struggle up the stairs. That was easy, it was just something we wanted to do and we were able to do it. The toilet was a problem. We have no facilities in the school whatsoever for the privacy of the incontinent, but it seemed to me to be something that wasn't that difficult to solve. We have the benefit of the Sports Centre on the same campus and they have toilet facilities in there which are normally used by adults, so it was a moment's work to negotiate with the Sports Centre to use their special facilities for John. It wasn't that difficult to arrange for people who deliver the sanitary towels for the girl's toilet to also deliver the pads that John needed. Then his diet. We had to get him to the dining room early, so we organised people to let John out of lessons with his chair a few minutes earlier than everyone else.

At lunchtime he would go down on his little ramp into the dining room and the ladies in the kitchen would serve him first, and make sure he got to a table. Shortly after his first few months he solved it and was able to look after himself. The point I'm making is that the problems of getting John around the school were easy to resolve. They just needed somebody to cut through the red tape. What we were worried about was how the rest of the children would take to John with his wheelchair. Now John has a very high profile, we could all see him and knew obviously what his problems were. As far as friendship was concerned, that too was easy, because basically he is a typical boy. However I realised that the first time I treated him as an integrated member of the school was the first occasion that I was actually able to shout at him. Because he can be quite naughty with his chair!! That's John. He is now in the third year and he is going to proceed through the National Curriculum and take the entire series of subjects.

I will now tell you about Samantha. She is a little girl who joined us having never been in a mainstream school. She has been hospitalised for all of her young life and she had recently undergone heart and lung transplant. Now having a heart and lung transplant attracted a lot of publicity and when she came into the school, she came in something of a blaze of publicity. She had not been in a school of any sort. This girl was 16 years of age, but she looked like a second/third former, 13 years of age and in terms of what she actually knew, she was about there too.

She was extraordinarily intelligent, we were convinced of that, and we placed her in the second year just rising into the third year although she was actually probably nearly four years older than some of them. We wondered about that and there was a considerable act of faith in doing that. The friendship thing worked very well. She became adopted by her form and friendship was easy to sustain. The problems that we had with Samantha were of a fragile child who could not, of course, do physical education. She was tired very easily and quite often had to go home from lessons. She has a high profile in the school, not just because of the publicity that surrounded her when she came here, she did look different, you could identify Samantha at a glance really. As far as diets were concerned, this was easy. The catering officer was quite happy to prepare a separate diet for her and I used to let Samantha go alone early to the dining room too. She needed regular medication. That was easy too. She had to administer some of those complex things and we used to let her do that in the school office. All the problems seemed to be technical and were again easy. My anxieties were around relationships and how she would fit socially into the school. There was about Samantha something that my nephew, whom I will tell you about shortly, has coined a phrase. He is now 19 and he calls this the "Ah Bless Her" syndrome. When she came into the school, there was a great danger that throughout her life in the school people would say "bless her". Now what we had to try and do in her school life was to achieve a balance between those times when we need to praise and complement for something really special, and our desire to make her integrate and merge. That's what happened to Samantha - bless her!

Tracey is the third one in my school whom I am going to tell you about. She came in the first year with an illness that we only later had diagnosed as the Prader Willi syndrome. It's certainly not a metabolic syndrome, it causes the children to be very often sexually mature, behaviour is often difficulty as a rule and they often have dietary problems. Tracey came in at the age of 11, on her mother's knee, to secondary school. There were problems about diet, because she would be devious. She was a compulsive eater - this is in fact part of the syndrome. She would eat when she wanted to and put on weight. The problem with Tracey was forming relationships. The other two that I have described to you had no difficulties whatsoever. People would adopt them readily and they were very much liked in the school. Tracey was easy to get along with. One moment she would hug you. The first time she saw me, she actually got off her mother's knee and came and put her arms around me. Now people don;t do that with head teachers! It was one of the endearing qualities that Tracey had because she could be very lovable at times. The people who liked her best were some of the toughest boys in the fifth year. She would put her arms around them and they would be very protective of her.

When Tracey's parents first brought her to the school, their hopes were for Tracey to be able to survive in a normal comprehensive school and to be socially integrated with the other pupils. As she passed through the first and second years, with obvious success, so the hopes and expectations for the future were modified. Her parents wanted her to do GCSEs. Tracey had learning difficulties, but she did do GCSEs and she left this year with a package of GCSEs (she has a job). I mention this though because it's the change of expectation that these parents had as their child went through the school. It started modestly - all they wanted was that she would come in, have a happy school life, in a mainstream school, and have friends. They weren't too interested in her school work and her progress. They soon were!

Now to the author of this phrase "Ah bless her!" It's my nephew David, who perhaps has been the trigger in my concern for introducing children with special needs into the school.

David was born blind. He is now 19 and went to the school for the blind in Liverpool. At the age of 12, when he was ready to be transferred to Secondary Education, this coincided with the wonderful 1981 Act. We talked as a family about the tremendous act of faith of inviting the local education authority (Clwyd as it happens) to take David into a neighbourhood Comprehensive School. They were very eager to help. They took him into the school.

They invested massively - in a teacher of Braille, in a mobility officer, in a room for him and they made that personal investment too, that took all those difficulties on board. He was the first in the school. The reason that I am mentioning David is that he is an example of somebody with a conventional disability really, in a mainstream school following the 1981 Act, who has passed through it and has now just done "A" levels at sixth form college. He is also beginning to articulate to me some of the things that I wish he had been mature enough to share with me before, because I now understand more about the life of somebody like David. People were expecting of him things we never would have expected of children without a handicap or physical disability. I'll give you an example. They have been spending ages teaching him how to butter bread. You will know that for a blind child buttering bread is incredibly complicated, as you can't see if the knife is on the bread and he has spent ages struggling with this. It's very difficult. He said to me only last week, "Peter, when you went to university, how often did you have to butter bread when you were up there?" Actually, I never once buttered bread! He is able now to try and identify what he himself needs. He said "There are so many people around me now who are determining my destiny and I am anxious that they should ask me about it". I wish he'd been able to say things like that to me at 11 when we had been studying him and some of the other children I'd taken on board.

These are the four children, very different.

I won't believe that all of the problems of integration into a main comprehensive school cannot he handled. The problems that they bring are soluble. Cutting through red tape, determination, saying to the Education Authority "do it". Those are soluble easy targets. The ones that I have always had more anxiety about are the ones about relationships. I am delighted to retain these pupils in the school. They have strengthened it, enlightened it and enriched it. My school is a better place because I have these pupils with me.

First published in RT MDC News Vol. 3. No. 7 1/91. Reprinted with permission Research Trust for Metabolic Diseases in Children, 53 Beam St, Nantwich, Cheshire, CW5 5NF.

HOW TO HELP SOMEONE WHO IS SUFFERING FROM LOSS

DO let your genuine concern and caring show.

DO be available . . . to listen or to help with whatever else seems needed at the time.

DO say you are sorry about what happened and about their pain.

DO allow them to express as much unhappiness as they are feeling at the moment and are willing to share.

DO encourage them to be patient with themselves, not to expect too much of themselves and not to impose any "shoulds" on themselves.

DO allow them to talk about their loss as much and as often as they want to.

DO talk about the special, endearing qualities of what they've lost.

DO reassure them that they did everything that they could.

DON'T let your own sense of helplessness keep you from reaching out.

DON'T avoid them because you are uncomfortable (being avoided by friends adds pain to an already painful experience).

DON'T say how you know how they feel. (Unless you've experienced their loss yourself you probably don't know how they feel.)

DON'T say "you ought to be feeling better by now" or anything else which implies a judgement about their feelings.

DON'T tell them what they should feel or do.

DON'T change the subject when they mention their loss.

DON'T avoid mentioning their loss out of fear of reminding them of their pain (they haven't forgotten it).

DON'T try to find something positive (e.g. a moral lesson, closer family ties, etc.) about the loss.

DON'T point out at least they have their other . . .

DON'T say they they can always have another . . .

DON'T suggest that they should be grateful for their . . .

DON'T make any comments which in any way suggest that their loss was their fault (there will be enough feelings of doubt and guilt without any help from their friends).

DIVORCE AND SEPARATION 1.6

HOW THE SCHOOL CAN HELP

Background Reading   — Section 1   'Understanding Loss',
    'Why Teach Loss and Bereavement',
    'Statistics for Britain'.

    — Section 2   'Living With Loss'.

    — Section 3   'Unhappy Ever After',
    'Caught in the Middle'.

One in 5 children experience the loss of a parent through divorce or separation. In many cases the effect on their psychological development may be more traumatic than the death of a parent.

HELPFUL HINTS FOR TEACHERS

Parents often discuss their marital breakdown with teachers.

- Be aware of the agencies available in your area, and advise parents to go for help as soon as possible. (See 'Useful Addresses' in Section 3).

HELPFUL HINTS FOR PARENTS

Professor Caplan, the Scientific Director of the Family Center for the Study of Psychological Stress, makes the following suggestions for parents:

"Parents intending to divorce should discuss the issues with their children before the separation to prepare them for what is about to happen in a manner geared to their ages and developmental levels. With pre-school children this discussion should take place a week or two before the family's break up; with 5—8 year olds the discussion should be a month or two beforehand; older children should be given longer notice.

If possible parents should talk to their children together to show that they agree. They should expect that, after this first discussion, they will need to continue talking about the issues with children as a group or individually depending on the children's reactions and the questions they raise. The initial discussion should cover the following 10 points:

- The parents intend to end their marriage, live in separate homes, and no longer be husband and wife, because they have stopped loving each other and cannot live peacefully with each other; the divorce has not been caused by anything the children have done.

- The couple intend to continue as parents of their children, to love them and care for them throughout childhood. They promise this without regard to what may happen in the future, when one or the other may remarry and have additional children.

- The children will live in the home of one parent and visit the other parent regularly. The parents know that the children need continuing contact with both of them for healthy growth and development, and both want the children to maintain close links with each parent.

- The parents realise that the children will probably oppose the divorce because it breaks up their home, but the children cannot alter their decision and should not try to do so. It has been made by the adults because of adult problems.

- The parents know that the children may feel angry, upset or insecure. They have taken these reactions into account and are sorry about them. They will help the children master these feelings; most children succeed in this after a few months.

- Divorce is common; every second or third marriage ends in this way. Thus the children should not feel different from others; they should not feel ashamed because their parents have divorced. Like other family matters this is private, but the children should feel free to talk about it to their close friends and their teachers. It often helps to share such matters with others who can provide support in times of difficulty. If, for a few weeks, thoughts about family troubles interfere with the children's capacity to concentrate in the classroom or in homework it would be good for their teachers to know what is happening and help the children overcome their temporary difficulties.

- The children should stay out of the quarrels between the parents; they should definitely not take sides. Even though the parents have stopped loving each other they continue to love their children and will always do so. They each want the children to love the other parent. They will do their best not to say bad things about each other to the children; if, beause of anger they do not always succeed, the children should forgive them.

- The parents do not wish the children to carry messages from one to the other, and promise to try not to send messages through the children. They do not wish the children to tell them what the other parent has been doing.

- The parents jointly or individually will talk to the children about these matters from time to time before and after the divorce. They know that it will be hard for the children to understand and come to terms with what is happening and that it will take a long time for them to adjust to the division of their family into two separate homes. The children should express their feelings in any way that is comfortable and should feel free to ask questions, which the parents will try to answer.

HELPFUL HINTS FOR CHILDREN

- Provide a caring atmosphere at school to help balance the disruption at home. (See 'The School as a Caring Community' in Section 1.)

- Involve the Educational Psychologist where appropriate to support the children and teachers.

- Read the two articles in Section 3 mentioned above.

TRACING WESTERN ATTITUDES TO DEATH

"Since men cannot cure death, they have made up their minds not to think about it" — Camus

In pre-Christian times there was little fear of death itself but fear of the 'spirits' of the dead returning to harm them.

From around the advent of Christianity onwards, a view of the world was formed with the earth at the centre, heaven above and hell below. However, early beliefs of an existence after death were accepted in the simple form of all those attending church would automatically go to heaven and those who did not would become extinct.

Life for nearly everyone at this time was rural-based with the church and manor being the centre of their lives. As local crafts developed with the subsequent trading of goods and the growth of towns, so beliefs started to alter, albeit slowly, in all areas of life.

Death had always taken place at home in the bedchamber with the family present, including the children. This continued into the 19th century, but during this time a change came in the way the Day of Judgement was perceived. At first it was thought all would sleep until the final day and, on awakening, be judged. A long way off. Then the Day of Judgement was thought to occur at the time of death itself, mainly due to a reinterpretation of the Bible, whereby death came to be seen as 'a symbol of the disastrous alienation between men and God due to sin' (Ninian Smart). Hence the element of 'fear' of death was introduced and reproduced in art and literature of that period (13th–14th century). On the whole though, death remained familiar and was an accepted part of everyone's life. This long chain of centuries when death was familiar is called "Tamed Death" by the historian Philippe Aries.

From the mid 18th century onwards, all this started to change with the emergence of new radical thought whereby individualism replaced collectivism, rationalism, scientific discoveries, industrialisation and eventual mass migration of people to live in towns.

Two aspects of this made a great difference to the attitude towards death. One was the change in religious perceptions. Darwin's theory of evolution brought with it a questioning of all previously-held beliefs and, as this century has progressed, all beliefs have been re-examined and analysed by many in varying ways. Now the central beliefs of the Virgin Birth and the Resurrection are under scrutiny, causing a rift in the institution of the Churches. Initially a 'Second Coming' and the Resurrection was expected within a comparatively few years. Now that 2000 years have almost passed, many are wondering — Why so long? They are uncertain, so little is spoken. This ambivalence of thought causes a difficult state of affairs for the dying and the bereaved. There is no set belief and code of behaviour to follow because accompanying this the rites of mourning have been discarded.

The second reason for a change in attitude was the advent of hygiene, hospitals, medical advances and technology. It was not considered hygienic for the dying person to be lying at home surrounded by family and friends. If a person does die at home, then the body is instantly removed. Unless death is caused by an accident, most die in hospital, with the situation being controlled by strangers in an alien atmosphere where we have little control, so apprehension and fear ensue. Sometimes no family member is present at the time of death. The professionals handling the situation are often as unused to the emotional aspect to death as everyone else. To many death is regarded as a failure within an environment geared for returning people to health. Many are not taught about death and its effects on loved ones. In conjunction with this there is a general expectation that, due to medical and technological advances, a cure will be available. That something can be done. Leading on from this we, as parents, do not expect children or younger people to die, whereas this is an acceptable fact in Third World countries.

The reality of death is constantly ignored but the unreality is too pronounced. Death is witnessed in films, plays, news and documentaries on television. "A child may see 15,000 deaths before reaching puberty", says Michael Simpson. The awareness of what death actually means to the families is ignored or glossed over so few have any idea what to expect when they find themselves bereaved.

Philippe Aries calls this "Forbidden Death".

by MARGARET HAYWORTH
The Compassionate Friends

Sources: *Man's Concern with Death* edited by Arnold Toynbee
             Western Attitudes towards Death by Philippe Aries
             The Facts of Death by Michael A. Simpson

HELPING YOUNG PEOPLE GRIEVE

by Dr. Dora Black, MB., FRCPsych. DPM
Consultant Child and Adolescent Psychiatrist,
Royal Free Hospital, London.
'Member of CRUSE Council'

Attachment and Loss

When humans and the higher primates lose someone or something they love, they grieve. In order to understand the processes of grief and mourning we must first understand how we become attached to people and objects. Our understanding of the biological and psychological roots of attachment has been illuminated by John Bowlby, whose eightieth birthday was celebrated in 1987. Basing his ideas on the work of animal ethologists, he has suggested that the processes whereby a newborn baby and his caretaker become attached are biologically based and serve an important function to protect the infant until he is able to care for himself. Babies, he suggests, come into the world with a repertoire of attachment behaviours, a sort of "suitcase of wiles" which enable them to attach a caretaker to them. One only has to think of the infectious nature of a baby's smile, a smile that is present from the very first day of birth and which by three weeks or so of age is produced readily at the sight of a human face, to understand what he means.

As children grow older they develop attachments to other people and the strength of their primary attachment is attenuated. When they reach adolescence these bonds weaken further in order to prepare them for making adult relationships. Many of the difficulties of adolescence can be understood in terms of attachment theory.

In order to understand what happens when a child loses a parent through death we must first turn to the effects of loss on adults.

Parkes has made a study of the effects on widows of losing their husband by death. He and others have described the processes of normal grief. On first realizing that her husband is dead a woman goes into a state of shock, may even deny that this has happened. This phase is usually short and gives way under the impact of recognising the truth to a phase of protest. Usually she is agitated and restless, may cry loudly and call upon the dead person. When the searching does not produce him and the calling is not responded to, the gradual realisation that he is gone leads to the third phase of grief which has been called despair. The crying now becomes quieter and more sad and the agitated searching subdues to a quieter rocking and keening. The individual finds it difficult to sleep or to eat, is often racked with guilt and sometimes by anger. At this time the comfort of friends and relatives is important and with their help the individual, in normal grief, moves into the fourth and final phase which is a kind of reconstitution of one's behaviour, a discovery of a new identity and acceptance of the state of widowhood which enables her to function. In normal grief this whole process may take up to two years from the loss of the spouse although some kind of functioning is possible long before then. Although grief is a process it is not a smooth progression from one phase to the other but rather a moving back and forth so that even many years after the loss of a husband a widow may be stung into tears of grief by, say, a chance encounter with an old friend of her husband's or the sight of an old home they shared, or one of his possessions come across accidentally.

The analogy of the processes of grief with the observed behaviour of a small child lost in a supermarket when accidentally parted from her mother is striking. After the first shocked realisation that she is lost the child will start agitatedly running up and down all the aisles of the supermarket seeking for her mother, crying loudly to attract her attention. If she fails to be reunited eventually the agitation ceases and tears of grief begin. During the reunion much anger is expressed. In order to explore these processes of grief in children, James Robertson, a colleague of Bowlby at The Tavistock Clinic in the 1950's, made a film "A Two Year Old Goes to Hospital". This film made hospital administrators and doctors aware of the harm that

was being done by separating young children from their parents in hospital and led to the more enlightened practices of admitting mother to hospital with her young child.

In order to grieve, however, one needs to be aware of the loss. One of the difficulties for children is that their limited conceptual understanding makes it difficult for them to understand about the permanence of loss or about the phenomena of death.

I have described the processes of normal grief but in a proportion of cases in adults grief may be pathological, that is, it may be absent altogether, it may be delayed, it may be prolonged or it may be distorted. There is much evidence that if we do not grieve at the time we are likely to be affected throughout our lives in all kinds of subtle ways. If children do not mourn, their personality development may be constricted. Adults who fail to mourn are likely to deal with issues of loss, even minor loss, in maladaptive ways. If grief is delayed we cannot make use of the normal community response to loss and important supports may not be available when we finally succumb to the pangs of grief. Interminable grief goes over into a depressive illness which may then require specialist treatment. However, there are some people who cannot express grief directly and this can lead to bodily symptoms such as arthritis or gastric ulcers, or even to heart disease. It is indeed possible to die of a broken heart.

There are certain features in the type of death, the kind of relationship and in the survivor's own character and background as well as in social circumstances which make a pathological outcome more likely.

Type of death:

1) Survivor may be to blame

2) Sudden, unexpected or untimely

3) Painful, horrifying or mismanaged.

Characteristics of the relationship:

1) Dependent or symbiotic

2) Ambivalent

3) Death of a spouse

4) Death of a child under 20

5) Death of a parent, especially mother.

Characteristics of survivor:

1) A grief-prone personality

2) Insecure, overanxious with low self-esteem

3) Previous mental illness

4) Excessively angry or self-reproachful

5) Physically disabled

6)   Unable to express grief

7)   Previous loss.

Social circumstances:

1)   Family absent or seem unavailable

2)   Certain cultures and religions

3)   Other losses (bereavement overload)

4)   Unemployed

5)   With dependent children at home

6)   Other losses.

It can be seen from this list that children are more at risk from pathological grief than adults.

Children and Loss

Children as young as five or perhaps a little earlier if they have personal experience of death, can have a quite well developed understanding of the concept of death including the fact that it is permanent and irreversible, happens to everyone, has a cause, and that dead people differ from live ones in a number of respects. They are immobile and cannot see or hear or taste or feel. Teachers have an important part to play in helping children to develop a cognitive understanding of death. Young children, before the age of five, have a very egocentric view of the world. If something's happened, it's because they caused it. If a death happens then, they often blame themselves. This is the time of concrete thinking so that it is very difficult for them to grapple with abstract concepts such as heaven or spirits. Religious explanations of death, which are often given to children, confuse them more than adults or older children.

Children need parents, young children especially cannot look after themselves and the loss of someone to whom they are deeply attached and on whom they are dependent can be even more devastating than in adult life.

Children who lose a parent by death have a five-fold increase in psychiatric disorder. School refusal is the single most important syndrome in school-aged children. This is a form of separation anxiety and there are understandable fears that the surviving parent might disappear unless the child keeps an eye on him. We know from the work of Brown and others that adults bereaved as children are more likely to become depressed, especially when they are subjected to other stresses.

Prevention

In order to prevent some of the morbidity associated with childhood bereavement we need to consider giving children coping strategies and I see the GOOD GRIEF Pack as a very important source of both cognitive and emotional strengthening. Keeping pets is another way to help children to understand something about the life cycle. When a child is bereaved it is important that he spends time with an adult who is not too preoccupied by the loss and who can help him to make sense of it. He may need an opportunity to play and to talk about his distress and confusion and to go over and over again the tragic event.

Children who are subject to various traumas including bereavement sometimes develop symptoms of post-traumatic stress disorder. They have recurring nightmares about the death, there is an inability to mourn accompanied by denial and withdrawal as well as other

symptoms. It is important to try and help them immediately, getting them to draw and paint what they have seen or what they imagine has happened. Teachers can do much to help such bereaved children.

In my own research study we offered a very short intervention to bereaved families where there was a child or children under sixteen which involved family meetings for four to six sessions. When we followed the families up over a one year period those that we had given such help were significantly healthier than the group to which we did not offer any help although they were matched in other respects. The surviving parent, too, was less depressed and sought less help elsewhere.

Our finding was that children tended to get left out of family grief. They are often not allowed to attend funerals and are sent away to play when they really should be joining in the family rituals. Again, a teacher can be of great help here, by visiting the family and helping them to understand the child's needs. However, it is difficult for adults to face their own mortality and they find the distress of children particularly painful. Before the material in this pack is used by pupils teachers may need to discuss its contents with their colleagues and friends in order to feel comfortable enough to discuss the subject honestly and openly with their pupils. Children should be monitored following a significant loss and who better to do this than the teachers who meet them daily? What must be looked for are changes in behaviour, in school performance, absenteeism, physical symptoms and, in some cases, even suicidal thoughts and actions. The child needs to be reassured that their feelings are understood, that they are normal and that they will improve in time. Suicidal ideas demand prompt action and medical attention should be sought. To do so may save a life. Counselling and support systems are available in some schools but the teacher should not hesitate to call on their local child psychiatric services if any of the pupils, following a bereavement, is showing signs of difficulty in functioning which is more than transient.

Little losses which are mourned at the time are preparations for greater losses in future. To help a child to mourn a death of a pet or loss of a school friend who moves away is not only rewarding in itself but helps to lay the foundation of a rich and varied repertoire of coping responses which will come to the aid of the child for the rest of his life.

. . . .

For details of Supporting Bereaved Children and Families: A Training Manual from Cruse Consultant Editor, Dora Black, see Section 3.

Further Reading:

Bowlby, J.: Attachment and Loss (3 Volumes), Penguin, Harmondsworth 1969, 1973, 1980.

Brown, G. and Harris, T.: Social Origins of Depression, Tavistock Publications, London 1978

Parkes, C.M.P.: Bereavement: Study of Grief in Adult Life, 2nd. Edition 1976, Penguin.

Grollman, E.: Explaining Death to Children, Beacon Press, Boston 1967.

Black, D.: Bereaved Children - Family Intervention. Bereavement Care, Volume 2, No. 2 Summer 1983

Forrest, G.: Mourning the Loss of a New Born Baby. Bereavement Care, Volume 2, No. 2 Spring 1983.

Pincus, Lily.: Death and the Family: The Importance of Mourning. Faber & Faber, London 1976

WORKING WITH YOUNG PEOPLE FACING DEATH 1.9

Richard Lansdown
Consultant Psychologist Great Ormond   Street Hospital for Sick Children

So often when one is working with people around the time of death there is a conflict between what is known intellectually and what is felt emotionally. In everyday conversations with families I often ask what they think in their heads and what they think in their hearts. Young people facing death, like so many adults as well, may find that at an intellectual level they understand the end of their life is near, whereas in their hearts this fate in inconceivable. A sixteen year old once said that he thought he would die within the next couple of weeks and they went on to tell me about the course he was hoping to do in college that autumn, Simply bringing out that we can hold two ideas in our heads at the same time may in itself be helpful.

The preoccupations of the young child who is dying are usually two fold: first they are upset at the thought of separation from their parents, second they may be apprehensive about heaven, what it will be like, how they will get there and so on. Older children tend to have preoccupations as well but their anxiety is often for their parents rather than themselves. "I don't care about myself, it's my mum and dad I worry about." "I've got to stay strong; my mum's had one nervous breakdown, if I crack she'll have another."

Such desires to protect parents can contribute to the phenomenon of mutual pretence, in which children pretend they have no worries in order to save their parents and parents carry out the same charade to protect their children. In the long run this can be harmful for it blocks both questions and mutual expressions of love, sorrow and anger.

A teenager is likely to have less certainty about an afterlife than younger counterparts and may need to explore ideas in this area. Or there may be certainty but considerable, justified worry about the moment of death: will it be painful, will it feel as I do when I hold my breath?

Expressions of love can be blocked if there is no recognition that time is short. "I wish I'd said sorry to my parents for all the trouble I've caused them" said a fourteen year old who died alone, at night, in hospital.

Sorrow and anger at what children may see as a terrible waste of a life should also be articulated if this is appropriate. "I'm so angry....I'm going to die and I haven't even taken my GCSEs." The girl who said that was helped to give some meaning to the last few months of her life by encouraging her to make a plan to do many of the things she had been wanting to but had not managed to achieve, So she visited friends, went to certain films and places of interest and generally had a sense of being in control right to the end.

There are two key phrases in the last paragraph. One is "if this is appropriate." Some young people desperately need to talk through their feelings, others cope by pushing thoughts away. We should respect both extremes, and those in the middle.

The second key phrase is "being in control." When someone is first ill there is a sense in which control is more or less handed over to the medical and nursing staff, Parents can feel that they are no longer truly parents, children and young people that they have had to give up much autonomy. In the last phase of an illness the medical staff have relinquished much of that control and it returns to the family. This can be a source of strength to the families, offering an opportunity to plan the end as they feel it should be.

For further reading:-

Jeffrey P. & Lansdown R. (1982) The Role of the Special School in the Care of the Dying Child. Developmental Medicine and Child Neurology, 24, 693-697.

Koocher J. (1974) Talking with children about death. American Journal of Orthopsychiatry, 44, 404-411.

Lansdown R. (1987) The Development of the Concept of Death and its Relationship to Communicating with Dying Children. In E.Karas (ed) Current Issues in Clinical Psychology London: Plenum Press.

Lansdown R. and Goldman A. (1988) The psychological care of children with malignant disease. Journal of Child Psychology and Psychiatry 29, 555-567.

Nitschke R., Humphrey G.B., Sexauer C.L., Catron B., Wunder S. & Jay S. (1982) Therapeutic choices made by patients with end-stage cancer. Journal of Paediatrics, 101, 471-476.

Rando T.A.(ed.) (1986) Parental Loss of a Child Champaign, Illinois; Research Press Company.

Wass H. & Corr C.A.(eds) (1984) Childhood Death Washington; Hemisphere Publishing Corporation.

EXPLAINING DEATH　　1.10

by Margaret Hayworth
newsletter Editor and Member of the National Committee of Compassionate Friends'

Preceptions and Explanations of Death

**The most meaningful help that we can give
any relative - child or adult - is to share
his feelings before the event of death and
allow him to work through his feelings,
whether they are rational or irrational.**

Elisabeth Kubler-Ross

There are particular aspects about young peoples perceptions of death that need special considerations:

1)　We all feel 'deprived' when a loved one dies but this emotion goes very deep in the young and it goes hand in hand with much 'fear'. Parents experience a fear and vulnerability about the safety of other loved ones but are more consciously aware of a world beyond their family network. Younger children's lives revolve completely around their mother, father, sisters and brothers. So not only do they feel 'deprived' of the family member who has died but the 'fear of death' for the rest of the family and themselves is heightened and becomes a paramount emotion.

2)　The actual thoughts that this age group have on 'death' is, in all probability, a distorted view. Those living in rural areas will have more of an idea about the cyclical rhythms of nature and will have witnessed the death of creatures in the wild. The town child will not have had these experiences and the main portrayal of death for the twentieth-century child is through the media — especially television — which gives an unreal picture of the event. The nineteenth-century child would have witnessed at first hand a death or deaths within its own immediate circle from an early age but it is a sad occurrence that now the death of loved ones usually happens away from most, if not all, of the family. This induces an anxiety and fear springing from a fertile imagination about an unknown event and the false pictures fed by the media. It has been noted that children often use the word 'kill' when describing death.

3)　Pre-adolescent children have great difficulty in grasping 'abstract' concepts about death. They are at the 'concrete' thinking stage in their development. Hence the difficulty in trying to explain the death of a loved one in a spiritual context.

So how do we explain death? For many of us, living in an age where any view if not scientifically provable is automatically considered suspect, the difficulty in understanding death for ourselves is great. Let alone explaining it to young people! This uncertainty within parents and teachers usually means the subject is ignored or explained without real conviction, i.e. "Granny's gone to heaven", but we are unable to follow on from this except in further vague, unconvincing abstract remarks which many of us query ourselves! No wonder our children experience 'deprivation and fear'.

Marjorie Mitchell say that "neither dogmas of immortality nor that of death being the final end are likely to create positive attitudes in the child and adolescent". Neither is "I don't know" very helpful, but to say "NO ONE YET KNOWS" is in keeping with the natural urge of the exploring child, who from babyhood is bent on finding out what life is all about. She suggests saying "People are still trying to find out, just as they are trying to find out what is in space. Probably when you are grown up you'll go on trying to find out too, but the brain is limited and can't find out everything."

There are two aspects of death. One, the lifeless body and two, the spiritual aspect.

1) **The Body.** What happens to the body is an aspect on which primary school children tend to concentrate. Jenny Kander explains it in this way:

"Tommy does not feel as you do because he is dead and that means that he does not have feelings anymore; he cannot feel hot or cold, that he is hurting or sick or well. He cannot think anymore either; not about nice things or scary things or good or bad things . . . And he does not need to be held or hugged or fed or played with anymore either because being dead means that his body is no use to him now. Remember how the tree's leaves die and then fall off the tree onto the ground? They are still beautiful but they are not alive and green after they have died. We will always remember and love Tommy even though we cannot see him or play with him anymore.

"There are two things we can choose between to do with Tommy's body. We can have it put in a special box called a coffin and bury it in the ground in a place called a cemetery which is just for that purpose, or we can have it turned into ashes and that is called cremation. That is what we have chosen to do and so we will ask/ have asked a man called a funeral director to take Tommy's body and put it in the special box, which is then put in a very small room — not like any room that we have in our home, all that is in it is a very hot fire, which changes that body into ashes. Then, when we are ready, we can bury them in the ground at the cemetery or we can scatter them in a place that we choose . . ."

For the 'concrete thinking' younger child, Marjorie Mitchell talks about a lesson with 9 year olds in which atoms and electrons were being explained as the basis of all matter. It was pointed out that electrons are still moving in the chemicals of the ashes of the cremated and they go on 'circling like tiny planets'. These children found this objective observance meaningful. One child, who had expressed a fear of death, said, "They (the tiny planets) *could* go on for ever; bits of me can go on for ever and ever and ever!!"

2) **The Spiritual Aspect** can be subdivided into three viewpoints:

a) There is no continuance of the individual spirit.

b) That there is a continuation of life in some form. One mother quoted in Marjorie Mitchell's book said to her child, "People usually die after they have done the work they had to do. As to what happens, nobody really knows, but many people believe that life continues in a different way."

This different way is often likened to the butterfly emerging from its chrysalis. The small story book "*Waterbugs and Dragonflies*" by Doris Stickney puts over this concept of a living being's continuance in a completely different form delightfully.

c) The religious aspect of soul/spirit. The explanation for this is a personal family matter but it is felt that children should be told that there are differing views.

Three observations about the spiritual aspect are:

i) The religious content in the media presentation of death is minimal so children do not readily connect death with a spiritual meaning.

ii) There is no evidence showing that religious attitudes make children feel more secure or console them. The abstract quality of them can frighten children.

iii) Children tend to grasp theories on reincarnation and pantheism easier than Christianity, whose concepts are difficult.

Quoted below are three questions and answers taken from the book "*A Child's Questions About Death*" by Neville A. Kirkwood. They bring together some of the aspects spoken about. The first one deals with the difference between sleep and death. The difference needs to be made clear to a child, who could become anxious about sleeping.

Is a dead person sleeping?

When we sleep we are resting our bodies. Our heart and other parts of our body do not work as hard. Sleep gives us strength for another day at school or play. When a person dies, his body stops working. There will be no waking up. The body's work is finished. So sleep and death are different.

What happens to dead people?

We live in a house. The people living inside make a house a home. For our bodies to be a home, we have a spirit which lives in the house — our bodies. When a person dies, the body becomes an empty house. Most people believe that the spirit which was living within the body goes to heaven. Our spirit is not a part of the body. It is with our spirit that we are able to give love and receive love. The spirit or soul nevers wears out. We cannot see someone's spirit, nor can we see heaven. We believe that we have a spirit and that there is a heaven. This is what we call faith. People of all religions believe that we have a spirit that lives on after our bodies have died.

What is heaven like?

We do not know what heaven looks like. We cannot tell you where heaven is. We know our bodies on earth wear out and die. Because it is our spirits that live on, we believe that we shall not again experience the sadness, the troubles and difficulties we have on earth. We believe heaven is the place where God is. Because God is love, heaven will be a place full of love.

Teenagers, like adults, realise the permanence of death and so become involved in looking for a meaning. The eternal 'whys'. Grief superimposed on the normal adolescent search for personal identity whereby family and societal values and views are all being questioned must make a confusing situation almost unable to communicate their feelings!

The conclusions of a survey of 6–15 year olds about their perceptions of the meaning of death were:

1) They wished to discuss death and have no 'unspoken barriers'.

2) The best explanations especially for under 8 year olds were those that "are simple, direct and draw as much as possible from the child's own experience".

3) It suggests that especially for those in the 'magical thinking' stage, it would be wise to ask the child to explain back again what he has been told so that gross distortion and misconceptions can be corrected.

A realistic, healthy understanding of death is required by society as a whole. This would remove much of the fear and anxiety that surrounds it and go a considerable way to easing the grief process for adults as well as the 'under twenties'.

SUICIDE   1.11

by Norman Keir
formerly Chairman, Samaritans.

The Incidence of Suicide

Those who have never felt suicidal have difficulty in imagining how anyone can seriously contemplate self-destruction. For most of us life is precious, something to be preserved rather than rejected. In the words of George Borrow's gypsy, Lavengro:

There's night and day, brother, both sweet things; sun, moon and stars, brother, all sweet things; there's likewise a wind on the heath. Life is very sweet, brother. Who would wish to die?

The sad fact remains, however, that many people do take their own lives. Each year in the United Kingdom some 5,000 deaths are attributed to suicide. The true figure is almost certainly higher, because coroners often lack sufficient evidence to establish suicide as the cause of death. A much larger number of people, in the region of 200,000, make what appear to be suicide attempts, usually by taking drug overdoses. Because the majority of these acts are not intended to be fatal they are called "parasuicides" to distinguish them from those which are meant to succeed.

Not all those who harbour suicidal thoughts act upon them. No-one knows how many there are who have survived periods when they have been preoccupied with thoughts of ending their lives as a way out of their unhappiness, when like Keats they "have been half in love with easeful Death." Some notion of how large their number might be can be gleaned from the fact that The Samaritans, a voluntary organisation set up to help those in danger of taking their own lives, receives two and a half million calls each year. A high proportion of these come from people with suicide on their minds.

Views of Suicide

There are many ways of looking at suicide. The Christian Church, for example, regards it as a sin, a deliberate destruction of a gift from God. Some philosophers, Kant for example, have agreed that suicide is wrong; others, notably the Stoics, have regarded it the right of everyone to terminate his or her own life. Sociologists tend to see suicide in the context of social conditions. Indeed the French sociologist, Emile Durkheim, wrote a study of suicide which was the first example of a methodical examination of statistical data as a means of exploring the social factors at play in human behaviour. Psychiatrists seek the cause of suicide in mental illness, though neither they nor anyone else would argue that the two invariably go together. The victims of some kinds of mental illness are prone to suicide, but a great many suicides are committed by people of sound mind.

In the past the law has reflected people's revulsion to suicide by treating as criminals those who commit or attempt it. All this was changed, however, in 1961, when The Suicide Act established that suicide was no longer a crime nor attempted suicide a misdemeanour. It made a criminal offence, however, the aiding, abetting or counselling of suicide by another person.

What Makes People Suicidal?

A great deal of research is done on the causes of suicide. Scientists can point to interesting relationships between its incidence and various sociological and biological factors. No effective way, however, has been found to predict who will and who will not commit suicide. One reason for this is that every suicide is unique.

We can start from the assumption that no-one wants to be suicidal. Those who are feel compelled to be so. From the individual's point of view his or her suicide is never an irrational act. It has a purpose, which is to bring to an end some unendurable psychological pain. The journey towards suicide may be short or long. It is an ever-narrowing path strewn with discarded options. The victim eventually reaches a point at which there seems to be only one way forward and that is suicide. There may be little thought of death. The prime objective is not to be dead but rather to escape. Being dead may be nothing more than an unavoidable byproduct. There may even be a kind of double-think: "I want to wake up dead" was how one man put it.

People seldom reach the end of the path for any one simple reason. More often than not there will be a multiplicity of reasons: bereavement, breakdown of an important relationship, loss of employment, financial problems, stress, poor health, terminal illness and others. A common feature is a sense of isolation. This may have nothing to do with the absence of contacts - the victim may be surrounded by family, friends and colleagues. The problem lies more in the realm of communication. The victim feels unable to share his or her feelings with anyone. There may be a feeling that no-one can help, or indeed should help. A common precursor to suicidal feelings is depression, which may result from some event in the victim's life or from some mental disturbance. It may be, as the writer William Styron described it, a failure of self esteem.

Whatever the reasons for suicide, it is never a good method of coping. Much as we must accept that people have the right to decide what to do with their own lives, much as we must avoid making moral judgments on those who take their own lives, we must stop short of suggesting that suicide is "an OK thing to do". It is not. One of the leading "suicidologists", Professor Shneidman, has suggested that

one should never commit suicide while disturbed. It is not a thing to do while one is not in one's best mind. Never kill yourself when you are suicidal. It takes a mind capable of scanning a range of options greater than two to make a decision as important as taking one's life.

The Effect on Others

The news that someone we know or love has died is always disturbing. When the person concerned is someone close to us the effect can be devastating. When death has been by suicide a whole new dimension is involved. All the feelings of normal bereavement will be there, though anger and guilt are likely to be even more severe. In addition there will be a deep sense of rejection and of the impossibility of making sense of the loss. Such feelings can last a lifetime.

The Need for Help

People who have suicidal thoughts and those who have been bereaved by suicide need to talk to someone who will accept their feelings and who will try to understand what the sufferer is going through. That is who organisations like The Samaritans and The Shadow of Suicide group of the Compassionate Friends have been set up.

(see activity 'Suicide' in Controversial Issues Sec (2))

"SHADOW OF SUICIDE"

'Shadow of Suicide' (SoS) is a group within The Compassionate Friends (TCF) for the parents, and families, of children who have ended their lives. (In TCF, the terms `parent' and `child' have no age limit.) The SoS group was founded in 1986 by Audrey and Ken Walsh, following the suicide of their daughter Jill. To lose a child, from whatever cause, is a terrible tragedy, but the parents of children who end their own lives have to cope with the police, an inquest and possibly the media. There is too, the unending and unanswerable `Why' that torments so many parents and families.

Suicide: what it means. When suicide occurs within a family, the shock is overwhelming. No-one expects the event, although parents may have been very fearful for the child.

Often the parents and family are treated differently from other bereaved people. There is a strong taboo in our society about talking of suicide. SoS parents are judged, ignored, shunned; they feel they are blamed for their son's or daughter's suicide. Very subtly, they can be made to feel they have loved too little, or too much. But, says Adina Wrobleski (an American writer on suicide whose daughter died in this way), "There are many 'bad' parents whose children do not kill themselves. There are many `good' parents whose children do. Our society has too often fostered the belief that suicide occurs in `bad' families". There is far to go until the rest of society treats the families of suicides with the sensitivity and compassion shown to other bereaved people.

Survival: how to begin. The shock of suicide has a disrupting influence on family and friends. It can tear the family apart. Grieving sisters and brothers can retreat into themselves, their isolation causing further pain and fear to their parents. Friends are at a loss to know what to say or to do, feeling helpless and inadequate.

This is where a group such as SoS can be of enormous support, because every family has endured a similarly devastating experience. Sometimes the SoS group is the only lifeline available to those stricken by the shock of suicide. The bond in a group of parents of suicides is strong. Children and their memories can be shared, sad and happy stories can be told without fear of rejection, and experiences can be exchanged.

Parents may 'meet' by corresponding through TCF's Newsletter. Letters, and then telephone numbers, are exchanged, and often a meeting between two families will take place. The experience of being able to reach out and help others, even in the midst of our own extreme pain, is very healing. In some areas, active groups are increasing, meeting regularly, with members both giving and receiving support and strength. The annual TCF Residential Weekend includes a group meeting for the SoS parents with the opportunity of meeting others from across the country, as well as parents bereaved in different ways.

The Newsletter, mentioned above, is published quarterly, and is a very great support to members. It is produced for the whole organisation and therefore has contributions from parents whose children may have died through illness, accident or murder, as well as suicide. There is, too, a range of leaflets available.

The future. The lives of parents and families are irreversibly changed by suicide. At first, and probably for some time, the hope of future happiness seems unattainable. However, almost imperceptibly, acceptance does eventually come, and it is possible to rebuild and enjoy life. We must give ourselves time to heal the deep wound and to learn to survive. The SoS group can be a great and positive help.

Further copies of this leaflet are available from The "Compassionate Friends" (see useful addresses).

MY FATHER DIED   1.12

by Susan Wallbank - Cruse Counsellor
(Article "My Mother Died is also available)

The Early Days

Sometimes people die suddenly, sometimes after a long illness but however it happens it nearly always takes us by total surprise. Shock affects all the members of the family for a while.

In the early days there is so much to do; decisions to be made, relatives to be told. When all this is happening it can be hard to believe that your father has really died.

The funeral service is so important because it publicly marks the ending of a person's life. Everyone may be a little anxious beforehand and it helps to know what the arrangements are and what lies ahead. The funeral is the time when all those who loved or knew your father come together to show how much they cared about him and care for you.

You may find that your feelings are very confused and change from moment to moment. It takes quite a long time for your mind to take in what has happened and begin to work out how this will affect you and the rest of your family in the months to come.

All kinds of questions that are hard to ask may come into your mind - How will we live? Who will drive the car? Even, will we still go on holiday this year?

During the first weeks your mother may be worried over money. It can take several months for all the paper work to be sorted out and until this is done she will not know exactly how much you will all have to live on in the future.

The worst period is usually the early one when you do not quite know how you stand and how much it is fair to ask your mother for. Try not to worry too much about the future. Many practical problems which seem large now sort themselves out quite naturally later on.

How did he die?

You will probably have to face this question from others sooner or later and it helps to have an answer prepared. With younger children, a mother may give a very simple explanation. "He was very sick and the doctors couldn't make him better". But you are old enough to understand more about how and why he died. You may find this painful to talk about and to some people you will want to give a very brief answer but, to others, find that it helps you to talk a little more about his death.

How do I feel?

Numbness, pain, sadness, anger and guilt are all perfectly natural feelings to have when you have lost one of the most important people in your life.

The sense of numbness, of not feeling anything at all, is part of the shock of

those early days. In a way it can be our mind's way of protecting us from toomany painful feelings all at once. It is natural that we should want to forget that it has happened whenever we can. Like most things that we hide away, at some
point they do come to the surface and then it is better to admit your feelings and allow them to show because in this way you get over them quicker.

You may hear people talk about 'working through grief' and this is what they mean. Grief is what we feel on losing someone very close to us. There is a kind of pattern to how we feel afterwards - the shock, not quite believing what has happened, the changing moods and emotions. Grief does not last for ever. Being able to say how you feel and talk about the past and what is happening to you now are ways in which you work through this sad time in your life.

If you were asked before you lost your father to describe somebody who had lost someone they loved, you probably would not have said that they would feel angry. Most people do not think about this side of grief and yet it is there and quite naturally so. When you think of what you have lost and how this affects your life now and for a long time to come, it is understandable that you should feel angry. Angry with life for letting this happen to you, even angry with your father for leaving you and not being there to look after you. These angry feelings can explode quite suddenly against yourself, your mother, perhaps your brother or sister or when you are with a friend or teacher.

Feeling guilty is another emotion which other people often do not understand. After all - what have you to feel guilty about? Nearly all people who have lost someone they are very close to do feel this from time to time. You may find you are feeling guilty because you do not seem to care enough or because you are not feeling what you should be or because you think in some way you are letting your father down or because you did not care enough or showed you cared enough about him when he was alive. It is hard to remember when someone dies that before that happened you were just parent and teenager and at this time of your life it is normal to have quarrels in the family and differences of opinions.

Sometimes grief can be felt physically. Sadness can be like a pain inside you. It can actually hurt to think of all you have lost. And grief can feel like fear, making your stomach turn over. These feelings do pass in time.

There may be times when everything seems just too much to take. Many people who have lost someone very close to them do, at certain times, feel that life is unbearable and think about ending it. Not because they want to die but because they feel that the strain and distress is so great and it feels as if it will never get any better. These periods of deep depression do pass. Adolescence is a time when your emotions can change rapidly from day to day. This change of how you feel is something that also happens when you are grieving, and the combination of these two forces within you at the same period of your life can lead to quite rapid swings of mood. If you feel depressed and can't talk about it at home, do go and see your doctor. There may be a Child and Adolescent Guidance Clinic, or Counselling Service, in your area. Being able to tell someone what is going on can help a great deal.

Your place in the family

If you are an only or the eldest child in your family you may find that your

41

mother naturally turns to you for support at this sad time. Younger brothers and sisters may also want to talk about what has happened.

"Well, thank goodness your mother has got you to help her." It can be rather a frightening prospect suddenly to be seen as the one who looks after someone, instead of being the one who is looked after.

Because your father has died, it does not mean that you will not have all the same needs as any other teenager. You still need to find yourself and to work gradually towards the point when eventually you are able to leave home and build a life for yourself. If people are depending on you for support this can be a difficult period, when it may seem as if your needs and those of your family are very different.

Grandparents and older brothers and sisters can be a great help at this time as can all relatives and close family friends who live near you. Sometimes they can help by just talking to you and your mother; sometimes by doing practical jobs in the home until you are all beginning to feel a little stronger again. In the early days quite a lot of people offer help of one kind or another. At this time it can be hard to know what you need. Don't be afraid to ask if you feel there is something they could do that you know would help your family.

When an important member of the family dies there are always quite a few jobs and tasks to be shared out among the remaining members. Some of these you may be able to take on alongside your work at school. Even little children can help if they are encouraged to do so by making their beds and tidying their rooms. At times all of you may feel tired out. Until a new pattern is built up this is a very exhausting time for all of you.

Fathers have a unique place in the family. They may be the main wage-earner or the person who made the rules. Your father may have been a major part of your growing up, perhaps encouraging you at sport or school or sharing a hobby with you. Or maybe he was away from home a lot but was still very important in your life. Even if you did not always get on well with him, as sometimes happens for a time with teenagers and their fathers, he was still part of you.

Your father will have been important to different members of your family in different ways. Your grandparents have lost a son and your uncles and aunts have lost a brother, so they too will be grieving. To your mother, your father was the person she had chosen to share her life with. As well as her husband, he may have been her colleague and best friend. When such a close partnership is ended by death, the loss can seem overwhelming. Even if the relationship went through bad patches, as is likely to happen sometimes, or even ended in separation or divorce, the loss can still be devastating and cause many painful and confused feelings.

In the first months everyone who knew and loved your father will be deeply affected by what has happened. Like you, they may feel sad, numb, angry or guilty. Some people, however sad they are feeling, try to hide their feelings. Others need to cry and talk about the past, again and again. We need to accept that everyone grieves in their own way, and at their own pace.

School or College

Except for the holidays, school makes up quite a large part of each day. You may find it a relief to go somewhere where everything is going on just as normal;

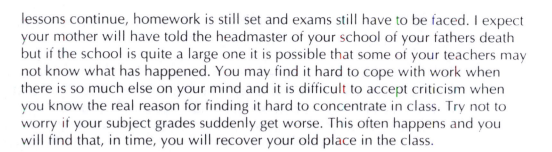

lessons continue, homework is still set and exams still have to be faced. I expect your mother will have told the headmaster of your school of your fathers death but if the school is quite a large one it is possible that some of your teachers may not know what has happened. You may find it hard to cope with work when there is so much else on your mind and it is difficult to accept criticism when you know the real reason for finding it hard to concentrate in class. Try not to worry if your subject grades suddenly get worse. This often happens and you will find that, in time, you will recover your old place in the class.

If you do not feel you can approach a particular teacher yourself, ask a friend to do it for you or, better still, ask your mother to write a letter to your form teacher. When you go into a higher class it is also worth making sure that your new teacher is aware of what has happened.

I am sure that, out of all the teachers you have one or two will be only too willing to talk if you feel you would like to do so. Your school may have a school counsellor whom you could see.

It does help enormously to talk to someone about how you feel and about any difficulties you may be facing. If you feel like crying please do remember that this is not a sign of weakness, it is a natural way of letting feelings come out and showing how sad you are and it often helps other people to show their sympathy for you. People are often worried about talking about it with you in case they upset you or say the wrong thing.

Friends and how you can help them to help you

It can seem that friends quickly forget what has happened to you. In some way this is a help because when you are with them you can forget too. If they are close friends they do not really forget just as you cannot forget either. In a way they are waiting for you to show them how they can help. Of course, the most important thing they can do is just to be there and continue to include you in their lives.

When they heard about your father all of them must have asked themselves, "Suppose it was my father, what would I have done?" It will have made them think very hard about you and what you are going through and about themselves and their own parents. You may not want to bring the subject up with them but if you do I am sure they will have a lot of things to say and will want to know what you are feeling.

Seeing them with their fathers and hearing them talk about them can be very painful for a while. At times you may feel very different from them and in a way, this way only, you are. However hard they try there is no way they can really understand what it is like to lose a parent unless they too have lost one. You are not really alone. In Britain today there are 200,000 children under the age of sixteen who have lost a parent by death.

Life Changes

The years between 11 and 18 are times of great change. During them we pass from the relative security of the small primary school to the larger secondary one and from there onto further education or into a job.

During these years you will be asked to make decisions. What do you want to do when you leave school? What subjects should be given up and which carried

on? And there will be exams to be taken, each one seeming to carry with it more importance as the terms pass.

This is a time of physical change as you grow from childhood into being an adult. Again there are decisions to be faced. When should you start going out with members of the opposite sex? How late should you be allowed to stay out at night? How do you balance your time between friendships and the need for school work and helping in the home? As you change, so will the relationship between you and your mother. You are both learning a new set of rules and trying to find solutions to these new problems that arise.

All adolescents face these changes, but you may find that others arise in your life after the death of your father.

Your mother may decide that it is necessary to move home to be nearer relatives or à new job. There may be less money now to live on, and money may be needed to pay someone to help look after younger children if your mother goes out to work. As well as coping with her grief, your mother may get very tired if she is doing a job as well as running the home and trying to do the things your father did.

Your mother may find that, like other widowed people, her friendships will change now that she is a "single" person once more. As well as her existing friends, she will begin to make new friendships with other single people. Some of these may be men. You and your brothers and sisters may find that you have mixed feelings over these new relationships. Do try to discuss how you feel with your mother.
The whole of the first year of bereavement is one of change as everyone tries to find a way of living in very different circumstances. At times you may feel that there is a conflict between the changes you need to make in your life and the needs of your family. An example of this may be if you have reached the point in your life when you wish to leave home, but are worried about the effect this may have on your family. This is where older friends and relatives may be able to help you reach a decision.

Memories

Make sure you have something special of your father's to remember him by; perhaps a watch, a pen or a pipe, something that makes you think particularly of him. Looking at photographs of him may make you feel a little sad now but later on you will be so glad that you have them. In the first year that follows your father's death, each birthday and anniversary can bring back sad memories and make all of you in your family miss him. Later on it is easier to remember the happier times, the things you used to do together. It is hard to believe in the early months that anything good can come out of so much sadness and distress but often, when one member of the family is lost, the others join together in a very close and caring way. You will grow up and leave home knowing so much more about your feelings and yourself than others who have not been through bereavement. Your father has been with you for all your childhood and he will always remain a very important part of your growing up and your past. No one can ever take that from you.

If you feel it would help you to write to Cruse about any particular difficulty you may be facing, please do so.
Copies of this leaflet are available from Cruse House (see Useful Addresses in Sec. 3).

TEENAGERS 1.13

By the Compassionate Friends

The teenage years reveal a multitude of emotions. Due to the release or increase of hormones in the body at this time, the see-saw emotions have a very unsettling effect upon both the teenagers and their families. There is the struggle for independence, the difficulties of relationships all round, and adolescents can be agonizingly self-conscious. Every choice and decision is of monumental importance, and beset by perpetual consideration of "what the others will think". Given the tensions that can be present in a family with teenagers, they often only feel at ease with their friends, the gang, the group. For teenagers who are also struggling with bereavement and grief, life can seen insurmountably difficult and painful. Some teenagers are well supported by their friends at a time of bereavement, but others may feel themselves isolated from everyone around them - unable to turn to the family from whom they are trying to separate, and unsupported by their friends who do not know how to help them.

Friends

Their friends may make jokes about death and everything surrounding it, simply as a way of dealing with something they do not understand. They do not know how to comfort, and their bereaved friend might not know how to accept any comfort that was offered. So it is a time of conflicting emotions, with something like an emotional tug-of-war taking place within them.

Boys may feel it is not masculine to be affected by grief, that they have to put on a brave front and almost laugh it off with their friends; but this does not ease the torment of grief within them. (They may welcome the suggestion that they 'cry in the shower' and thus in privacy).

Girls may find their friends' chatter about clothes and make-up and boys desperately trivial in the face of their grief, but, as with the boys, their friends may not know how to respond to the situation or how to comfort and support them.

Communication

The bereaved teenager may seek refuge from grief by turning to alternative preoccupation in an effort to shut themselves off from the pain and confusion of their emotions and the sadness within the family. These preoccupations may be sports, clothes or music. Some may retreat into their headphones or spend hours on the telephone or seek to stay away from the home. Some may turn to alcohol or drugs to dull the pain and avoid acute feelings. This apparent denial can be upsetting to those around them.

Other youngsters will want to help and protect their parents, and may shoulder responsibilities beyond their years. Some take on 'parental roles', others seek to carry out the responsibilities of their older brother or sister. Teenagers may postpone their own grieving in an effort to help those around them. They may then come to their grief when those others have moved ahead, and find themselves 'out of step'.

The difficulties may not only lie within the teenager - many parents find it difficult to communicate with their teenage offspring. In some families the bereavement may help parents and teenagers to talk with each other, but in others it may become a barrier.

Try to involve them in the discussions and decisions that necessarily take place at this time - about the funeral, about their brother or sister's room, their belongings, about Christmas, birthdays, and other special occasions. They will have their own views and feelings about all of these, and due consideration needs to be given to them.

It can be helpful too if your teenage son or daughter has another adult outside the family to whom they can talk freely and unburden themselves; they may even welcome someone who can act as go-between or 'interpreter' for them to their family (and vice versa).

Talking to other adults around them, such as teachers, club or sports leaders, employers, doctor or minister, may be a way in which you (or others) can help them.

TCF publishes a wide range of leaflets, including some that are helpful to the family, friends and others. They are listed on the back cover.

Survival guilt and other stresses

Teenagers can experience 'survival guilt' (feeling that they should have died instead of their brother or sister); can be aware if their parents' marriage is under stress; and be conscious that their dead brother or sister may have been put on a pedestal. Any of these concerns will add to their turmoil and distress. 1Some relief can come through talking openly about them; this may be with you, or with another trusted adult.

Concentration

As with younger children, concentration can diminish, and their performance - at school, college, work - may suffer. Their won expectations, and those of people around them, may need to be redefined (if temporarily) to allow them time to recover from the initial shock and grief. The knowledge that this will improve with time will be ann encouragement. (It might be necessary to consider whether to take imminent exams, or it may be appropriate for the head-teacher to write a letter to the examining body, explaining the situation.)

The meaning of life

The teenage years are often the time when very profound discussions take place as young people try to sort out for themselves the meaning of morality, ethics, spiritual issues, ideological standpoints, etc. The death of a brother or sister brings a sense of the reversal of nature and of expectations (which parents experience also). This can cause fear and confusion, and a sense of meaninglessness.

Discipline

Disciplining teenagers usually causes parents many 'headaches', but it is particularly difficult after a bereavement because of not knowing whether the problems are due to grief or whether they would have occurred anyway. There are no easy answers, as teenagers are so individual. Talking through the difficulties with other bereaved parents helps to defuse the situation and may produce some ideas on 'what to say' to the teenager or what action to take. It is also a way of releasing the stress within a parent.

Leaving home

Where there were two children and now there is one, it can be particularly difficult for that one to leave home - to go to college, to emigrate, to marry, even to go on holiday - knowing that their parents are now alone. For the parents, it can revive the feelings of bereavement. Talking this through together, recognising each other's needs and fears, deciding how contact will be maintained (by telephone, by letter, by visits) and how often, will help ease the difficulties of another separation.

Books and penfriends

Reading books where teenagers have expressed their feelings after a bereavement may help a teenager to feel less isolated. The TCF Postal Library has suitable books.

Contact with others in similar circumstances can also be reassuring and supportive. The TCF Newsletter has a penfriend section, and we are endeavouring to find other ways of offering support to bereaved sisters and brothers. If you have any suggestions, please do contact our National Office. (See Useful addresses, Sec.3).

The Compassionate Friends

BROTHERS' and SISTERS' CREED

We are the surviving siblings of The Compassionate Friends. We are brought together by the deaths of our brothers and sisters. Open your hearts to us, and have patience with us. Sometimes we will need the support of our friends. At other times we need our families to be there. Sometimes we must walk alone, taking our memories with us, continuing to become the individuals we want to be. We cannot be our dead brothers or sisters; however, a special part of them lives on with us.

When our brothers and sisters died, our lives changed. We are living a life very different from what we envisioned, and we feel the responsibility to be strong even when we feel weak. Yet we can go on because we understand better than many others the value of family and the previous gift of life. Our goal is not to be the forgotten mourners that we sometimes are, but to walk together to face our tomorrows as surviving siblings of the Compassionate Friends.

The Compassionate Friends - USA

PREPARATION FOR A CHILD'S FUNERAL

Suggestions for Parents

This has been written by members of The Compassionate Friends, an organisation of bereaved parents. Some of us wish that we had known, at the time of our child's death, of the choices available to us; with hindsight, we might have done things differently. This is not a detailed list of such choices, but some pointers along the way which you can think over, and then discuss with family and friends, and with your funeral director.

Take as much time as you need over making these choices — there is no reason to feel hurried; the decisions you make now will have long-lasting effects. You may wish to talk to others in your family, to a minister of religion, or other people outside the religious field.

The first choice you will have to make is between burial and cremation. (If you choose cremation, you do not have to make an immediate decision on the dispersal of the ashes.)

Following that decision, you may then want to choose what your child will be dressed in, and whether this is something you want to do yourself (with help), or would prefer others to do. If the funeral director is doing this, it will be helpful to give him a photograph of your son or daughter. You can ask for a lock of hair, or to have a photograph taken.

There is too the question of whether you want to see your child's body again, and whether others wish to do so. This can be very helpful in coming to accept the reality of what has happened. You may, where appropriate, want to place a favourite toy in the coffin, or your other children may wish to do so.

If you have young children you will want to discuss — with them or with others — whether they are to be present at the funeral. Children of all ages can take part in the discussions and arrangements at their own level.

A religious service is not a requirement, you can plan and shape the funeral that you want for your child. You may want to invite people who have been important in your child's life to lead the funeral; this could be a teacher, a leader in a voluntary organisation, a friend or employer. Forms of service, both religious and non-religious, can be made available to you by your funeral director.

Music and readings can be of your own choice, and you may like to have photographs of your child in the chapel. You may wish to suggest members of the family, or friends, as coffin-bearers; you may wish to do this yourself. You can ask your funeral director to list the names of those attending the funeral, and those who sent flowers.

Consideration can also be given to questions such as flowers, or charitable donations instead, to memorial funds and other similar ideas. There can be the possibility of a memorial or thanksgiving service which could take place some weeks or months later.

Discussing the possible alternatives, and making the choices that are necessary, can reduce the feelings of helplessness and loss of control that arise at this time. Your involvement in these decisions, painful as it is, will ultimately help you to mourn the death of your daughter or son.

You may be offered drugs or alcohol 'to help you through'. If you can manage without these it will be better, because using them can impede your ability to make important decisions, and delay the grieving process too.

This has been written in a brief and simple way, to help you to consider carefully something that none of us ever wanted to consider. It is intended to widen your horizons about the different ways of preparing a funeral so that it will be meaningful for your child, yourselves and your family.

(Further copies of this leaflet are available from the Society of Compassionate Friends.)

THE EFFECTS OF DISASTERS ON CHILDREN

1.15

William Yule
Professor of Applied Child Psychology
University of London Institute of Psychiatry
(co-author of wise before the Event - Coping with Crises in School)

Following major disasters, a high proportion of children experience a number of distressing reactions, including anxiety, fear, depression. It is now recognised that many show Post Traumatic Stress Disorder and without treatment such disorders can last for a considerable time.

Schools get directly and indirectly involved in the aftermath of many disasters. At Aberfan in 1966, 116 children and 28 adults died when a huge coal slip slid on to the school. 143 primary school children survived. Schools can be directly involved when there are life threatening fires, fatal accidents in the playground, road traffic accidents involving children walking to and from school or during school journeys. Many of us recall our distress when learning of the party of children swept off the rocks in Cornwall, those who slid to their deaths on a skiing trip in Austria, or the 400 children and teachers who survived the sinking of the cruise ship Jupiter in 1988, 22 years to the day after Aberfan.

Children get caught up in other mass disasters outside school - in the stands at Bradford football stadium, watching the crush at the Hillsborough football ground, travelling on the Herald of Free Enterprise, living in towns like Lockerbie where major accidents happen. Sadly, they can also be the direct victims of malicious events such as the shootings in the school at Hungerford.

It is important that teaching staff prepare themselves to deal with the emotional aftermath of such disasters. The large, dramatic ones fortunately happen infrequently; smaller ones happen with great regularity.

Recent studies find that teachers report less psychopathology among child survivors than do parents, and that both report far less than the children themselves. One reason for the failure to recognize and report the severity of the effects of disasters on children is the understandable but misplaced reaction of adults who do not want to consider the horrors the children have faced. After some disasters, people in authority have prevented researchers interviewing children; schools have ignored the event or paid it cursory attention, arguing that children are getting over it and no good is done by bringing it all up again. The result is that children quickly learn not to unburden themselves to teachers who then take a long time to link the drop off in standards of work and impaired concentration with the intrusive thoughts the children are experiencing.

Based on my own recent studies of child survivors (under 16 years) from the Herald of Free Enterprise and 334 teenagers from the "Jupiter", the following are some of the common reactions shown in the first few months after such life-threatening disasters:

SLEEP DISTURBANCE Almost all children have major sleep problems in the first few weeks. They reported fears of the dark, fear of being alone, intrusive thoughts when things are quiet, bad dreams, nightmares, waking through the night. Problems persisted over many months. Use of music to divert thoughts helped.

SEPARATION DIFFICULTIES Initially, most wanted to be physically close to their surviving parents, often sleeping in the parental bed over the first few weeks. Some distressed parents found their clinginess difficult to cope with.

CONCENTRATION DIFFICULTIES During the day, children had major problems concentrating on school work. When it was silent in the classroom they had intrusive memories of what had happened to them.

MEMORY PROBLEMS They also had problems remembering new material, or even some old skills such as reading music.

INTRUSIVE THOUGHTS All were troubled by repetitive thoughts about the accident. These occurred at any time, although often triggered off by environmental stimuli — e.g., movement on a bus, noise of glass smashing, sound of rushing water, sight of tables laid out like the ship's cafeteria. Thoughts intruded when they were otherwise quiet.

TALKING WITH PARENTS Many did not want to talk about their feelings with their parents so as not to upset the adults. Thus, parents were often unaware of the details of the children's suffering, although they could see they were in difficulty. There was often a great sense of frustration between parents and children.

TALKING WITH PEERS At some points, survivors felt a great need to talk over their experiences with peers. Unfortunately, the timing was often wrong. Peers held back from asking in case they upset the survivor further; the survivor often felt rejected.

HEIGHTENED ALERTNESS TO DANGERS Most were wary of all forms of transport — not willing to put their safety into anyone else's hands. They were more aware of other dangers. They were affected by reports of other disasters.

FORESHORTENED FUTURE Many felt they should live each day to the full and not plan far ahead. They lost trust in long term planning.

FEARS Most had fears of travelling by sea and air. Many had fears of swimming, of the sound of rushing water. Most of the new fears were specifically related to their recent bad experiences rather than being just a general increase in fearfulness.
It helps to say to children that they are experiencing normal reactions to an abnormal situation. Of course, one must also constantly remember that other disorders may also follow a disaster — particularly anxiety disorders and depression, the latter when bereavement has occurred.

Some Developmental Issues

Younger children may show all sorts of regressive behaviour or anti-social behaviour. There are many reports of children repeatedly drawing what they experienced or incorporating it in their play. Parents may avoid talking to the child about what happened, mistakenly thinking they will not remember or understand. However, even 4 year olds can sometimes describe vividly what they had experienced, much to their parents' surprise. Some pre-school children have very adult concepts of death and dying and it is important that we remember the range of individual differences in cognitive awareness when discussing (or not discussing) the effects of disasters with children.

Children over 10 years of age have usually a very good understanding that their lives were threatened. Young teenagers often report a sense of foreshortened future — what is the point of planning anything when the fates can be so capricious? This realisation is very difficult for parents to cope with.

Indeed, parents are often at a loss to know how best to react.
If they were directly affected by the same disaster, they are having to cope with their own reactions at the same time as trying to support their children. Following the Australian bush fires, McFarlane (1987) found that 8 months on, the families showed increased levels of conflict, irritability, and withdrawal, with maternal overprotection quite common. The

adjustment of the parents themselves was an important determinant of the adjustment of the children. In particular, he comments that "...families who did not share their immediate reactions to disaster may have had more trouble with their long-term adjustment ... and experienced a greater degree of estrangement". Equally important, the child's reaction to the fire affected the adjustment of the family, emphasizing the reciprocal interactions among members of a family system.

Teenagers who survived the Herald of Free Enterprise capsize often found it very hard to share their feelings with their parents. They would go out of the house a lot to avoid talking about it. Parents were often frustrated that they wanted to reach out to their children but did not know how to. Behaviourally, the children looked as if they had developed lots of interests outside the home; in reality, they were avoiding dealing with the effects of the trauma.

When children have returned from a traumatic school outing, they may well have enormous problems concentrating in class and in doing their homework. If they are not sleeping properly, all this gets exacerbated. Children are sensitized to a wide variety of stimuli, mention of which may trigger an emotional reaction, as in the child who had to read about the evacuation from Dunkirk. Teachers need to make arrangements for child survivors to leave the classroom when such events occur.

For example, children returning to a very caring school after the sinking of the Jupiter entered a geography classroom where the walls were covered with projects on "great disasters of the world". Their upset was immediate and the connection obvious. Less obvious was the pressure put on a boy whose GCSE project had not survived the sinking of the Herald. Unable to concentrate on new learning, he was still pressurised to rewrite his missing project, until the problem was drawn to the school's attention. The teacher had, understandably, focused more on the impending exams than the current problems and these were then very quickly resolved. Overall, children who survived the "Jupiter" sinking performed significantly less well academically over the following two years, with the less able children taking longer to recover.

Teachers need to be aware, too, of the reactions of other pupils towards the survivors. One eight year old suffered silently for weeks after a classmate said, "I wish you'd died in the ferry". A 12 year old girl had to cope with taunts about being orphaned. These episodes only came to light during a group run for the child survivors (Yule and Williams, 1990).

Treatment Needs

In the immediate aftermath, children usually need to be reunited with their parents and family. Even teenagers may go back to sleeping in their parents bed. Tolerance and understanding are called for. Survivors need to talk over what happened so as get the sequence of events clear in their minds as well as to master the feelings that recall engenders. Repetitive retelling is not enough alone. Professionals can help by creating a relatively safe environment in which such recounting can take place. Experiencing that the world does not come to an end when feelings are shared can be very facilitating. Learning that other survivors share similar, irrational guilt about surviving can help to get things in perspective. Learning how to deal with anxiety attacks, how to identify trigger stimuli, how to take each day as it comes — all are important therapeutic tasks.

However, these things should not be left to chance. Mental health professionals are rapidly learning that formal psychological debriefing can help victims of disaster. Ayalon (1988) emphasizes the need to help children make sense of what happened to them and to gain mastery over their feelings. To this end, many practitioners agree that children should be treated in small groups. They might be asked to write detailed accounts of their experience and to be helped to cope with the emotions that brings up. In addition, they may need specific treatment for fears, phobias and any other avoidant behaviours. They should get practical help with sleep disorders. Given that intrusive thoughts seemed worse at night just before dropping off to sleep, I advised many children to use portable tape-recorders to play music to distract them and blot out the thoughts. With better sleep, they were better able to face the thoughts in the safety of daylight.

Conclusions

Events of recent years have forced on us an awareness of the emotional effects of disasters on children. It is clear that children as young as 8 years can suffer PTSD that is almost identical in form to that presented by adults. The effects can go on for one to two years, and cannot be considered transitory. Parents and teachers often underestimate the anxiety reactions that children report. Normal screening instruments will not pick up all the psychopathology.

There are developmental changes in children's reactions, but as so few young children have been studied, we cannot yet be clear of the nature of these changes. Children's reactions are intimately bound up with effects on the family, but some distress is directly caused by the trauma. Teachers, especially, need guidance on how to deal with the aftermath in schools. There is a great need for good treatment studies. Because disasters occur unexpectedly, we need to plan in advance how to conduct and evaluate all forms of intervention.

REFERENCES

Ayalon, 0.(1988) Rescue! Community Oriented Preventive Education for Coping with Stress. Haifa: Nord Publications

McFarlane, A. C.(1987) Family functioning and overprotection following a natural disaster: The longitudinal effects of post-traumatic morbidity. Australian and New Zealand Journal of Psychiatry 21:-210

McFarlane, A. C., Policansky, S., Irwin, C. P. (1987) A longitudinal study of the psychological morbidity in children due to a natural disaster. Psychological Medicine 17:727-738

Raphael, B.(1986) When Disaster Strikes: A Handbook for the Caring Professions. London : Hutchinson

Yule, W. (1991) Work with children following disasters. Chapter in M. Herbert (Ed.) Clinical Child Psychology: Theory and Practice. Chichester: John Wiley.

Yule, W., Udwin, 0. and Murdoch, K. (1990) The "Jupiter" sinking: effects on children's fears, depression and anxiety. Journal of Child Psychology and Psychiatry, 31, 1051-1061.

Yule, W., Williams, R.(1990) Post traumatic stress reactions in children. Journal of Traumatic Stress, 3, 279-295.

THE MANAGEMENT OF TRAUMA AND BEREAVEMENT: an INSTITUTIONAL RESPONSE 1.16

John Shears
Head Teacher, The Streetly School

STREETLY SCHOOL - 11 - 19 co-educational county comprehensive school of 1100 pupils in Streetly which lies on the eastern edge of the Walsall M.B. The catchment area could be described as a N.E. suburb of Birmingham and is of mainly middle class owner occupiers.

TRAGEDY and TRAUMA

> In life there are occasional moments that remain with you for ever. Many of my generation can remember vividly what they were doing at the moment in time of :
>> the Manchester United aircrash at Munich
>> the assassination of John F. Kennedy.
>
> To me, October 2lst 1988 will live on in the same way.

At midnight on the Thursday evening (October 20) 20 excited children and two teachers plus one other adult left Streetly School for the experience of a lifetime - a week long cruise of the Eastern Mediterranean. Eighteen months of planning and much saving had gone into preparing for the cruise which was to take place over the following half-term week. With pupils from two other Walsall schools, the party left Gatwick and flew to Athens where they transferred to the port of Piraeus and embarked on the S.S. Jupiter in the early evening of Friday October 2lst. One mile out of Piraeus harbour, the S.S. Jupiter was in collision with an Italian freighter just at the moment when the pupils were in the large dining room being briefed. The vessel sank within twenty minutes. Thanks to an outstanding rescue effort some 470 persons were saved, but sadly two Greek seamen, Bernard Butt a teacher from T.P.Riley School, Walsall and a 14 year old pupil Vivienne Barley from Streetly School were lost, presumed drowned. No bodies were ever found.

The news broke to me at about 7 o'clock on the Friday evening when a parent rang to inform me of a newsflash on Channel Four of the sinking of the S.S. Jupiter. An emergency procedure was instituted but getting through on the telephone was very difficult. The local police set up a network as well linking to the British Embassy in Athens. The evening was spent by the telephone trying to calm and re-assure parents. Much was shown on the - television news but information was confused. By ten o'clock my teacher in charge of the cruise party had telephoned to say 18 of our pupils were safe but at that time two were unaccounted for. An hour later another pupil was found in the local hospital but no one had seen Vivienne.

To make the situation worse, the Barley family had seen a news item on the sinking and were convinced they had seen Vivienne being helped ashore. A long evening of telephone calls went on into the early hours when I was able to confirm to most parents that all was well. At 3 a.m. after many searches, I was given the news that Vivienne could not be found. With a police officer friend, I visited the Barley's and together we went to Central Television in Birmingham to check the news footage in the hope that it was Vivienne coming ashore. Sadly it was not to be.

The following day was spent preparing for the pupils' return. Much of the time was given over to supporting parents and trying to shelter them from the unreasonable attention of the media.

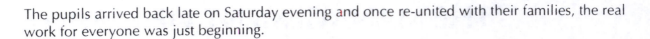

The pupils arrived back late on Saturday evening and once re-united with their families, the real work for everyone was just beginning.

MANAGEMENT STRATEGIES -

The school now had a duty to meet a vast range of very different needs:

- Pupils on the Cruise
- Staff on the Cruise
- Parents of cruise pupils
- The Barley family and 12 year old brother, Alastair, at the school
- Close friends of Vivienne
- Pupils and staff at the school
- the local community

all had needs to be provided for.

Some of the early concerns included:

PUPILS on CRUISE - emotion, anxiety associated with trauma and bereavement. Lack of concentration, nightmares, fear of water.

STAFF on CRUISE - Deep guilt and feeling of failure, especially by the man who did not have to enter the water.

PARENTS - Feelings of guilt on letting their children go. Did not understand their children's emotions. Anger, Sad at what seemed a sudden loss of childhood.

BARLEY FAMILY - Obvious emotion at the loss.
and
VIVIENNE'S FRIENDS

PUPILS/STAFF
LOCAL COMMUNITY - Lacked information, unsure how to respond?

The good fortune of the half-term, created a little space for planning. It allowed some very immediate needs to be met and some family healing to take place. It was clear, however that the tragedy had to be managed sensibly and sensitively. During half-term the school's senior management team met and devised a strategy:
Several important decisions were taken:

1. INFORM EVERYONE
2. ESTABLISH KEYWORKERS
3. Try to be NORMAL

In order to make the decisions work, a number of strategies had to be implemented.

1. A STAFF MEETING was held in half-term. This was used to:
   - accurately inform of the tragedy
   - explain the system of CARE being established
   - stress the importance of normality
   - establish guidelines so that not everyone was counselling, guiding, caring as that could lead to well intentioned difficulties and confusion.
   - to offer advice on what to do in practical terms
   e.g. how to manage, tears, hysteria.....

2. A PARENTS MEETING was also held in half-term. The LEA were able to supply a social worker, an educational and clinical psychologist. Parents and children on the cruise were given good information on what is "normal" in trauma and how to help their children and how to seek help. Children need to be allowed to show emotion. Their lives would never be the same.

3. The senior management team re-adjusted some roles to create time for the Head and Deputy to take on their new tasks. The S.M.T, also took a high profile and a crucial one in ensuring that the school functioned well. The plan was to cancel nothing and to keep a busy school running.

4. The pupils on the cruise were seen together. A strong bonding had developed and they were told -
    a)   of the KEYWORKER IDEA
    b)   of the "FLAT" - a quiet, comfortable place to use whenever necessary
    c)   that they would experience all sorts of emotions and anxieties and this is normal.
    d)   Psychologists offered help, and suggestions were made on how to face the problems that might develop.

They then chose a KEYWORKER.

The success of the strategy depended on the KEYWORKER. Pupils had to chose, because mutual trust, respect, care were essential. Appointing keyworkers would not have been so successful. Even with this there were problems. One young teacher was chosen by 6 pupils - she could not cope. The aim was no more than 2 cruise pupils to a keyworker, and ideally only one: it was to be a draining experience. The keyworker had to be always available and a system was needed for this. The keyworker liaised with the Deputy Head who could then seek professional advice or just communicate to other staff as appropriate. The focus role of the Deputy allowed a whole overview and enabled common problems to be tackled jointly.

The flat - a part of the Home Economics suite, was to be very valuable. It was made cosy - coffee, tea was available. It was in a quiet part of school. It was manned by a cover teacher so if a pupil arrived they could be calmed and then their keyworker fetched. The cover teacher looked after the class while the keyworker looked after the pupil in the flat. Early on, the flat was used a lot as pupils needed to find some space and to escape for a little while. It was not abused and most pupils once through a bad spell went back to lessons. Pupils needed a lot of support and reassurance. Often this came from others on the cruise - there was much peer support. The flat became a meeting place - fears, anxieties shared and talked through. Issues were brought to our attention and professional help sought when appropriate.

On the Monday after half-term when school returned, a series of assemblies were held in the morning at which;
    a)   Accurate information was given. The media had created a number of "myths" about the sinking.
    b)   Pupils were told of the need for sensitivity. They were briefed on asking questions, jokes, the value of talking ...... Permission was given to grieve, but advice was supplied so that a bout of morose hysteria did not set in. Schools must allow their pupils to express their grief, but it requires delicate handling. They had to be told that being normal, happy etc. at this time was not wrong.
    c)   Advice was given on how best to help friends and peer group healing was crucial.
    d)   Prayers were said for Vivienne and the Barley family as well as in thanks fore the safe return of the rest of the group.

The management strategy chosen meant a heavy investment of time, but in a caring community such as ours it was freely given. For a time there was a steady use of the flat and the keyworkers as well as a series of regular meetings for pupils and parents with professionals to

assist with relaxation, sleep, concentration spans, emotions and so on. By the late Spring a clear pattern had emerged:

1. Some children appeared to have mended. They naturally took on a supportive role in the group.
2. Many children had good spells and regression.
3. Vivienne's friends found her loss hard to take.
4. Keyworkers were able to relax their involvement and the flat was less used for "meetings" - only occasionally for an individual.

Some eighteen months on, there is still need for support. 15 of the group appear to be through the worst of the trauma, as do most of Vivienne's classmates. Three of the 20 need occasional help. The flat is no longer in use and the role of keyworkers is now minimal. Two of the children are having psychological support and their problems are longer term. It is interesting to note that their parents were the most difficult in coming to terms with the trauma, and for a long time refused their children permission to grieve. Too often they were told - "come on, snap out of it, you are alright"!

It is important to allow children to show emotion and feelings - if these can be channelled into a constructive role, all the better. Memorials, tree planting etc can all help. At the request of the family, an evening of Music and Dance was arranged: Vivienne was a keen singer. This enabled a lot of children and adults to be involved in a moving tribute, but one that emphasised the positive. This was followed some months later by a small service in the school, when Vivienne's class unveiled a plaque as their special tribute. They had raised the funds and they contributed readings to the occasion. Vivienne Barley lives on in our memory and despite the sadness of her loss, the care that has shone through the experience has made the school community a stronger one.

THE SIXTH OF MARCH 1987   1.17

For this article, I did not need to use notes to help me plan it out, because all the information that I needed was still very vivid in my mind. It is about the night of Friday, the sixth March 1987, the night when the 'Herald of Free Enterprise' (owned by Townsend Thoresen) sank off the coast of Belgium, along with my Father, who was a forty-one year old steward (he worked in the kiosk where the magazines and confectionery were sold).

My Mother's friend told me after the tragedy what my Father was doing in the last few moments of his life. She knew because she worked in the Bureau de Change, which was just opposite where my Father worked. She said that at the time the ship capsized, everyone on my Father's shift was getting ready to go up to the messroom for their evening meal (this was at about a quarter to seven) and my Father was explaining to Linda (the woman who took over from my Father) that the till was not working properly. That was the last thing she remembered until she was rescued.

Meanwhile, at about ten to seven, I was upstairs doing my homework. My Mother was downstairs doing the ironing. Then there was a newsflash on the radio, saying that a ferry had hit a sandbank in the Channel, nobody was sure which one it was, and that all the emergency services had been put on red alert; more news at seven o'clock. My Mother just carried on with the ironing; she did not really think twice about it.

At seven o'clock, I was still doing my homework, and the news came on. They said the ferry concerned was the "Herald of Free Enterprise", and it had capsized. My Mother screamed, "Oh my God!" and dropped the iron. I rushed downstairs, and she told me what had happened.

We tried to phone anyone that we knew, but of course, everyone was trying to phone out at once, and the lines were overloaded. Eventually, my Mother got through to my auntie in Sittingbourne. My auntie knew what had happened as she had watched the Channel Four news. She and my uncle drove down to our house, and they stayed all night keeping my Mother company and praying for news of my Father. Nobody slept that night.

The next day was the longest of my life. My Mother's friend went over to Ramsgate to fetch my Gran and also took my Mother down to the Townsend Thoresen offices to try and find out if my Father had been rescued. My Gran stayed with me and we watched videos of old comedy shows. It did not cheer us up, of course.

At one o'clock in the morning on Sunday, the doorbell rang. Two policemen stood there. One slowly told my Mother that there had been no news, and he was missing, presumed dead. My most vivid memory of that night is of hearing my Mother crying herself to sleep.

My Father's body was flown back to England, and his funeral took place on the eighteenth of April 1987. Surprisingly, I cannot remember much about it, only the coffin covered in a Union Jack.

This March it will be three years since it happened, and I like to think that I am almost over the tragedy. My Mother became anorexic afterwards, but with medical help and much support of friends and relatives, she had now almost recovered to her old self. We both still cry when the pictures come up on the television, and dearly wish that Anthony Graham Spink was still with us today.

Pupil at Dover Girls Grammar School

Coping with a major personal crisis

cruse – bereavement care

126 Sheen Road
Richmond, Surrey TW9 1UR

Tel: 081-940 4818
Fax: 081-940 7638

Patron Her Majesty The Queen

Where to find help

Your Family Doctor.

The Social Services Department of your Local Council.

Cruse — Bereavement Care
126 Sheen Road
Richmond
Surrey TW9 1UR
Tel: 081-940 4818
and branches nationwide.

Local Representatives of:
British Red Cross
Relate
Samaritans

Your Citizens Advice Bureau will have the addresses of these and other voluntary organisations that can help you.

This leaflet was first produced in Australia and various versions have been issued after recent major disasters in this country. It is aimed to help people affected by disaster or violent and sudden loss. We hope it will also help anyone faced with a major personal crisis.

Cruse — Bereavement Care is a national charity dependent on voluntary contributions Many of its services are provided entirely free. It helps anyone who has been bereaved, through counselling, advice and social contact. There are over 175 Branches nationwide. Cruse welcomes donations from all who can afford it and can provide further details of gifts by covenant or legacies. These ways of giving enable us to continue to offer

When to seek help

1. If you feel you cannot handle intense feelings or body sensations.

   If you feel that your emotions are not falling into place over a period of time, you feel chronic tension, confusion, emptiness or exhaustion.

2. If after a month you continue to feel numb and empty and do not have the appropriate feeling described.

   If you have to keep active in order not to feel.

3. If you continue to have nightmares and poor sleep.

4. If you have no person or group with whom to share your emotions and you feel the need to do so.

5. If your **relationships** seem to be suffering badly, or **sexual problems develop.**

6. If you have **accidents.**

7. If you continue to **smoke, drink** or take **drugs to excess since the event.**

8. If your **work** performance suffers.

9. If you note that those around you are particularly vulnerable or are not healing satisfactorily.

10. If as a helper you are suffering exhaustion..

DO **REMEMBER** THAT YOU ARE BASICALLY THE SAME PERSON THAT YOU WERE BEFORE THE EVENT.

DO **REMEMBER** THAT THERE IS A LIGHT AT THE END OF THE TUNNEL.

DO **REMEMBER** THAT IF YOU SUFFER TOO MUCH OR TOO LONG, HELP IS AVAILABLE.

Coping with a major personal crisis

Someone close to you may have died. You may have been injured yourself or you may have witnessed the death and injury of others. Your experience was a very personal one but this leaflet will help you to know how others have reacted in similar situations. It will also show how you can help normal healing to occur and to avoid some pitfalls.

Normal feelings and emotions you may experience

Fear — of damage to yourself and those you love.
— of being left alone, of having to leave loved ones.
— of 'breaking down' or 'losing control'.
— of a similar event happening again.

Helplessness — Crises show up human powerlessness as well as strength.

Sadness — for deaths, injuries and losses of every kind.

Longing — for all that has gone.

Guilt — for being better off than others, i.e. being alive, not injured, having things.
— regrets for things not done.

Shame — for having been exposed as helpless, 'emotional' and needing others.
— for not having reacted as one would have wished.

Anger — at what has happened, at whoever caused it or allowed it to happen.
— at the injustice and senselessness of it all.
— at the shame and indignities.
— at the lack of proper understanding by others and their inefficiencies.
— WHY ME?

Memories — of feelings, of loss or of love for the other people in your life who have been injured or died.

Let Down — disappointment for all the plans that cannot be fulfilled.

Hope — for the future, for better times.

Everyone has these feelings after a disaster and they are normal. Nature heals through allowing their expression. They usually last only a short period at any one time and can be controlled in an emergency. Experience has shown that they may be particularly strong if many people died; their deaths were sudden or violent or if no body was recovered. Feelings do not lead to loss of control of the mind but blocking them may lead to nervous and physical problems. **Do remember**, crying can give relief.

Physical and mental sensations

You may feel bodily sensations with or without the feelings described. Sometimes they are due to the crisis, even if they develop many months after the event.

Some common sensations are tiredness, sleeplessness, bad dreams, fuzziness of the mind including loss of memory and concentration, dizziness, palpitations, shakes, difficulty in breathing, choking in the throat and chest, nausea and diarrhoea, muscular tension which may lead to pain e.g. headaches, neck and backaches, dragging in the womb, menstrual disorders, changes in sexual interest.

Family and social relationships

New friendships and group bonds may come into being. On the other hand, strains in existing relationships may appear. The good feelings in giving and receiving may be replaced by conflict. You may feel that too little or the wrong things are offered, or that you cannot give as much as is expected. Accidents are more frequent after severe stress. Alcohol and drug intake may increase due to the extra tension.

The following make the event and the feelings about it easier to bear

Numbness — Your mind may allow the misfortune to be felt only slowly. At first you may feel numb. The event may seem unreal, like a dream, something that has not really happened. People often see this wrongly either as 'being strong' or 'uncaring'.

Activity — Be active. Helping others may give some relief. However, over activity is detrimental if it diverts attention from the help you need for yourself.

Reality — Confronting the reality, by attending funerals, inspecting losses, returning to the scene, will all help you come to terms with the event.

Going over the event — As you allow the disaster more into your mind, there is a need to **think** about it, to **talk** about it, and at night to **dream** about it over and over again. Children play and draw about the event.

Support — It can be a relief to receive other people's physical and emotional support. Sharing with others who have had similar experiences can help.

Privacy — In order to deal with feeling, you may find it necessary at times to be alone, or just with family and close friends.

Healing

Activity and numbness (blocking of feelings) may be over-used and may delay your healing.

Remember that the pain of the wound leads to healing. You may even come out wiser and stronger

Some Do's and Don'ts

DON'T bottle up feelings.

DO express your emotions and let your children share in the grief.

DON'T avoid talking about what happened.

DO take every opportunity to review the experience.

DO allow yourself to be part of a group of people who care.

DON'T expect the memories to go away — the feelings will stay with you for a long time to come.

DON'T forget that children experience similar feelings.

DO take time out to sleep, rest, think and be with your close family and friends.

DO express your needs clearly and honestly to family, friends and officials.

DO try to keep your life as normal as possible after the acute grief.

DO let children talk about their emotions and express themselves in games and drawings.

DO send your children back to school and let them keep up with their activities.

DO make sure their teacher knows what has happened.

DO DRIVE MORE CAREFULLY.

DO BE MORE CAREFUL AROUND THE HOME.

Warning:

Accidents are more common after severe stresses

HELPING SCHOOLS TO DEAL WITH DEATH AND DYING

Adapted with permission from Sandra S. Fox Ph.D. "Good Grief Program (C) USA."

In order to facilitate an agreed approach to death and dying, schools need to plan the steps they will take and make sure staff are aware of them. To this end the following areas need to be considered.

Dissemination of Information

*   Is there one member of staff who will be responsible for putting a plan of action into motion?

*   Information about a death may come in an 'obvious' way, e.g. a letter to a Head of Year, or less directly, e.g. a remark by a pupil. In either case, does the recipient know to whom to pass the information?

*   Once information is received, how will members of teaching staff be told?

*   Who else in the school community should be told and how?

IMMEDIATE ACTION

*   What arrangements need to be made to allow teaching staff, students and others to express their feelings?

*   Who would be available to help those needing support?
    [Finding this out in advance often brings to light more resources in the school community than is immediately obvious].

*   Is there space in the school that could be used for groups to share feelings or individuals to talk one to one.

*   Is the school prepared to allow time to those who need it?

*   What realistic level of support can be offered at the end of the school day?

*   If the death is of a member of the school community, who will be responsible for dealing with any of their belongings and make sure appropriate written information is amended (lists, registers, etc.)?

FURTHER ACTION

*   What will the school's position be about students and/or staff attending a funeral in school time?

*   How can the school help students find an acceptable way to remember the life of someone who has died - is a formal or informal commemoration at the school appropriate?

*   How will the school deal with anniversaries of a particular death?

*   How will the school assist staff or students who are having difficulty in coming to terms with the death?

EVALUATION

*   How will the school assess how well their protocol responded to the needs that arose following a death that affected the school?

HOW ONE SCHOOL COPED WITH THE DEATH OF A STUDENT

A student, who I will call 'Peter'. from a school in West London, was knocked down crossing the road on the way home from school. He was taken to hospital critically injured and put on a life support machine.

The school was made aware of what had happened and the next day had to start a process that would enable staff and students to come to terms with Peter's accident (and probable death).

1. At the morning briefing, all the staff were told of what had happened and that many children would be upset - staff were asked to accept this but to ask for help if they felt they couldn't cope.

2. Pupils in the same year (yr 8) as 'Peter' were assembled together and told by the Year Head, supported by experienced staff, exactly what had happened and what 'Peter's' condition was, as far as we knew. Some of the students who were near the scene of the accident added their bits of the story. Many students were upset and shared their feelings with the staff.
    This took considerable time.

3. Other year groups also had assemblies and were told of 'Peter's' accident - they were also asked to be aware that some pupils, particularly in Yr 8, would be very upset during the day.

4. The year 8 pupils were then given a choice - they could either go with some of the staff to continue to talk about 'Peter' or they could go to their lessons (also if they chose to go to lessons but then got upset they could come back to the other group).

    About 30 students (from a year group of about 120) mostly close friends, and those from his tutor group, formed the group that did not go to lessons. Staff gave up free time, or offered to cover lessons for others, in order to be with this group. The year head offered their room as a suitable meeting place and cups of tea/coffee/fruit juice were rustled up.

    It became clear at this time that there were about 10 pupils in other year groups who the pupils felt should be allowed to join in. These pupils were identified and found in their lessons (many very upset) and most chose to join the group in the Year Head's room.

    Staff allowed the pupils to talk as they wanted, which they did volubly, and cried, and laughed and joked and reminded each other of Peter's exploits. They decided to make 'Get Well' cards for Peter - although they were aware that he was unlikely to live.

5. The school contacted the hospital, who said that many pupils had been to see 'Peter' and that some were still there - a few accompanied by parents but several who were not. A member of staff went to the hospital and sensitively sorted out who had parents with them, who had parental permission to be there, who wanted to go home and who

61

wanted to go back to school.

The hospital told this member of staff that Peter was brain dead and that they would take him off the machine in the afternoon.

(Many of the pupils who saw 'Peter' in hospital either on the night of the accident or the next day, said how helpful it had been for them.)

6. By lunchtime quite a few of the students in the year heads room decided they would return to lessons in the afternoon. A core of close friends of 'Peter' stayed and finished the messages and then started to make a tape recording to play to Peter in case he was in a coma.

7. Mid-afternoon the school re-contacted the hospital and were told that 'Peter' had been taken off the life support machine. All the students who were in the original group were collected together and told that Peter had died - this meant they knew what had happened before they went home and didn't have to rely on rumour.

    Enough time had been left for expressions of grief and for some messages of condolence to be put together for 'Peter's' parents.

    Staff offered to take home, or contact the parents of those pupils who were very upset. Staff also discussed with pupils when it would be best for them to visit 'Peter's' parents, phone them etc.

    The 'get well' messages were kept - later they were given to 'Peter's' parents.

8. A letter from the school expressing sorrow and support, along with the pupils contributions, were sent to the parents.

9. Students and staff kept in close touch with 'Peter's' family.

10. 'Peter's' family invited his close friends and some staff to the funeral. They also arranged that the hearse would come past, and stop briefly, outside the school on the way to the funeral. Those students who wished to gathered outside the school whilst it went by.

11. The pupils had collected money, initially for flowers, and ended up with about ú60. They decided this was too much to spend on flowers and that they would send some money to the local hospital and spend some on a permanent memorial to 'Peter'.

12. After about 2 months, the pupils bought a flowering tree which was to be planted in the school garden.

    A ceremony of commemoration was held at the school, during which some of 'Peter's' friends planted the tree. 'Peter's' parents and sister were invited and attended this ceremony. One of the staff took photographs and later a book was compiled which contained the photographs, poems and anecdotes written by 'Peter's' friends and classmates. This was given to 'Peter's' family.

    A small plaque was put with the tree.

13. From the day the tree was planted 'Peter's' friends put flowers by it and continued to do so throughout the year.

    On 'Peter's' birthday they hung cards on the tree.

14. On the anniversary of 'Peter's' death, the school marked the date by holding a special assembly for 'Peter's' year group (then Yr. 9). The school also sent a card to 'Peter's' family, saying they were thinking of them.

15. The students still sometimes put cards or flowers by the tree, but their feelings seem very positive. A lot have kept in touch with 'Peter's' family who have told the school how much their involvement has helped.

This might sound a time-consuming course of action, but apart from the first day's counselling, most events fitted into normal school routine. The students did NOT become hysterical, sentimental or morbid, but were able to understand that their feelings were O.K. Not just the feelings of sadness and loss, but also those of anger, hate and inadequacy, and that the adults involved felt the same range of emotions. Out of this sadness came a genuine learning and growing experience, for both students and staff. All those involved felt a little more able to cope with losses in the future.

N.B. No amount of teaching about loss and bereavement will benefit our students unless the losses that they and the staff incur are recognised.

- We must show students that they have worth, this means not labelling them but seeing each as an individual.

- We must LISTEN to their stories of friendships breaking / articles being lost - these are meaningful to them, even if we have 'heard it all before'.

- We must acknowledge the pain of young people whose parents are divorcing or separating and be ready for the effect this might have on their work and/or relationships.

- We must support staff and students who are new or moving on.

- We must support staff who have suffered loss, particularly those who are bereaved - they need to talk as well.

- We must provide ongoing support for young people whose parent dies and not assume all will be O.K. after 6 months,

- We must give OPEN and OBVIOUS support for any death from within the school community:
  * member of staff
  * pupil.

ANOTHER APPROACH - PEER COUNSELLING

"I know people's Mums and Dads die all the time, but up to now it's just been me". David Quarmby reports on how talking and a teddy-bear helped bereaved teenagers.

Helping teenagers to cope with the death of a parent or someone else close to them is a difficult subject for schools. With the best will in the world, teachers share the common misconceptions about grief in adolescence.

I came across two typical reactions earlier this year, when I was trying to set up some practical research to help young people who had been bereaved. There was no point coming into school, a senior teacher told me, because only one pupil had been bereaved. He meant "in the last six months".

In fact, Government statistics show that about 180,000 children under 16 have lost a parent through death. So, on average, a secondary school of 800 can expect to have two dozen such pupils who at some time have been bereaved.

In addition, recent research suggests that three out of five teenagers consider that they have experienced a "major" bereavement, even through this may not be the death of a parent. So the problem is far from insignificant, even in purely numerical terms.

The second misconception was shown by a deputy head who protested that her own father had died when she was a child, and she was sure that she would have been deeply disturbed if anyone had tried to get her to talk about it. Death was best left unmentioned, she said. People would get over it if they were left alone.

She was right. Children can in time "get over" bereavement. But it is open to question whether being "left alone" is a requirement for "getting over".

Bereavement in childhood or adolescence needs to be understood on two levels. There are the "normal" effects of grief on any human being. In a child, these will inevitably affect everyday life, at least during the year following the death, in terms of anxiety, depression, learning difficulties, behaviour problems, and so on. But what is often overlooked in a culture which finds it difficult to look death in the eye, is that if mourning and grief are not given adequate expression immediately after the death, the effects can become deep-seated and long-term. A recent Canadian study looked at adults aged 25 to 35, who between the ages of 6 months and 16 years had lost a parent. Feelings of guilt, low self-esteem, and a tendency to depression were in many cases found to be still at work in adulthood.

In my own research, I ran peer counselling sessions with a small group of teenagers, either one or both of whose parents had died in the previous three years. My work was funded by Lancashire education committee and based at Manchester University's centre for educational guidance. The children were pupils at Counthill High School in Oldham.

Previous research had suggested that an effective way of helping bereaved teenagers to overcome their pain is for them to counsel each other. Only in other bereaved teenagers will they find the understanding which will enable them to accept the pain, and to develop the capacity to face life fully again.

Agreement to take part in the sessions, both from pupils and from their surviving parents, was hesitant, and the degree of participation in the first two sessions was cautious. But the use of group games - and perhaps the presence of Geoffrey, my daughter's therapeutic teddy-bear -

helped to break down barriers. From the third session onwards, the children increasingly found the courage to talk.

Mark aged 15 at the time, told the group about when he had been abusive to his Dad. Having struggled as a parent of teenagers myself, it sounded to me like a fairly normal, verbal confrontation between a rebellious teenager, and a parent desperately trying to retain some disciplinary hold. But in the light of his father's death Mark clearly regretted what he had said.

He nodded when I said, "You look back now and regret that." There was silence and Mark was close to tears. I added, "And you perhaps wish you could say to him... "He ended the sentence for me, "Sorry - I didn't really mean it."

There was a sense that he was speaking directly to his father. Previously, he might have thought about wishing he had said sorry, but acting it out in the group had a visibly cathartic effect.

Though only Mark and I spoke, it was the attention of the other group members which gave the moment its power. The everyday, conversational approach to someone's problem is to try and solve it, so that the listener can rid him or herself of the pain and responsibility. The counselling approach is to listen, and, when necessary, to accept the pain of a problem which perhaps cannot be solved. Nobody told these young people about this approach, and yet their bereavement seemed to have given them a natural capacity for this kind of sensitivity.

During individual interviews after the counselling sessions had come to an end, all the children agreed that listening to others describe their painful experiences had made it easier for them to bear their own hurt. "It sort of helped me, and helped them at the same time," as one said.

They agreed too that it was the element of shared experience which gave the meetings their value. Donna, aged 14, said that she had talked to her other friends about her Mum. "They've been really sympathetic, and it's made it worse! I think to myself, "What do they know? They've still got theirs." But with Claire [another group member], she'd not say, "Are you OK?" - she knew."

It was Donna too who summed up the effect of the meetings. "I know people's Mums and Dads die all the time, but up to now, it's just been me - I've been different from everyone else.

"But when we were in that room - I didn't think there'd be that many kids that had actually lost a parent at our school. With everybody else having the same sort of feelings as me, it made me think - Well, you're not to only one, so you've just got to carry on."

Teacher's impressions were positive too. Head of year John Sanders said that 12-year-old Leslie's self-confidence and initiative had noticeably improved after the meetings. "He took it on himself to go and find not one, but three part-time jobs, which were a great contribution to the money problems which had hit the family after the father's death."

The staff and pupils' perceptions were confirmed by objective psychological tests, which showed statistically significant improvements in the children's self-concept and relationships.

All the pupils also expressed a strong fellow-feeling for other bereaved youngsters. This contrasted with another area of teachers' hesitancy, some of whom felt that this type of research was using already vulnerable children as guinea pigs. But the pupils themselves seemed to value the experimental aspect of the research. They were concerned that our work should help others, and hence their willingness for this article to be printed.

The problem of how to handle bereavement in schools can be tackled from two angles - prevention, and cure. In terms of prevention, personal and social education needs to cover the

emotional and social consequences of bereavement. Packs such as "Good Grief" can help to prepare children (and, indeed, staff) for times when they have to come to terms with bereavement - in their own lives, or in the lives of those around them.

In terms of "curing" children, bereavement should be considered a special need of the kind envisaged by the Warnock Committee, and embodied in the 1981 Act. School records should therefore give details of any bereavement, and staff should be encouraged to give careful consideration to these children's educational and pastoral needs.

More staff training in basic counselling and listening techniques is needed. Counselling is such a vital skill to have in schools, that the task of arranging such training should be the stated responsibility of a particular member of a secondary school's senior management team.

However, even with such training, few schools are likely to be able to provide in-depth counselling of the kind described above - not only for bereaved pupils, but also for pupils with problems, such as aggressiveness, truanting, and so on. Schools should therefore recognize the need to bring in counselling expertise from time to time. We bring in specialists in speech therapy. Why not for counselling too?

David Quarmby was formerly head of religious education at Norden High School, Rishton, and is now a part-time counsellor at Huddersfield Polytechnic.

First Published by the Times Education Supplement 22.6.90. Reprinted with permission.

WHEN A CHILD   1.19
IN YOUR SCHOOL IS BEREAVED

Children can be bereaved in different ways - of their parent, grandparent, friend, brother or sister. The Compassionate Friends is an organisation of bereaved parents and therefore this leaflet is based upon the loss of a sister or brother. Much of it will, however, be applicable to other forms of bereavement.

Children's understanding of, and reactions to, death alter with their age and experience, personality and family circumstances. Under-sevens have little conception of the permanence of death, and may think their brother or sister can come back to them. Others may fear that any separation - even for the school day - can be a forerunner of death.

Children aged approximately seven to eleven gradually understand the irreversibility of death and begin to concern themselves with the rituals associated with it; 'playing funerals' is one way of expressing this.

From the age of eleven or so, children have a more adult understanding of death.

Reactions

Some of the normal reactions of grief are withdrawal, aggression, panic, anxiety, guilt, fear, regression and signs of stress (scratching, fiddling, repetitive visits to the toilet, etc.).

Bereaved children may express their feelings in a variety of ways. They may 'act out' some of their stressful experiences, may become aggressive, withdrawn, morose; they may 'put on a brave face' or become the 'class clown' or giggle a lot. They may become nervous or fearful. Any of these, and any mixture of these, can be described as 'normal'.

Grieving is very tiring in itself. In addition to this can be the fear - especially in younger children - of going to bed, and difficulty in going to sleep. This may be because of the 'separation' referred to earlier, and they may be particularly frightened of going to bed if their brother or sister died in bed, or if the death has been referred to as 'fell asleep', or 'died in their sleep' or 'just didn't wake up'. The attention spans for many grieving children are shortened and they may have trouble in concentrating, thus affecting their school work.

Encourage expression of feelings

You may be able to help the child in different ways. One is by being available personally to the child on a one-to-one bases, allowing and encouraging him or her to talk of their brother or sister, of their feelings about the death, of their loss. Where there were two children, the survivor is now an only child and may be terribly lonely. The two may have shared a bedroom, and going to bed is now a nightly hurdle. They need to talk of how they felt about the child who has died - they may be experiencing strong and conflicting emotions, of loss and sorrow, loneliness for themselves, grief for their parents, fear of their own death or their parents' deaths. The dead child may have been ill for a long time, or always, and jealousy, resentment, guilt and remorse may be complicating their feelings, causing inner turmoil. The child may find the effect of grief on their parents' normal behaviour very unsettling. Sudden death may leave feelings of injustice, of disbelief. And always, as in any death, there are the "If onlys".

If the child breaks down while talking, be prepared for them to cry or shout, to beat their fists or stamp their feet. Their feelings need to be expressed in these physical ways, especially where they do not have the vocabulary to express them. To repress their emotions could be much more harmful than allowing them a 'safe place' in which to express them. Perhaps the school

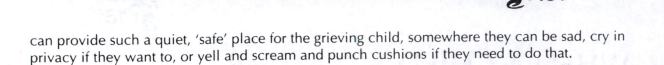

can provide such a quiet, 'safe' place for the grieving child, somewhere they can be sad, cry in privacy if they want to, or yell and scream and punch cushions if they need to do that.

Supporting the bereaved child

Talking about the dead child helps the grieving process. Try not to stop or divert the child's conversation if it includes their dead brother or sister, whether this is in private or in class. Death can then become a normal part of conversation, and everyone's fears may to some extent be allayed. The dead child will always be part of the surviving child's family, and it is healthier if he or she openly remains an integral part of the family.

You may have known the dead child yourself, and so experience your own grief over this tragedy. The grieving child will be touched, and in some measure comforted, by knowing of your sadness, by your tears, by the knowledge that his or her sorrow is shared by others.

Try not to single out the grieving child for special attention. He or she needs to feel part of the group or class, and it helps if you expect him or her to continue to perform, though for a time at a different level. Perhaps there is another bereaved child in the school; the two may be able to help one another through their sad, shared experience. Only those who have suffered a similar loss can truly say they know how the child is feeling.

To use the phrase "I know exactly how you feel" is not helpful unless you have lost a brother or sister. You may have had close and personal experience of grief; if so this will enable you to share your feelings with a bereaved child.
You may be able to help also by talking with the child's special friends. They are likely to be upset themselves, and may not know how best to help their friend.

Parents

The parents will be grateful for the sympathy of the school staff, and will welcome any support and understanding the school can give. They are experiencing tremendous pain and bewilderment themselves in trying to cope with their loss. They may not understand their child's pain or know how to help them.

Years of adjustment

The time taken by each child to move through the stages of bereavement (rather than 'get over it') is entirely individual. The initial stages of shock and disbelief generally pass quite quickly, but the more complex stage of adjustment can take a long time, perhaps many years. Try to ensure so far as possible that there is someone aware and available to that child for a long as is needed, perhaps all their remaining years at the school (It is important to ensure that knowledge of the bereavement is passed from primary to secondary school.)

In time, and with help, the child will be able to reach a stage of acceptance and to go forward with joy in the knowledge that they were fortunate to have had a brother or sister who enriched their lives.

Created and written by the Compassionate Friends
(part of the original has been omitted)

Leaflets published by The Compassionate Friends are available through your local contact or from the office in Bristol. Donations towards the printing and distribution costs are always welcome. (See Useful Addresses Sec.3).They also have a postal library of more than 400 books suitable for parents, teachers and young people.

LOSS OF A CHILD – HELPING THE PARENTS

When a child dies it upturns the natural order of things. We expect old people to die one day, but no parent is ready to accept the death of a child cut off by an accident or illness from all their dreams and aspirations. Every year there are some 15,000 deaths under 20 years of age.

Certain types of loss such as stillbirths or that of a young baby can be particularly hard to grieve over. In these types of loss, there is apparently no one to remember or talk about.

The other main cause of death in children and young people are accidents, cancer, and suicide in the teen years.

What can we do to help the parents? Please see the list below.

A REMINDER OF HELPFUL THOUGHTS

DO let your genuine concern and caring show.

DON'T let your own sense of helplessness keep you from reaching out to a bereaved parent.

DO say you are sorry about what happened to their child and about their pain.

DON'T avoid them because you are uncomfortable (being avoided by friends adds pain to an already intolerable painful experience).

DO allow them to express as much grief as they are feeling at the moment and are willing to share.

DON'T change the subject when they mention their dead child.

DO encourage them to be patient with themselves, not to expect too much of themselves and not to impose any "shoulds" on themselves.

DON'T avoid mentioning the child's name out of fear of reminding them of their pain (they haven't forgotten it).

DO talk about the special, endearing qualities of the child they've lost.

DON'T point out at least they have their other children (children are not interchangeable; they cannot replace each other).

DO reassure them that they did everything they could, that the medical care their child received was the best or whatever else you know to be true and positive about the care given their child.

DON'T say that they can always have another child (even if they wanted to and could, another child would not replace the child they have lost).

Section 2

Activities

SETTING THE SCENE

Objectives

To make the course as relevant to the needs of students as possible.

To include students in the course planning from the beginning.

To create a safe environment for students to explore feelings and attitudes.

Resources

Flip paper and pens. Prepared task.

Method A

1) Divide students into small groups.

2) Tell them a new subject is to be introduced and you would appreciate their ideas.

3) Read out the task below.

Decide if we should teach about loss and death. Write down the reasons for and against doing so.

4) Ask groups to share answers, discuss and clarify.

Method B

1 and 2 as above.

3) Ask groups to brainstorm the advantages and disadvantages of learning about loss and death.

4) As above.

5) Ask students to make own ground rules or discuss the ones below and ask if they have any alterations or additions.

Ground rules for the group

AIM - A safe stress free atmosphere - clear communication.

1) Each person speaks for themselves. Try to use the first person "I feel" "I tend to" rather than "one feels/you/people tend to" etc.

2) Choice - everyone can choose to opt in or out of any discussion/activity - that's OK. Group pressure (even as a joke) is to be avoided.

3) Each person has the right to their own opinions/feelings - no value judgments or put downs.

4) Tears are fine - crying is natural when we are sad.

5) Confidentiality - anything "personal" shared is confidential.

6)   There are no right answers, only alternatives!

7)   (Add any others) n.b. Ground rules could be put on overhead projection.

Extensions

Ask group to brainstorm what they would like included in course - discuss and add any suggestions you may have and your objectives.

MAKE YOUR OWN GLOSSARY

Objective

To familiarise students with words associated with death and to help them feel more comfortable with their use.

Resources

List of words associated with death, flip paper and felt pens for each group.

Method A

1) Explain to the Group the meaning of the word Glossary and that there are many words to do with death with which they may not be familiar. It is important for them to understand the different terminology in case they experience death of someone close to them.

2) Divide the students into small groups or pairs.

3) Tell them you will call out a word - they are to brainstorm what they think the meaning is.

4) When all the words have been brainstormed, re-form the large group, share and clarify the lists.

Method B

As above but use dictionaries.

Method C

Resources

A copy of the Activity Sheet - Make your own Glossary (1) for every student.

1) Discuss what a Glossary is.

2) Provide everyone with a copy of the Activity Sheet and reassure them that this is not a test and that you will give them the correct answers.

3) Go through the instructions for whichever sheet is used.

4) Read out the correct answers and clarify points that are not understood.

N.B. These activities could also be used in groups of two to three people.

GLOSSARY OF WORDS ASSOCIATED WITH DEATH

BEQUEATH — to leave behind.

BEREAVEMENT — to be deprived by death, loss or parting.

CREMATORIUM — a place where cremations are held.

DEATH — the act of dying.

DECEASE — the end of life on this Earth.

EPITAPH — words inscribed on a tombstone or monument.

EULOGY — to speak or write well of someone.

EUTHANASIA — a way made easy for people to die.

FUNERAL — a ceremony.

GRIEF — distress — great unhappiness.

HEDONIST — someone who believes pleasure is the chief thing.

IMMORTAL — living forever.

LAMENT — to express grief passionately.

MAUSOLEUM — a magnificent monument.

MEMORIAL — that which serves to keep remembrance.

MOURNING — dark clothes worn as a sign of bereavement/to feel or express sorrow about something.

OBITUARY — the printed announcement of a person's death.

ORPHAN — a child whose parents are dead.

REINCARNATION — to live again in a different body.

RESURRECTION — to rise from the dead.

THANATOLOGY — the scientific study of death and the process of dying.

WIDOW — a woman whose husband is dead.

WIDOWER — a man whose wife is dead.

WILL — deed showing disposal of one's possessions — usually called a bequest — at death.

MAKE YOUR OWN GLOSSARY (1)

Write the correct word in the space provided

Hedonist	Immortal	Crematorium
Bequest	Bereavement	Deceased
Eulogy	Death	Euthanasia
Obituary	Epitaph	Grief
Widow	Funeral	Mausoleum
Orphan	Memorial	Resurrection
Reincarnation	Widower	Will
Lament	Mourning	

a) .... Someone who believes pleasure is the chief thing.

b) .... To leave behind.

c) .... To be deprived by death, loss or parting.

d) .... A place where cremations are held.

e) .... The end of life on this Earth.

f) .... Living for ever.

g) .... The act of having died.

h) .... Words describing a dead person on a tombstone or monument.

i) .... A way made easy for people to die.

j) .... To speak well of someone.

k) .... The ceremony.

l) .... Distress - great unhappiness.

m) .... To express grief passionately.

n) .... A magnificent monument.

o) .... That which serves to keep remembrance.

p) .... Dark clothes worn as a sign of bereavement/to feel or express sorrow about something.

q) .... The printed announcement of a person's death.

r) .... A child whose parents are dead.

s) .... To live again in a different body.

t) .... To rise from the dead.

u) .... A woman whose husband is dead.

v) .... A man whose wife is dead.

w) .... Deed showing disposal of one's possessions at death.

5)   Correct answers are:-

a. Hedonist   m. Lament
b. Bequest   n. Mausoleum
c. Bereavement   o. Memorial
d. Crematorium   p. Mourning
e. Death   q. Obituary
f. Immortal   r. Orphan
g. Deceased   s. Reincarnation
h. Epitaph   t. Resurrection
i. Euthanasia   u. Widow
j. Eulogy   v. Widower
k. Funeral   w. Will
l. Grief

Method D.

Resources

1 and 2 as Method C, using Activity Sheet (2).

3)   Ask the students to put the words into pairs that belong together.

4)   As Method C.

CORRECT ANSWERS ARE:-

Bequest	–	Legacy	Mourning	–	Sadness
Bereavement	–	Loss	Obituary	–	Statement
Cremate	–	Burn	Orphan	–	Parentless
Death	–	Termination	Reincarnation	–	Re-live
Deceased	–	Dead	Resurrection	–	Revival
Epitaph	–	Inscription	Widow	–	Husbandless
Euthanasia	–	Death	Widower	–	Wifeless
Eulogy	–	Praise	Will	–	Legal document
Funeral	–	Burial			
Grief	–	Sorrow			
Hedonist	–	Pleasure Seeker			
Lament	–	Regret			
Mausoleum	–	Tomb			
Immortal	–	Forever			
Memorial	–	Monument			

MAKE YOUR OWN GLOSSARY (2)

Put the words into the pairs that belong together

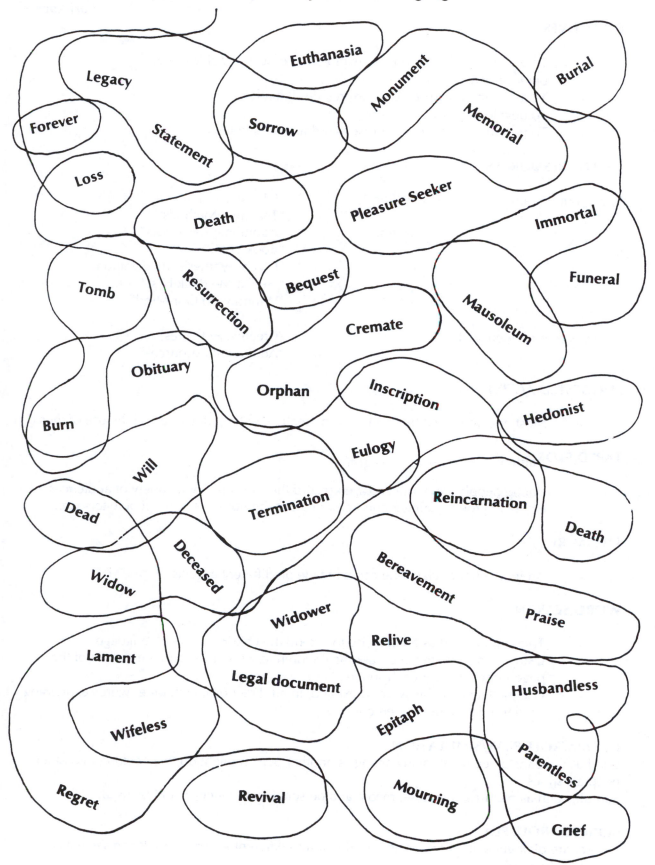

Legacy

Euthanasia

Monument

Burial

Forever

Sorrow

Statement

Memorial

Loss

Death

Pleasure Seeker

Immortal

Tomb

Resurrection

Bequest

Funeral

Mausoleum

Obituary

Cremate

Orphan

Inscription

Hedonist

Burn

Will

Eulogy

Dead

Termination

Reincarnation

Death

Widow

Deceased

Bereavement

Widower

Praise

Lament

Relive

Legal document

Husbandless

Wifeless

Epitaph

Parentless

Regret

Revival

Mourning

Grief

CREATIVE ACTIVITIES   2.3

"I know I cannot teach anyone anything. I can only provide an environment in which they can learn."

Carl Rogers

OBJECTIVES

- To encourage discussion and exploration of feelings of loss and bereavement.
- To allow the unconscious to express itself freely.
- To develop creativity and choice.
- To use art, music, poetry, prose and drama as stimulus.

USEFUL RESOURCES

Background reading   -   in Section 1   -   "Educator's Notes"
                                          -    "Teaching Methods"
                          in Section 3   -   "Additional Resources"
                                          -    "Book List".
                                               "Psychosynthesis in Education"
                                               "He Hit Me Back First"
                                               "Windows to Our Mind"

See selection of poems/articles   -   "Creative Activities"
                                               "Additional Resources".

SUGGESTED ACTIVITIES

- Most educators will be familiar with creative writing, drawing and the use of music

TAPED STORIES

- Young people can write and then record their stories. For a variety of audiences e.g. peer group, younger children or record memories of older people to share.

THESAURUS

- An individual or class one can be made on different aspects.

WORD SEARCH

- This can be used as an exercise to extend the children's use of language.
- Using 1 cm. square paper, ask the children to write a word in the middle of the page - one letter for each square.
- Use the letters of this word to expand, in all directions, with other words expressing similar/ related ideas or emotion.

DRAMA/ROLE PLAY/SIMULATION

Used as a means of feeling/thinking/acting as another person might do, e.g. 'getting into other people's shoes'.
Stimuli, such as pictures, literature, media and personal experiences could be used.

SCRIPTED ROLE PLAY

To prepare dialogues/situations as an introduction to different experiences. It can serve as a model for 'free role play'.

N.B. Role play needs careful handling and should only be used if the teacher/educator is experienced and confident in this method.

The importance of a careful introduction and debriefing cannot be emphasised too much.

FREE DRAWING

This follows naturally after 'Guided Imagery' or 'Creative Imagination'. It is important to emphasize that i has nothing to do with 'Art'. (I often show my own basic drawings to reassure the students before they start).

This method is ideal for troublesome feelings helping to free people for learning.

Method A - Encourage students to draw freely and spontaneously.
Method B - Ask to draw the particular image/s, received during 'guided imagery'.

N.B. See also article:"Value of Hospitalized Children's Art Work" in Section 3.

ART/ENGLISH/HISTORY
Look at how loss and death has been portrayed throughout the ages and in different cultures.

INFORMATION TECHNOLOGY
. . . is now part of a cross-curricular requirement.

Possible uses of IT:
The use of a word processor to express and clarify thoughts and ideas. The drafting and editing facilities allow the thought process to be carried out at the computer, with the advantage of immediately deleting all unwanted text. This could act as a catharsis and help people to work way through personal grief. A printout can be made but is not necessary id a individual doesn't want a hard copy of their thoughts and feelings.

Specific programs:
Wordplay (BBC and Nimbus computers) This program allows the individual to create 'poetry' on the computer. A theme is chosen e.g. LOSS and the person is asked for nouns, adjectives, adverbs and verbs associated with the theme. This process can be very thought-provoking especially in the next stage of its use when the computer strings elements together and the user decides whether he/she feels they are appropriate. A printout can be made of the final 'poem', as below.

Loss
Terrible incomprehensible guilt,
Help help quickly,
Unbelievable unbelievable loneliness,
Terrible incredible fear,
Slowing,
Shout fear quickly,
Loneliness painful weep unthinkingly.

Intro-tray, Developing Tray (BBC) Expose and Developing Tray (Nimbus)

This family of programs allows the user to create pieces of text on related themes. The text can then be set up with letters or words removed for groups or individuals to disclose.

```
H o w   c _ n   w e   h _ l p ?
K _ n _ _   _ _ _   j u _ _   m o v _ _   i n _ o   _ _ _   _ _ _ _
_ n d   _ _ _   p _ _ _ n _ _   _ _ _   d i v _ c _ d .
_ _ _   i _   l i v i n g   w i _ _   _ _ _   m o _ _ _ _   i n   _
_ m _ l l ,   _ _ n _ _ d   f l _ _ .   W _ _ _   _ _ _ o u _ c _ _
c o u l d   w _   _ u g g _ _ _   _ o   _ u p p o _ _   _ _ _   ?
```

FILENAME: KANTA

How can we help?
Kanta has just moved into the area and her parents are divorced. She is living with her mother in a small, rented flat. What resources could we suggest to support her?

LETTER FREQUENCY:

e:19	a:13	t:13	r:12
s:11	h:11	o:9	n:8
i:7	l:6	d:6	u:5
w:5	p:4	c:4	g:3
v:3	m:3	k:1	f:1
j:1	b:0	q:0	x:0
y:0	z:0		

MUSIC,SINGING, DANCING

Examples can be found in all types of music and songs e.g. songs such as "The streets of London' could be used to illustrate feelings. Requiems could be used to open discussion on death. Many types of music can be used to dance to in order to express feelings e.g. sadness and anger

MUSIC THERAPY

Music as therapy, and in relation to 'bereavement and loss' is a tool, and one which can be used to communicate with children at their own level - "Music can be the only key that unlocks the inner child" (Lea 1984). Active participation with the controlled use of music, acts as a link between the inner world of the child with unresolved problems and difficulties, and the outward expression of those difficulties. The child is helped back to perceptive and emotional reality and becomes more able to express hidden feelings.

Percussion instruments are generally used by participants, with the therapist often at a piano, and sessions can be on an individual or group basis. Some therapists use music exclusively while others use a combination of music and discussion.

The use of rhythm, the beating of drums, tambourines, chime bars and so on, can be echoed on the piano; the use of the voice, of tonality, of pitch and timbre, can be improvised or echoed; there can be a 'dialogue' or duet in sound and rhythm.

Music can be happy or sad, descriptive of a situation, feeling or a scene. Therapy can be extended into drawing/word association or stories - the experienced therapist deciding how to guide each child/young person.

MUSICAL EMOTIONS

Choose one of the following feelings and make a sound or group of sounds to describe the feeling.

Anger   Excitement

Joy   Sadness

Loneliness   Fear

Happiness   Love

Can you make your sound using a musical instrument?

Share your music with a partner.

Can they guess the emotion you are describing?

Can you make a musical emotions story?

Your story will begin with one feeling and move through other feelings until you reach an emotion that feels like the end of your story.

You may like to add some words to your musical story.

Methods, styles and emphases of therapy vary, but the basic process of 'unlocking' the child's emotions, and building links from 'inside' to 'outside', is the aim of music therapy.
(See activity "Musical Emotions")

N.B. Further information can be obtained from the British Society of Music Therapy -
see 'Useful Addresses' in Section 3.

Method

As a Music Therapist I work on an understanding of music and its effect on mind, body and emotions. As a mother, I worked on an understanding of my relationship with my three children.

Aim

-	Communication	-	vocally, rhythmically, and melodically.
-	Spontaneity	-	exploration of 'me', themselves, sounds and instruments.
-	Initiations and Responses		
-	Turn Taking		
-	Interactions	-	between the students and the students with me.
-	To play games and have fun.		

Instinctively I use my voice most of the time, plus the addition of drums, bells, autoharp, triangle, and guitar.

Creative Imagination

The purpose of this is, to focus and energise, to enhance imagination and intuition, and to increase the flow of ideas around a particular subject, e.g. loss or happiness.

Guided Imagery

Encourages creative imagination, choice and focuses attention. Invite the students to do the following:
- 'Close your eyes, and imagine an apple - see it as clearly as possible.
- Imagine the colour, shape, size.
- Move on to other objects and repeat the process.
- Then discuss it with the whole class or smaller groups.'

N.B. This can be repeated imagining smell, taste, hearing or feeling. Also this simple activity familiarizes the students with closing their eyes and using their imagination.

Expanded Guided Imagery 1

Integrates the creative imagination into the learning process. Encourages a positive attitude towards the individuals own creativity.
- Start with asking the students to close their eyes and spend a few moments becoming still and relaxed.
- (See Sections on 'Relaxation' and 'How Can We Help'.)

Directed

- Take the students on a journey, this could be subject specific.
- You choose where they go, and constantly ask them what they see, hear, smell, and how they feel.
- Remind them to notice colours, shapes, people/animals.
- Bring them back to their starting place and ask them to write, draw or act out their experience.

Undirected

Ask the students to:

- Imagine inside yourself a very quiet place that is special to you, where you feel very good, and at home.
- From this place think about the story you are going to write.
- See the story beginning - watch it unfold - notice all the details, the colours, sounds, and the characters - what they are doing, saying or feeling in it - imagine how it will end.
- When your story is finished - there is no need to hurry - come back into the room and begin writing.

N.B. This could also be adapted by using drama, drawing or other creative activities. (See exercise following).

A good initial introduction to this method is to stop at the 'special place' and to get the group to imagine it in detail. Then write a description of, draw, and finally talk about their 'place'.

Expanded Guided Imagery 2

This visualization can be used as a transition from one activity to another, or following a playtime held indoors because of wet weather.

Ask the students to close their eyes and lead them through a simple relaxation before suggesting that they:

- Go to that place in your mind where you can create or imagine.
- See yourself in your imagination, sitting at your desk/table, working comfortably and enjoying your work.
- Choose how you're going to be, what *attitude you're going to have.
- How will this *attitude help you?
- See yourself and the rest of the group working well together.
- Feel this comfortable feeling.
- When you are ready open your eyes.

N.B. * You need to have discussed 'attitude' previously.

WRITING

A) Journal

Recording thoughts and feelings in a written or pictorial form have a valuable place in the learning process. Also it is psychologically important to 'ground' experiences in this way and/or by talking about them afterwards.

Encourage the students to design the cover for their own journal, either with their own drawings or pictures from magazines that have special meaning for them. Reassure them that they don't have to share the contents unless they wish to do so.

A loose leaf folder will enable students to remove work they may not wish to show to anyone else. They should also be given permission to destroy any part of their work, if they want, in a way that has most meaning for them.

There is a temptation for educators to keep all the written work which students produce, as tangible proof that the course has been covered.

'Good Grief' provides many learning experiences that cannot be recorded, evaluated or measured in this way. They will be recorded in the mind of the student, and will remain there to provide a firm foundation upon which to build their experiences of the future.

   N.B. Students can make the journal up individually or in groups.

B) Diary

Alternatively a diary can be kept, to record events and/or experiences of personal significance. This can be particularly useful for students who have difficulty in talking about their feelings. It is important to emphasize to each student that the diary is for their own benefit and can be kept private. Ideally it should be loose-leaved so that students can remove information they don't want to share.

Expanded Writing

Objectives
   - To use poems to facilitate discussion and explore feelings of loss and bereavement.
   - To encourage creative writing.

Resources
   - Selection of poems and prose from a variety of backgrounds and cultures.
   - Flip paper and pens. See also 'Book Lists' & 'Additional Resources'.

Method
   - Read a poem or prose. This may be read by a volunteer.
   - Ask the students to write without discussion the first two or three words which came to mind from the reading.
   - List the words for the students.
   - Read the poem/prose again with the words displayed.
   - Form small groups to discuss the activity or discuss it with the whole group.

N.B. This 'Method' may be omitted for older students.

N.B. Drama and Art can also be expressed following this approach.

Suggested Discussion Points
(Depending on the chosen poem/prose)

Ask the students:
- What were the feelings of the people involved?
- How long did these feelings last?
- What happened to make them feel that way?
- What did they say or do?
- Can you think of anything, or anybody else, that could have been helpful at the time?
- Do you think the person or people involved gained anything from the experience?
- Do you remember a time when you felt like this?

Extensions

Ask the student to:
- Write a poem or short story using the words chosen in 'Methods' above.
  Write a poem or story about their own experience.
- Role play one of the poems or pieces of prose.
- N.B. Creative drawing/painting could also be used.
- Close their eyes and experience the feeling of the poem, then suggest that they draw a picture of the feelings that they have become aware of because of the poem.
- Alternatively ask them to paint a picture of something the poem recalled to mind. Perhaps there was one word or sentence which struck some chord within.

EXAMPLE OF POEM

Violet Oaklander in 'Window To Our Children' says: 'The poem, "There Is A Knot" in 'Have You Seen A Comet?' never fails to bring forth some feelings usually kept hidden'.

TRANSLATION OF A POEM BY A TURKISH GIRL

THERE IS A KNOT

There is a knot inside of me
A knot which cannot be untied
Strong
It hurts
As if they have put a stone
Inside of me

I always remember the old days
Playing at ou summer home
Going to gran lmother
Staying at grandmother's

I want those days to return
Perhaps the knot will be untied
when they return
But there is a knot inside of me
So strong
And it hurts
As if there is a stone inside of me.

After hearing this poem, a 10 year old girl drew a figure standing on top of a hill, a black dot in her middle, arms outstretched, with the words, "I hate you, I hate you" written around the figure. She dictated to me: "My knot is anger inside of me." Prior to this she had defensively denied feelings of anger, in spite of her rebellious behaviour at school and home.

THE HISTORY BEHIND THE POEM

Gresford is 3 miles from Wrexham and the disaster referred to occurred on 23 September 1934. Four hundred men were on a Friday night shift, many of them working so they would be free for Saturday afternoon football. The explosion occurred at 3 a.m. Saturday morning and the fire was so fierce that the rescuers could not get near to the men. The final death toll was even higher than the poem suggests - 264 - and it was 7 months before anyone was able to go down that pit.

The Gresford Disaster

You've heard of the Gresford disaster,
The terrible price that was paid;
Two hundred and forty-two colliers were lost
And three men of a rescue brigade.

It occurred in the month of September;
At three in the morning that pit
Was wracked by a violent explosion
In the Dennis where dust lay so thick.

The gas in the Dennis deep section
Was packed like snow in a drift,
And many a man had to leave the coal-face
Before he had worked out his shift.

A fortnight before the explosion
To the shot-firer, Tomlinson cried:
"If you fire that shot we'll all be blown to hell!"
And no one can say that he lied.

The fireman's reports they are missing,
The records of Forty-two days,
The colliery manager had them destroyed
To cover his criminal ways.

Down there in the dark they are lying,
They died for nine shillings a day;
They've worked out their shift and it's now they must lie
In the darkness until Judgement Day.

The Lord Mayor of London's collecting
To help both the children and wives.
The owners had sent some white lilies
To pay for the collier's lives.

Farewell our dear wives and our children,
Farewell our dear comrades as well.
Don't send your sons in the dark dreary mine
They'll be damned like the sinners in Hell.

ANON

GOING THROUGH THE OLD PHOTOS

Me, my dad
and my brother
we were looking through the old photos.
Pictures of my dad with a broken leg
and my mum with big flappy shorts on
and me on a tricycle
when we got to one of my mum
with a baby on her knee,
and I go,
'Is that me or Brian?'
And my dad says,
'Let's have a look.
It isn't you or Brian,' he says.
'It's Alan.
He died.
He would have been
two years younger than Brian
and two years older than you.
He was a lovely baby.'

'How did he die?'
'Whooping cough.
I was away at the time.
He coughed himself to death in Connie's arms.
The terrible thing is,
it wouldn't happen today,
but it was during the war, you see,
and they didn't have the medicines.
That must be the only photo
of him we've got.'

Me and Brian
looked at the photo.
We couldn't say anything.
It was the first time we had ever heard about Alan.
For a moment I felt ashamed
like as if I had done something wrong.
I looked at the baby trying to work out
who he looked like.
I wanted to know what another brother
would have been like.
No way of saying.
And Mum looked so happy.
Of course she didn't know
when they took the photo
that he would die, did she?

Funny thing is,
though my father mentioned it every now and then
over the years,
Mum — never.
And he never said anything in front of her
about it
and we never let on that we knew.
What I've never figured out
was whether
her silence was because
she was more upset about it
than my dad —
or less.

Michael Rosen

GONE

She sat in the back of the van
and we waved to her there

we ran towards her
but the van moved off

we ran faster
she reached out for us

the van moved faster
we reached for her hand

she stretched out of the back of the van
we ran, reaching

the van got away
we stopped running

we never reached her
before she was gone.

Michael Rosen

DAVID COPPERFIELD
(an excerpt)

"A mist rose between Mrs Creakle and me, and her figure seemed to move in it for an instant. Then I felt the burning tears run down my face and it was steady again. 'She is very dangerously ill,' she added.
I knew all now.
'She is dead'.

There was no need to tell me so. I had already broken out into a desolate cry, and felt an orphan in the wide world.

She was very kind to me. She kept me there all day, and left me alone sometimes; and I cried, and wore myself to sleep, and awoke and cried again. When I could cry no more, I began to think; and then the oppression on my breast was heaviest, and my grief a dull pain that there was no ease for.

And yet my thoughts were idle; not intent on the calamity that weighed upon my heart, but idly loitering near it. I thought of our house shut up and hushed. I thought of the little baby, who, Mrs Creakle said, had been pining away for some time, and who, they believed, would die too. I thought of my father's grave in the churchyard by our house, and of my mother lying there beneath the tree I knew so well.

I stood upon a chair when I was left alone, and looked into the glass to see how red my eyes were, and how sorrowful my face. I considered, after some hours were gone, if my tears were really hard to flow now, as they seemed to be, what, in connexion with my loss, it would affect me most to think of when I drew near home - for I was going home to the funeral. I am sensible of having felt that a dignity attached to me among the rest of the boys, and that I was important in my affliction".

Charles Dickens

ANGER!

Anger is black
Anger is red
Anger steams inside your head
Whirling round getting you mad
Getting you hotter, making you bad

You feel you want to be evil
To every one you see
And hatred and horrible
Is all you want to be

Anger gets you tight and tense
Your fists seem to tightly clench
You shout and scream and cry and howl
Then the anger's not there at all!

By Sophie Stevens

GRIEF

Deep sobs -
that start beneath my heart
and hold my body in a grip that hurts
The lump that swells inside my throat
brings pain that tries to choke.
Then tears course down my cheeks -
I drop my head in my so empty hands
abandoning myself to deep dark grief
and know that with the passing time
will come relief.
That though the pain may stay
There soon will come a day
When I can say her name and be at peace.

Norah Leney

DON'T DRINK

don't drink don't drive
don't take your boat out on the seas
take care beware unwind
watch light relief and comedies
exercise and you will find
death is an avoidable disease
grow old and old and old
along with me
keep death to the clinics
keep it in the wards
and cardboard posters tell us
to beware take care
don't drink don't drive
survive survive
Is it surprising we're surprised
when someone we love dies?

IF GOD HAD WANTED A GERBIL

If God had wanted a gerbil
He should have saved up like me
and gone to the pet shop and bought one
that's doing things 'properly'

If God had wanted a gerbil
then I think its awfully mean
to have made me drop mine and kill it
when I fed it and kept it so clean

If God had wanted a gerbil
He should have taken its cage and its straw
No. I won't have another gerbil
just in case God wants some more.

TO EMILY

To Emily at four
death is grandma
a Christmas tea party
and then no more

death is a rabbit
an uninhabited hutch
and a garden rose
growing through its bones

death is a bird
so many birds die
death is a word
she follows with WHY

So I tell her OLD
and I tell her ILL
she's too young for CANCER
or MURDER or KILL

and heaven at best
is somewhere to rest
when we're tired.
Emily says yes

she can see heaven
clearly she can
with grandma and rabbit and bird
and the leg from the one-legged man

Susan Wallbank

91

WHY ME?

Grieve for the loss, the separation,
- Why me, why me? -
Grieve for the loneliness, the rejection,
- Why me, Oh why me? -
Feel the shock, the desperation,
- Why pick on me? -
So stamp, so scream and shout, destruction,
- My fault, my guilt? -

Feel the gloom and the depression,
- No talk, no talk! -
The most unutterable opression.
- Don't speak, won't speak! -
Unspoken thoughts, so silent home. Home?
- Bursting, breaking -
Help me oh carer to mourn, to moan,
And in mourning, peace!

Sally Crosher

DEATH

I had him and cared
He ran from man but not from me.
I played with him when I was in a good mood
And I even gave him his food.
I cried when he died.
He could have survived.
But the pain was with him.
He died.
I cried for five days
But he was not alive to play.

Sateki Faletau
Aged 10

Death is nothing at all - I have only slipped away into the next room. I am I and you are you.
Whatever we were to each other that we still are. Call me by my old familiar name, speak to
me in the easy way which you always used. Wear no forced air of solemnity or sorrow. Laugh
as we always laughed at the little jokes we enjoyed together. Play, smile, think of me, pray for
me. Let my name be ever the household word that it always was. Let it be spoken without
effect, without the ghost of a shadow on it. Life means all that it ever meant. It is the same as
it ever was. There is absolutely unbroken continuity. What is this death but a negligible
accident? Why should I be out of mind because I am out of sight? I am waiting for you - for an
interval - somewhere near just around the corner. All is well.

Canon Scott Holland

92

LAMENT FOR GLEN
(Killed in a motor-bike accident, aged nineteen)

The splendid youth is dead and is no more,
And who shall comfort those who are left?
Who shall comfort the mother who has lost her son?
Who shall comfort the sisters who have lost a brother?
Who shall comfort the friends who have lost a friend?
And who shall comfort the father?
There is no comfort for those who are grieving
For faith is not enough
To assuage the tearing wound of sudden death.
O let me not drown in the flood of grief
For all young men who died before their time
And for this one so newly dead.
O let me catch the raft of life again
And not be swept away
Into the darkest depths of grief and loss.

Marjorie Pizer

THE EXISTENCE OF LOVE

I had thought that your death
Was a waste and a destruction,
A pain of grief hardly to be endured.
I am only beginning to learn
That your life was a gift and a growing
And a loving left with me.
The desperation of death
Destroyed the existence of love,
But the fact of death
Cannot destroy what has been given.
I am learning to look at your life again
Instead of your death and your departing.

Marjorie Pizer

REMEMBER

Remember me when I am gone away,
Gone far away into the silent land;
When you can no more hold me by the hand,
Nor I half turn to go yet turning to stay.
Remember me when no more day by day
You tell me of our future that you planned:
Only remember me; you understand
It will be late to counsel then or pray.
Yet if you should forget me for a while
And afterwards remember, do not grieve:
For if the darkness and corruption leave
A vestige of the thoughts that once I had,
Better by far you should forget and smile
Than that you should remember and be sad.

Christine Rossetti

GRIEF

*Why didn't someone tell me when I was growing up, that life was hard and hurtful, that I
would cry more than I would laugh?*
*Why didn't someone teach me instead of algebra that relationships break down and people
really cry?*
Why didn't someone tell me that loved ones really die and that grief is an eternal thing?
*First the unbelief, sitting there watching the body move even after death, convinced he's
coming back to life. Watching the body's motions continue into the catheter bag below. You
can't be really dead, the body is still functioning.*
*An hour later and still I'm holding a warm hand beneath the covers, the sun shines on your
face.*
You can't really be dead, you can't, you can't, you can't.
Then funeral: realisation, body racking tears,
Desolation you've really gone.
The tears go on and on and black despair just overwhelms.
Nothing matters any more, no future, no hope, no love.
Then months go by, I feel I'm getting better, I even laugh again.
But then suddenly it all overwhelms me again.
The need for you, the longing, aching desire to see your smile, feel the warmth of you.
The awful black despair clamps down again.
Once more the tears flow, spill over so easily, continually.
Why, why didn't someone tell me, that grief is an everlasting, fearful overwhelming thing?
Can someone tell me please, does it ever really end?

Sally Trow

He stayed for such a little while
So small, so complete but so frail
He stayed for so very short a time
That he hardly seemed quite real
But he stayed for just long enough
For you to know his touch, his warmth
He stayed just long enough
To know he was really yours
And when you felt you were getting
To know him
When you thought you were just making
friends
He heard the voice of a far greater friend
Calling him home from the struggle of living
To play in the sunshine of heavenly fields
There he can run without aids and crutches
There he can play and sing without tears
There he can wait in God's tender keeping
Until you can join him in coming years.

Anon

KATE

What do you see nurses
What do you see?
Are you thinking
When you are looking at me,
A crabbit old woman
not very wise,
Uncertain of habit
with far-away eyes,
Who dribbles her food
and makes no reply,
When you say in a loud voice
'I do wish you'd try'
Who seems not to notice
the things that you do,
And forever is losing
a stocking or shoe,
Who unresisting or not
lets you do as you will
with bathing and feeding
the long day to fill,
Is that what you're thinking,
is that what you see?
Then open your eyes nurse,
You're not looking at me.
I'll tell you who I am
as I sit here so still,
I'm a small child of ten
with a father and mother,
Brothers and sisters who
love one another,
A young girl of sixteen
with wings on her feet,
Dreaming that soon now
a lover she'll meet;
A bride soon at twenty,
my heart gives a leap,
Remembering the vows
that I promised to keep;
At twenty-five now
I have young of my own
Who need me to build
a secure happy home.
A young woman of thirty
my young now grow fast,
Bound to each other
with ties that should last;

At forty my young ones
now grown will soon be gone,
But my man stays beside me
to see I don't mourn;
At fifty once more
babies play round my knee,
Again we know children
my loved one and me.
Dark days are upon me,
my husband is dead,
I look at the future
I shudder with dread,
For my young are all busy
rearing young of their own,
And I think of the years
and the love I have known.
I'm an old woman now
and nature is cruel,
'Tis her jest to make
old age look like a fool.
The body it crumbles,
Grave and vigour depart,
There now is a stone
where once I had a heart:
But inside this old carcase
a young girl still dwells,
And now and again
my battered heart swells,
I remember the joys
I remember the pain,
And I'm loving and living
life over again,
I think of the years
all too few - gone too fast,
And accept the stark fact
that nothing can last.
So open your eyes nurses
Open and see,
Not a crabbit old woman
look closer - see ME.

'Kate', the writer of this poem, was unable to speak, but was occasionally seen to write. After her death, her locker was emptied and this poem was found.

A NURSES REPLY

What do we see, you ask, what do we see?
Yes, we are thinking when looking at thee,
We may seem to be hard when we hurry and fuss
But there's many of you, and too few of us.
We would like far more time to sit by you and talk
To bath you and feed you and help you to walk.
To hear of your lives and the things you have done
your childhood, your husband, your daughter, your son.
But time is against us, there's too much to do
Patients too many, and nurses too few.
We grieve when we see you so sad and alone
With nobody near you, no friends of your own.
We feel all your pain, and know of your fear
That nobody cares now your end is so near.
But nurses are people with feelings as well
And when we're together you'll often hear tell
Of the dearest old gran in the very end bed,
And the lovely old Dad, and the things that he said,
We speak with compassion and love, and feel sad,
When we think of your lives and the joy that you've had.
When the time has arrived for you to depart
You leave us behind with an ache in our heart
When you sleep the long sleep, no more worry or care
There are other old people, and we must be there.
So please understand if we hurry and fuss -
There are many of you, and too few of us.

Liz Hogben

KATE

First printed in the Sunday Post in 1973, it has appeared in newspapers and magazines all over the world, and read on radio and t.v. Over the years thousands of people have asked for copies and the poem written by a young nurse in reply.

THE SOLDIER
November-December 1914

If I should die, think only this of me:
That there's some corner of a foreign field
That is for ever England. There shall be
In that rich earth a richer dust concealed;
A dust whom England bore, shaped, made aware,
Gave, once, her flowers to love, her ways to roam,
A body of England's, breathing English air,
Washed by the rivers, blest by suns of home.

And think, this heart, all evil shed away,
A pulse in the eternal mind, no less
Gives somewhere back the thoughts by England
given;
Her sights and sounds; dreams happy as her day;
And laughter, learnt of friends; and gentleness,
In hearts at peace, under an English heaven.

THE DEAD

These hearts were woven of human joys and cares,
Washed marvellously with sorrow, swift to mirth.
The years had given them kindness. Dawn was theirs,
And sunset, and the colours of the earth.
These had seen movement, and heard music; known
Slumber and waking; loved; gone proudly friended;
Felt the quick stir of wonder; sat alone;
Touched flowers and furs and checks. All this is
ended.

There are waters blown by changing winds to laughter
And lit by the rich skies, all day. And after,
Frost, with a gesture, stays the waves that dance
And wandering loveliness. He leaves a white
Unbroken glory, a gathered radiance,
A width, a shining peace, under the night.

Rupert Brooke

LIFE IS A NONSENSE, DEATH THE END

Tomorrow, and tomorrow, and tomorrow,
Creeps in this petty pace from day to day
To the last syllable of recorded time;
And all our yesterdays have lighted fools
The way to dusty death. Out, out, brief candle
Life's but a walking shadow, a poor player
That struts and frets his hour upon the stage,
And then is heard no more; it is a tale
Told by an idiot, full of sound and fury,
Signifying nothing.

William Shakespeare

LIFE IS NOT ENDED BY DEATH

Death be not proud, though some have called thee
Mighty and dreadful, thou art not so:
For those who thou thinkest thou dost overthrow,
Die not, poor Death: nor yet can thou kill me.
One short sleep past, we wake eternal
And Death shall be no more:
Death thou shalt die!

John Donne

TURN AGAIN TO LIFE

If I should die and leave you here awhile
Be not like others sore undone, who keep
Long vigils by the silent dust, and weep:
For my sake turn again to life, and smile,
Nerving thy heart and trembling hand to do
Something to comfort weaker hearts than thine,
Complete these dear unfinished tasks of mine,
And I, perchance, may therein comfort you.

Mary Lee Hall

FOOTPRINTS IN THE SAND

The following was received from Canada, where it was broadcast by a sixteen year old girl dying of cancer..........................

One night a man had a dream
He dreamt he was walking along the beach with the Lord.
Across the sky flashed scenes from his life.

For each scene he noticed two sets of footprints in the sand.
One belonging to him - the other to the Lord.

When the last scene of his life flashed before him,
He looked back at the footprints in the sand
And he noticed that many times along the path of his life
There was only one set of footprints.
He also noticed that it happened at the very lowest and saddest times in his life.

This really bothered him and he questioned the Lord about it.
"Lord, you said that once I decided to follow you, you'd
walk with me all the way
But I have noticed that during the most difficult times in
my life,
There is only one set of footprints.
I don't understand why in times when I needed you most,
you would leave me".

The Lord replied:

"My precious, precious child,
I love you and I would never, never leave you
during your trials and suffering.
When you see only one set of footprints,
it was then that I carried you!".

Anon

DEATH IN THE FIRST PERSON

I am a student nurse. I am dying. I write this to you who are, and will become, nurses in the hope that by my sharing my feelings with you, you may someday be better able to help those who share my experience.

I'm out of the hospital now-perhaps for a month, for six months, perhaps for a year - but no one likes to talk much about such things. In fact, no one likes to talk about much at all. Nursing must be advancing, but I wish it would hurry. We're taught not to be overly cheery now, to omit the "Everthing's fine" routine, and we have done pretty well. But now one is left in a lonely silent void. With the protective "fine, fine" gone, the staff is left with only their own vulnerability and fear. The dying patient is not yet seen as a person and thus cannot be communicated with as such. He is a symbol of what every human fears and what we each know, at least academically, that we too must someday face. What did they say in psychiatric nursing about meeting pathology with pathology to the detriment of both patient and nurse? And there was a lot about knowing one's own feelings before you could help another with his. How true.

But for me, fear is today and dying is now. You slip in and out of my room, give me medication and check my blood pressure. Is it because I am a student nurse, myself, or just a human being, that I sense your fright? And your fears enhance mine. Why are you afraid? I am the one who is dying!

I know, you feel insecure, don't know what to say, don't know what to do. But please believe me, if you care, you can't go wrong. Just admit that you care. That is really for what we search. We may ask for why's and wherefores, but we don't really expect answers. Don't run away ... wait ... all I want to know is that there will be someone to hold my hand when I need it. I am afraid. Death may get to be a routine to you, but it is new to me. You may not see me as unique, but I've never died before. To me, once is pretty unique!

You whisper about my youth, but when one is dying, is he really so young anymore? I have lots I wish we could talk about. It really would not take much more of your time because you are in here quite a bit anyway.

If only we could be honest, both admit of our fears, touch one another. If you really care, would you lose so much of your valuable professionalism if you even cried with me? Just person to person? Then, it might not be so hard to die - in a hospital - with friends close by.

Anon

FROM JOYCE: BY HERSELF AND HER FRIENDS

If I should go before the rest of you,
Break not a flower nor inscribe a stone,
Nor when I'm gone speak in a Sunday Voice,
But be the usual selves that I have known.
Weep if you must,
Parting is hell,
But life goes on,
So sing as well.

Joyce Grenfell

THE LESSON

'Your father's gone,' my bald headmaster said.
His shiny dome and brown tobacco jar
Splintered at once in tears. It wasn't grief.
I cried for knowledge which was bitterer
Than any grief. For there and then I knew
That grief has uses - that a father dead
Could bind the bully's fist a week or two;
And then I cried for shame, then for relief.

I was a month past ten when I learnt this:
I still remember how the noise was stilled
In school-assembly when my grief came in.
Some goldfish in a bowl quietly sculled
Around their shining prison on its shelf.
They were indifferent. All the other eyes
Were turned towards me. Somewhere in myself
Pride like a goldfish flashed a sudden fin.

Edward Lucie - Smith
copyright © 1964

LONDON
(an excerpt)

When I returned from school I found we'd moved:
'53 Church Street. Yes, the slummy end' -
A little laugh accompanied the joke,
For we were Chelsea new and we had friends
Whose friends had friends who knew Augustus John:
We liked bold colour schemes - orange and black -
And clever daring plays about divorce
At the St. Martin's. Oh, our lives were changed!

John Betjeman

When my father died
I never cried.

When my plant looked sad,
I thought, I know,
I'll ask my dad.

And then I cried.

Anon

MY DAD

March 11th was when he died,
That's when we all cried.
something happened to his brain,
The thought of death drove me insane.
My heart was what no one could mend,
I couldn't sleep for days on end.

The next couple of days were really hard,
Somebody sent a bereavement card.
The day of the funeral suddenly came,
There was his coffin, inscribed with his
name.
We had a party, in memory of dad,
Everyone there, was so sad.

What I remember most about dad,
Are all the good times we had.
He knew how to play his cards right,
He always loved to fly his kite.
My dad was brainy, not a dope,
And since he died, I've learned to cope.

Boy of 13

POOR LITTLE JOE

Poor little Joe,
Stuck in your wheel-chair,
No one will talk to you
No one will care.
All day long
On your own
At school.
Poor little Joe,
Stuck out on your own!
Go join them, have some fun!
"They don't want to play, so what can I do?"
Just hang around
And wait;
Just talk to them
And hope;
Poor little Joe.

D. Norris

HIS LIFE AND HERS

I know a girl who's anorexic.
She vomits night and day.
I know a boy who isn't,
but he's dying anyway.

She longs to be a model,
Slim and slender as they say;
He longs to have plump arms and legs,
But he's dying anyway.

She haunts herself with visions
Of buttocks as they sway;
He's revolted by his body,
But he's dying anyway.

He sits amongst the shadows
Trying to recall his life,
But all that he remembers
Is hunger, drought and strife.

She's obsessed with thoughts of weight and size
Her whole life is a mass of lies;
He longs for love, food and care:
She's crying as he's dying.

Frances Maclennan (12)
Hewett School, Norwich, Norfolk

HOPE

The handicapped child sits tied to his wheel chair,
Gazing sorrowfully into the deep blue sky,
Watching the gusty wind move the clouds,
Across the watercolour turquoise heavens.
Children seem to shout and scream everywhere
In ignorance of the young cripple's plight.
Their rejoicing echoes the deep, cavernous
Thoughts of the boy.
"Come on, Michael, Eat up!"
His eyes return to the triangular head of the nurse,
Each eyeball swelling with the bottomless pit
Of emotion he holds,
A deep, sinking hope.
She bangs his spoon against the mashed potato.
A primeval sign to eat.
The two wells of self-pity and deprivation
Cut through the nurse.
She winces,
Emotion like a germ has been
Passed on,
A fleeting glance has said all.
The self anguish has been released from its cage;
The bell and mirror can be left to rot and decay,
There must still be hope.

D. Grant

102

GROWING UP

In Infancy
He finds it very hard to play
like other little boys;
He'd rather wreck the Wendy house
or smash the classroom toys.
Poor mite, he's from a broken home
and hasn't got a dad;
It's social deprivation,
he isn't really bad.

In Boyhood
It seems he lies and often steals,
and tends to be a bully.
He swears and cheats, he's insolent
and thoroughly unruly.
But being underprivileged
should earn him absolution
And so we have to help him
escape from retribution.

In Adolescence
Completely antisocial,
a vandal and a thug.
He reckons every working lad
is nothing but a mug.
Because we feel he's still a case
for pity more than blame,
We try to ease his passage through
the Courts to spare his name.

Manhood
And now he's holding hostages
but claims it's not a crime,
That when his 'just' demands are met
they'll be released on time.
He swears that it's the System,
which causes all the pain
And if he has to kill them,
Society's to blame.

He cannot win by argument
much popular support
And so he's turned to Terror which
he thinks will be great sport
Now we've begun to wonder,
recall and try to trace;
Did we help to convince him
that he's a special case?

M.H.L.

SOMETIMES IT HAPPENS

And sometimes it happens that you are
friends and then
You are not friends,
And friendship has passed.
And whole days are lost and among them
A fountain empties itself.

And sometimes it happens that you are
loved and then
You are not loved,
And love is past.
And whole days are lost and among them
A fountain empties itself into the grass.

And sometimes you want to speak to her
and then
You do not want to speak,
Then the opportunity has passed.
Your dreams flare up, they suddenly vanish.

And also it happens that there is nowhere to
go and then
There is somewhere to go,
Then you have bypassed.
And the years flare up and are gone,
Quicker than a minute.

So you have nothing.
You wonder if these things matter and then
As soon as you begin to wonder if these
things matter
They cease to matter,
And caring is past.
And a fountain empties itself into the grass.

Brian Patten

103

PAKISTANI

FUNERAL AT THE TRAFFIC LIGHTS

A corpse is passing, stiff in turquoise.
Mourners follow in a broken line.
It is my third corpse in a week.
These are the flowers of April and this is the red neon sign.

More like a sofa than man, woman, hermaphrodite in bright
upholstery. Beyond this, the corpse refuses to be named.
Like many others I simply drive my car.
A keen sun is shining. No one is ashamed.

It could have been anyone, a shady undertaker , a crook,
a waiter, or a wife. Now it lies, its lines jammed tight,
its eyes barbed, its tongue hooked, its tossing
stopped, its silly secrets buried overnight.

The mourners mourn in Arabic. They will carry
the body, as though it were a dead king,
down past the drugstore, though the fish-market, thinking maybe
since it died in April, it will dream of spring.

Dust to dust. The traffic sign turns amber.
Tier by Tier, the dead are cosy in the rustling loam.
Uncanny parcel, you have been sealed, stamped
and registered, ready for the journey home.

Adrian Hussain

GRANDMOTHER

The bright needles clicked;
The old woman's hands,
Quick, dextrous and expert,
Were a blur of colour.
"Your new gloves are finished."
She eased them on to
My short plum fingers.
"Now you can play in the snow."
I ran into the street, excited.
The gloves, soft, warm and dry
Were a magical source
Of safety and love.
Time drew on;
My winters grew colder;
The snow fell thicker.
Today my gloves
Are faded and thread-bare;
Her needles lie silent
And my hands are so cold.

Robert McGregor (15)
Debenham High School,
Stowmarket, Suffolk
(Highly commended)

LIVING WITH LOSS   2.4

The way we adapt to loss in our lives such as losing a favourite pet, a sentimental possession, a friend moving away, reflects the way we will adapt when there is a major loss fin our lives such as divorce or a bereavement. But remember what is a major loss for one person could be a minor one for someone else e.g. moving home

Here are some examples where there are changes in our lives that give us a real sense of loss:-

STARTING SCHOOL	
NEW BROTHER OR SISTER	
MOVING HOME	
CHANGE OF SCHOOL	
GRANDPARENT DIES	
PARENTS SEPARATE	
CHANGING TEACHER	
CHANGING FRIENDS	
PARENT LOSES JOB	
FAILING EXAMS	
CHOOSING ACADEMIC OPTIONS	
LEAVING SCHOOL	
BROKEN LEG, INFECTIOUS DISEASE	

LIVING WITH LOSS:

Life is made of joy and woe:
And when this we rightly know
Thro' the world we safely go.

From 'Auguries of Innocence' William Blake.

Objectives:

To help the students realize that loss touches everyone throughout life and that these experiences can be used as a process for growth.

To understand the grieving process and that the associated feelings can apply to all forms of loss and not just death.

To appreciate that grief is a necessary and important response to situations of loss. That 'Good Grief' accepts that loss is a natural and positive part of life and that avoiding painful feelings means we can also lose happy feelings to.

To show how prejudice can heighten the sense of loss experienced by members of the community.

N.B. Because of the nature of this subject it is important to establish ground rules* at the beginning of this section (*see 'Setting the Scene").

Resources:

Background reading found in Section 1.

INTRODUCING LOSS

Resources:

Writing Paper
Definition of 'Loss'

Method:

1) Hand out paper and ask the group to write the word 'Loss' in the centre of it.

2) Invite the group to write at random all the types of loss they can think of - (give examples from 'Understanding Loss' to demonstrate that loss can be of a significant person, part of self, situation, object or phase of life.

3) When the students have finished, ask volunteers to share and make a composite list.

4) Divide students into small groups and ask them to make an individual, and then group, definition of the word 'Loss'.

5) Reform large group and share the definitions and how they were arrived at - compare with the dictionary definition of the word 'Loss'.

106

FEELINGS ASSOCIATED WITH LOSS

Resources

- For Method A: Copies of Activity 'Feelings Associated with Loss'.

- For Method B: Flip paper and pens, copies of 'Loss, Grief and Mourning', and/or 'Stages of Grief'.

Method A:

1) Discuss and clarify the group's understanding of the word 'feeling'. Make a list of the common feelings they have experienced. E.g. happy, sad, angry, etc.

2) Hand out activity 'Feelings associated with Loss' and ask them to include any other feelings of their own choice.

3) Invite students to share their answers either in pairs, small group and/or volunteers in the large group.

Extensions:

- Ask the group to write a story, or poem, or to draw a picture, about a real or imaginary loss using some of the words they have circled.

- Explore colours which we somehow link with various feelings. E.g. black day, blue mood, rosy future.

- Explore ways in which music can reflect feelings associated with loss.

Method B:

1) a. Ask the students to shut their eyes and think about an object which is important to them (e.g. cassette player).

  b. Ask them to remember where they keep it and imagine going there to look for it.

  c. Tell them it has gone and let them become aware of the loss.

  d. Ask them to open their eyes and let volunteers share how they feel about the loss. Make a list of these feelings on the flip chart.

2) Tell them to imagine that it is now half an hour later and they still have not found the missing object. Ask the following questions:-

  a. How do they feel now?

  b. Have they told anyone? (If not, why not?)

  Share responses of the students.

3) Repeat question 2, but ask them to imagine the object has now been missing for a day, then a week, then six months and finally for a year.

4) Ask them to share how they feel about the loss at these different intervals.

5)   Depending on the age and ability of the group, hand out 'Loss, Grief and Mourning' and/or 'Stages of Grief' and/or 'Whirlpool of Grief'. Discuss how these relate to the loss situations they chose as well as death.

N.B. Grieving involves letting go of the identity we had with someone or something we love and rebuilding another identity without them/it. The sooner we learn to grieve the sooner we can begin to enjoy the life we still have. If we shut out painful feelings we generally shut out the good ones too.

Two of the most difficult emotions can be guilt and anger

Guilt - is generally about things in the past which we cannot change, only learn from "if only I had..........."

How to Help:

1) **Reality Test** - were we really guilty. Most of us did the best we could at the time, with the knowledge and the skills we had.

2) **Apologise** - to the person if possible, otherwise write a letter, even if the person is dead, it lets the feelings out..

3) **Learn from it** - If I were in the situation again what could I do differently "We all make mistakes, I always aim to make them new ones". (Professor M. Simpson)

Anger - often masks hurt. If repressed it can cause stress and/or depression.

How to Help:

1) **Recognise and acknowledge feelings**. You are less likely to act agressively if you accept anger as a normal response to loss. Say "I am angry because. . . . " <u>not</u> "You make me angry. . . . . "

2) **As in "Guilt" above.**

3) **Find outlets for anger**, e.g. stamping feet, shouting, thumping cushions, drawing, painting, dancing it out or playing music.

WORKSHEET

FEELINGS ASSOCIATED WITH LOSS

Circle the feelings you, or other people you know, have experienced at times of loss. You may like to add other ones of your own.

Bewildered

Dazed   Disorientated

Denial   Panic   Misunderstood

Self Pity   Distress   Disbelief   Apprehensive

Alienated   Unloved   Grief   Pain

Lonely   Burdened   Unwanted   Hopeless

Vulnerable   Hurt   Redundant   Tired

Anxious   Impotent   Helpless   Worthless

Insecure   Guilty   Shocked   Revengeful

Relief   Tearful   Powerless   Numb

               Freedom   Sad   Fear

                              Release   Unhappy

                                                Gratitude

LOSS, GRIEF AND MOURNING

We do not need to have lived long before we experience LOSS. For example, as little children we might have lost a special toy; we might have lost some friends when we moved from one school to another; a favourite pet might have died, and we feel this as a great LOSS. Sometimes the loss is only a little one, but sometimes it is more important and makes us sad or unhappy. From time to time we may want to cry about the losses in our lives, yet we will not always let ourselves do this - perhaps because we are afraid that we may be called a "cry-baby". In this way, we do not always have the freedom to express our feelings, and this can make things very difficult for us when we experience an important loss.

For many of us there comes a time when we experience a very big loss - the loss of one of our family who dies. It might be the death of a grandparent, whom we especially loved; it might be our mother or father, or a brother or sister. This kind of loss is known as BEREAVEMENT, and if one of our family dies, we are then BEREAVED. When someone very close to us dies and we feel sadness and unhappiness - that feeling is called GRIEF.

Feelings of grief may be very different for each of us, depending on how close we were to the person who died, on what our relationship was to him or her (was he a parent, or a brother?) and on the circumstances in which he or she died. The closer we were to the person who died, the greater we will feel our loss. As children and teenagers our parents play a vital role in our lives. We would probably feel, far greater, the loss of our father or mother whom we lived with and depended on to look after us, than we would feel the loss of a relative we did not see very often. However, for us the grief of losing a parent will be different to the grief felt by our mother who has lost a husband, or our father who has lost a wife. Also the way in which the person died may affect how we feel about it, for some time to come. For example, we might be in a state of shock for a long time, following a very sudden death.

The sadness of grief can be like a pain inside us. But grief does not last forever. The way in which we feel about our loss changes as time moves on. The process by which we express our grief is called MOURNING. When we are mourning we might have many different feelings - we might feel numbness, shock, pain, sadness, anger or guilt. There is usually a kind of pattern to how we feel. To start with, we will probably find it a great shock that the person we love so much is dead; it is very difficult to believe, and we feel numb. After a time we begin to understand that he or she is really dead and will not be coming back to us. We may begin to pine and long for him. We may also feel angry for many reasons, for example, angry that life has dealt us and our family such a cruel blow and perhaps for forcing on us responsibilities for which we may not feel ready.

When we are feeling grief, each of us have different ways of expressing what we are feeling. Some people seem to cry a lot; some people are very quiet and hide their feelings, and some people talk about it. Very often what we feel like doing and what seems "correct" to do can be quite different. When we feel like crying we are told to be "brave" or "strong". Traditionally in most western countries, we are expected to suffer our grief privately. In some parts of the world, however, people are encouraged to cry aloud and to share their feelings with the whole community. It is time that we (all of us - adults, teenagers and children alike) learned that crying is NOT a sign of weakness - instead it is a sign of deep feeling.

In Ireland, friends, relatives and neighbours often help bereaved families, more than they do in other western countries. Many bereaved families still have a wake before the funeral. This is a time when lots of people in the community mourn the death of one of their members and express their sorrow for the family. The wake can help us through that period of disbelief, numbness and panic, but it may also seem very strange and unreal to us. It is after the wake and funeral that most of us need help and support and sadly this can sometimes be difficult to find.

When a member of our family dies, we have lost something and someone very precious and in one form or another that loss will always be with us. We will not however always feel grief and be in mourning. But for the time being, we must realise that the pain of grief is every bit as much a part of life as is the joy of love.

Northern Ireland Cruse

STAGES OF GRIEF

Grief is a normal, essential response to the death of a loved one. It can be short lived or last a long time depending on the personality involved, the closeness of the relationship, the circumstances of the death and previous losses suffered. Death of a husband, wife or child is likely to be the most difficult.

In many cases, this grief can take the form of several clearly defined stages. Very often a bereaved person can only resume a normal emotional life after working through these stages.

1)   SHOCK and disbelief

This happens when our model of the world is upset. One not only loses the person but life also can feel that it has lost its meaning. Shock can take the form of physical pain or numbness, but more often consists of complete apathy and withdrawal or abnormal calm, in some cases even anger. Numbness can act as a defence so we are able to cope with the immediate jobs and needs.

2)   DENIAL

This generally occurs within the first 14 days and can last minutes, hours or weeks. In this stage the bereaved person behaves as if the dead person is still there, no loss is acknowledged. The dead person's place is still laid at meal times, for example, or a husband may make arrangements for both he and his wife to go somewhere together.

3)   GROWING AWARENESS

Many feel at this stage that they are abnormal because they have never before experienced the waves of savage feelings that surge through them and over which they temporarily have no control e.g. tears, anger, guilt, sadness and loneliness. Some or all of the following emotions may be experienced:-

a) Yearning and pining - urge to search, go over death, trying to find a reason for the death, visiting where it happened.

b) Anger - This can be against any or all of the following, the medical services, the person who caused the death, in case of accident. God for letting it happen, the deceased for leaving them

c) Depression - The bereaved person begins to feel the despair, the emptiness, the pain of the loss. It is often accompanied by feelings of redundancy, lack of self worth, and point to anything. If a person can cry, it usually helps to relieve the stress.

d) Guilt - This emotion is felt for the real or imagined negligence or harm inflicted on the person who has just died. People often say 'if only I had called the Doctor - not gone out' etc. There is a tendency to idealize the person who has died and feel they could have loved them better. The bereaved can also feel guilty about their own feelings and inability to enjoy life.

e) Anxiety - In extreme cases anxiety can even become panic - as the full realization of the loss begins to come through. There is anxiety about the changes and new responsibilities that are taking place and the loneliness looming ahead. There may even be thoughts of suicide.

4)   ACCEPTANCE

This generally occurs in the second year after the death has been relived at the first anniversary. The bereaved person is then able to relearn the world and new situations with its possibilities and changes without the deceased person.

WHIRLPOOL OF GRIEF

This broad pictorial approach may help to emphasise that the details of each persons experience of bereavement is individual. A conversation or an interview should begin with the recognition that we know nothing about this particular person until we have listened to what they have to say. Their previous experiences in life, the person they have lost, the manner of their dying and the reactions of the world are all different.

The "River of Life" which may previously have run smooth, the "Waterfall of Bereavement" in which one is suspended in shock, and the "Whirlpool of Grief" may be a little fanciful. However, it is less rigid than suggesting that there are Stages of Grief which must be completed. People cannot be healed by shepherding them through a fixed treatment plan; however we may be of some assistance as they make their way along their own difficult and personal journey.

Grief is a turbulent time, although there may be precious periods of calm, violent emotions which had seemed to be over can return. They are innumerable and all valid. In grief there is a disorganisation of life and thought and values, but most people are then able to reorganise their life in a new way. Although old emotions can always return in almost the same intensity, they do so infrequently and for much shorter periods of time.

Sigmund Freud wrote in a letter to a friend whose son had died "Although we know that after such a loss, the acute stage of mourning will subside, we also know that we shall remain inconsolable and will never find a substitute. No matter what may fill the gap, even if it be filled completely, it nevertheless remains something else."

A girl of about 8 years was talking to her longtime best friend about her baby brother who died 4 years previously. Her friend said, "Oh, but that was a long time ago." She said, "It's not a long time if you love somebody."

Richard Wilson
Consultant Paeditician
Kingston Hospital

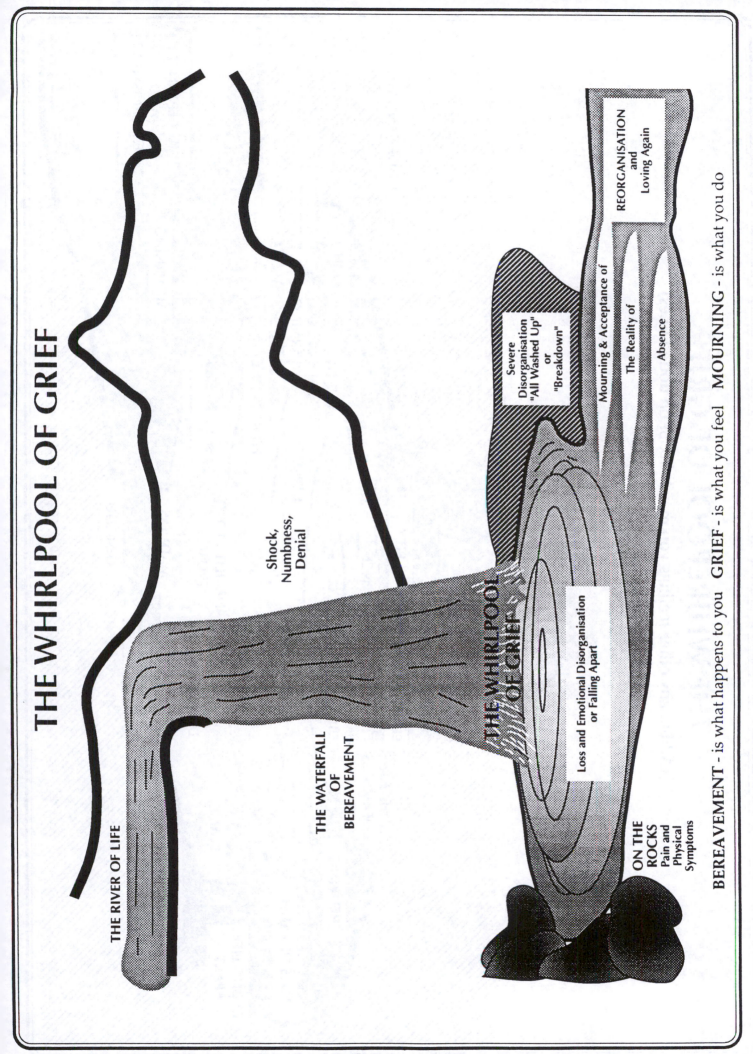

THE WHIRLPOOL OF GRIEF

THE RIVER OF LIFE

Shock, Numbness, Denial

THE WATERFALL OF BEREAVEMENT

THE WHIRLPOOL OF GRIEF

Loss and Emotional Disorganisation or Falling Apart

Severe Disorganisation "All Washed Up" or "Breakdown"

Mourning & Acceptance of

The Reality of

Absence

REORGANISATION and Loving Again

ON THE ROCKS
Pain and Physical Symptoms

BEREAVEMENT - is what happens to you   GRIEF - is what you feel   MOURNING - is what you do

THE WHIRLPOOL OF GRIEF

(Add in any other feelings you may think of on dotted lines)

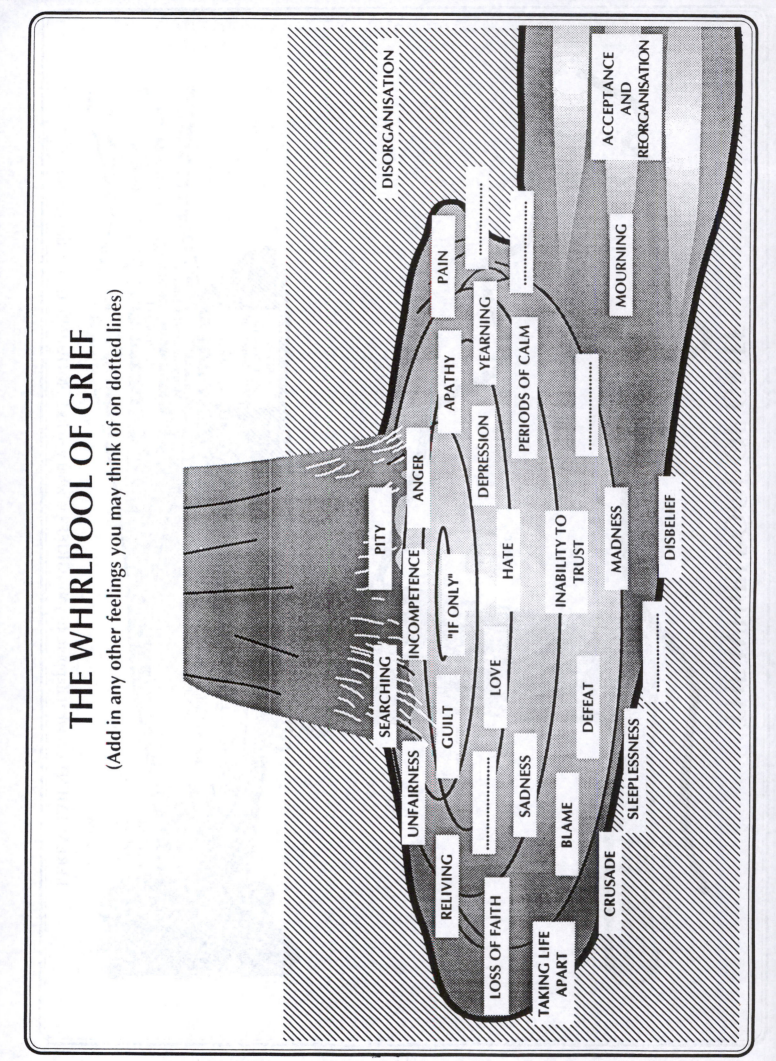

HOW OTHERS FEEL

Resources

Labels with names on

Explain that loss can affect us all in different ways and that the purpose of this exercise is to think how they would feel in this particular situation.

Method

1) One student at a time takes a label and puts it on and without the group interrupting states briefly:

    a. Their immediate personal reaction to the character they have been given.

    b. The reaction they think other people could have to this particular group.

2) The whole group then discuss and share their experiences with the particular group in question.

3) Each student repeats 1 - 3 until everyone has had a turn.

4) Debrief. It is essential to allow time to discuss the feelings aroused and to ask the students to re-establish their own identities e.g. I am not a redundant person of 45, I am John Smith.

SUGGESTED LABELS

Unemployed young person

Redundant person of 45

* A rape victim

Single parent with teenage children

* Girl of 14 who has been sexually abused

A disabled telephonist

Boy with downs syndrome

Add other labels of your own choice

Widowed person of 35

* Gay with AIDS

Senior citizen

Homeless person

Unmarried mother

Black policeman

* Only use with care with mature students and if you know your group well.

Extension/Alteration

- 'Agony column' use letters from popular magazines,
   This can allow distancing of feelings and anoymity for the more vulnerable.
- 'Photographs' The use of appropriate pictures can be used in a similar way to "Agony Column" above.

HOW WOULD I FEEL

Resources

Copies of different situations
'Stages of Grief' (Living with Loss)

Explain that loss can affect us all in different ways and that the purpose of this exercise is to think how they would feel in this particular situation.

Method

1) Divide students into pairs or small groups and give a situation to each.

2) Ask them to read and then either:-

    a) imagine what they would feel like if it happened to them

or b) imagine what they would feel like if it happened to someone else

      ((b) would be less emotional)

3) Re-group and ask volunteers to share experiences and relate to 'Stages of Grief'.

Extension

- These situations could be role played
  Remember the importance of debriefing

- Suggestions could be made of what would help in these situations
  See 'Helping Strategies' in Sec. 1.

SUGGESTED SITUATIONS

1) You are 16 and about to take your G.C.S.E. when your family have to suddenly move 200 miles away due to a change in your father/mother's job.

2) You break your leg just before you are to captain the school team.

3) The parent of a close friend has died.

4) Your Aunt has been told she is dying of cancer. You visit her in hospital.

5) A fellow student was killed in a motor-cycle accident. You speak to his parents at the funeral.

6) Your best friend's sister commits suicide.

7) Your pet cat is run over and killed.

8) Your child of 8 dies from leukaemia.

9) Your parents have suddenly told you they are separating/divorcing.

10) You are 5 years old and are lost.

11) You start a new school or college and don't know anybody.

12) Your family moves to a country where your mother tongue is not the main language.

COPING WITH LOSS

Resources

Copies of Activity 'Coping With Loss' and 'Time line'
Difficulties in Grieving (see 'Helping the Bereaved')
Understanding Loss in Section 1

Method

1) Remind students of the different types of loss. Tell them they could also be described as changes or transitions.

2) Hand out question sheet and 'Time Line' for 'Coping with Loss' Activity.
Give e.g.'s from own experience before asking students to complete.

3) Invite students to share in pairs or small groups and/or volunteers to share Time Line answers in the large group. On question (2) remind them that all change has potential for loss & gain.

4) Read *"There is no growth without pain and conflict and no loss that cannot lead to gain"* (Lily Pincus 'Death in the Family') or a poem or prose of your own choice. Then ask the group to list the negative and then the positive aspects of loss. (end by focusing on positive aspects, e.g. "Good Grief")

Extension

- Alternatively, the exercise may be done in pairs as an interview, with the interviewer filling in the answers.

- Read or hand out 'Difficulties in Grieving' and discuss.

- This theme could be continued with the "whole life with relationships grid" in chapter 8 of "FEEL THE FEAR DO IT ANYWAY".
See additional resources section '3'.

COPING WITH LOSS

1) Using the 'Time Line' write and/or draw in the different losses you have experienced in your life.

2) Do you feel all the losses on your 'Time Line' are causes for grief? Give reasons why -

....

....

....

....

3) Choose one of the loss situations and describe briefly what helped in that situation -

....

....

....

....

4) Describe briefly what did not help in the situation you chose in Q.3.

....

....

....

....

5) What did you learn about yourself and/or other people as a result of this experience -

....

....

....

....

....

6) On looking back would you have done anything different?

....

....

....

....

7) How do you think you could use your experiences of loss to prepare yourself for important losses in the future?

....

....

....

....

8) How could you use your experiences of loss to help other people?

....

....

....

....

9) The Chinese sign for "Crisis" means Danger and Opportunity. How does this relate to your experience of Loss?

. . . .

. . . .

. . . .

. . . .

. . . .

. . . .

. . . .

. . . .

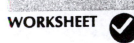

COPING WITH LOSS

My Time Line

Age

0 Years

e g. 4-5 yrs started School

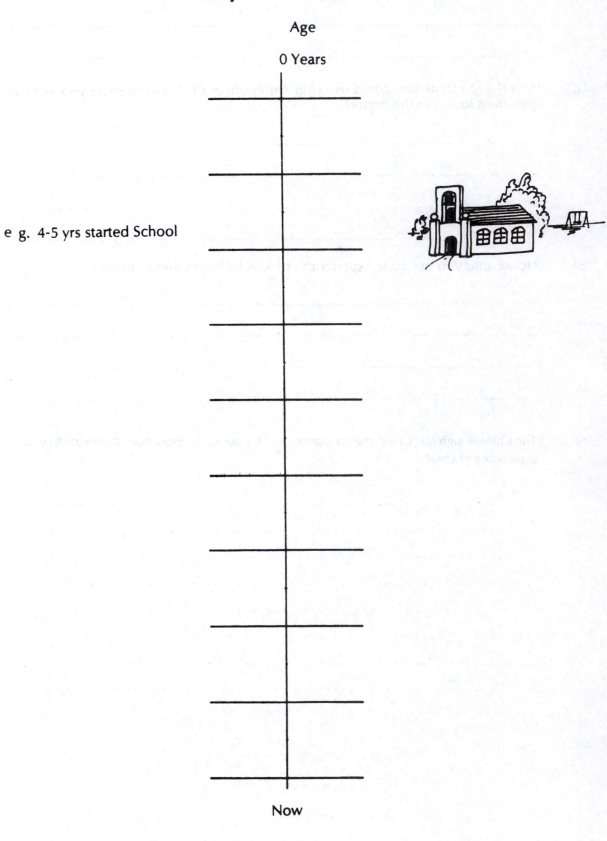

Now

LOSS AND HEALTH

Resources

Copies of SOCIAL RE-ADJUSTMENT SCALES for students, & for educators.
- see following pages
See 'Understanding Loss' in Section 1.

Notes for Educators

This scale was devised in 1968 by Americans Holmes and Rahe, and rates life changes according to the amount of re-adjustment needed.

The scale quantifies life change events in terms of the likelihood of illness resulting. People with a score of over 300 in any one year were found to have a 4 out of 5 chance of becoming ill in the following year.

Method

1)   Introduce and hand out the 'students' copy of the scale
     N.B. The 'Values' and 'How to Score' have been omitted from the student's copy as they can cause anxiety to people under stress.

2)   Ask students to rate the events from 1 - 100, in order of importance for them.

3)   Invite students to share their results in pairs, then to compare the top 5 of the students ratings with the top 5 on Holmes a Rahe scale. Discuss differences and suggest reasons why these occur.

Extensions

-    Ask students to imagine that someone has died and score all the other events that could affect them as well.

-    As above but use a loss situation instead - (e.g. moving house).

SOCIAL RE-ADJUSTMENT SCALE

Stress Test
(Educator's Copy)

Event	Value
Death of spouse	100
Divorce	73
Giving up "Hard Drugs"	71
Marital separation	65
Prison sentence	63
Death of a close family member	63
Personal injury or illness	53
Marriage	50
Sacked or made redundant	47
Marital reconciliation	45
Retirement	45
Change in family member's health	44
Pregnancy	40
Giving up 40 or more cigarettes a day	40
Sex difficulties	39
Addition to the family	39
Business re-adjustment	39
Change in financial state	38
Death of a close friend	37
Change to a new line of work	36
Change in number of arguments with spouse	35
Foreclosure of mortgage or loan	31
Mortgage over 20,000	30
Change in work responsibility	29
Son or Daughter leaving home	29
Trouble with in-laws	29
Outstanding personal achievement	28
Wife begins or stops work	26
Children start or stop School	26
Change in living conditions	25
Revised personal habits	24
Trouble with boss	23
Giving up smoking - fewer than 40 a day	21
Change working hours or conditions	20
Change in residence	20
Change School	20
Change recreation	19
Change Church activity	19
Change social activity	18
Mortgage or loan under 20,000	17
Change in sleeping habits	16
Change in number of family get-togethers	15
Change in eating habits	15
Holiday	13
Christmas	12
Minor law violations	11

_____
Total

Adapted from Holmes & Rahe

How to Score
Below 60: your life has been unusually free from stress lately.
60 to 80: you have had a normal amount of stress recently. This score is average for the ordinary wear and tear of life.
80 to 100: the stress in your life is a little high, probably because of one recent event.
100 upwards: pressures are piling up, either at home or work, or both. You are under serious stress, and the higher you score above 100 the worse the strain.

SOCIAL RE-ADJUSTMENT SCALE

Stress Test
(Students Copy)

Event	Your Score
Death of spouse	
Divorce	
Giving up "Hard Drugs"	
Marital separation	
Prison sentence	
Death of a close family member	
Personal injury or illness	
Marriage	
Sacked or made redundant	
Marital reconciliation	
Retirement	
Change in family member's health	
Pregnancy	
Giving up 40 or more cigarettes a day	
Sex difficulties	
Addition to the family	
Business re-adjustment	
Change in financial state	
Death of a close friend	
Change to a new line of work	
Change in number of arguments with spouse	
Foreclosure of mortgage or loan	
Mortgage over 20,000	
Change in work responsibility	
Son or Daughter leaving home	
Trouble with in-laws	
Outstanding personal achievement	
Wife begins or stops work	
Children start or stop School	
Change in living conditions	
Revised personal habits	
Trouble with boss	
Giving up smoking - fewer than 40 a day	
Change working hours or conditions	
Change in residence	
Change School	
Change recreation	
Change Church activity	
Change social activity	
Mortgage or loan under 20,000	
Change in sleeping habits	
Change in number of family get-togethers	
Change in eating habits	
Holiday	
Christmas	
Minor law violations	
	_____ Total

Adapted from Holmes & Rahe

DIVORCE AND SEPARATION
ONE PARENT FAMILIES

"Relationships are there to grow a part of us. When we've grown that part, we need to either deepen the relationship or move on".

Anon

OBJECTIVES

To help students recognise that divorce and separation are an important form of loss that can affect all those involved in different ways.

To recognise that those involved in divorce and separation need to grieve.

To enable students from single parent families to feel less alienated.

N.B. All groups will include students who have been or are involved in such situations, so particular sensitivity will be needed.

INTRODUCING DIVORCE & SEPARATION

Resources - Background reading on Divorce, Separation and Loss in Section 1. Suggested books and articles in Section 3. Have library books available for follow up.

Pieces of paper.

Method A

Use the activity "Feelings associated with Loss" on Page 110. Method A and extensions, but use the topic"Divorce?Separation" in place of "Loss".

Method B

Use the Worksheet "Social Re-Adjustment Scale" students' worksheet on page 126? Ask students to mark other events that could happen at times of divorce & separation. Discuss in pairs/small groups and then a larger group.

WHAT IS A FAMILY

Tell the students that more than one in three marriages end in divorce. One in three children are born outside marriage and that one in five children will experience a parental divorce by the age of sixteen (see "Statistics for Britain" in Section 1) and that you are going to introduce an activity to look at what a 'family' is.

Method

1) Divide students into groups of five and give each person a piece of paper.

2) Ask each group to choose a surname, then one of the following roles: father, mother, son, daughter,grandparent.

3) Give the students five minutes to write down the following details of the person they have chosen to represent: Christian name, surname, age, occupation, income,hobbies/interests, favourite magazines/books/television programmes.

4) When finished ask students to share details with other members of their group.

5) Ask all groups to fold their pieces of paper in four. Then ask the students to stand in a circle and pass the pieces of paper around until you tell them to stop.

6) Ask the students to unfold their pieces of paper, read the details, then find a family by comparing the details with other members of the group.

7) When all students have found a "family" ask them why they chose those particular roles. This leads into a useful discussion of what constitutes a "family. Ideally there should be a mixture from single parents to extended families. In one class one boy was asked why he was on his own. He said "because I'm an orphan".

Extensions

- Ask a member of "Relate" to talk about the work of the organisation.

- Debate e.g. "It is better for children if their parents stay together or "Families are no longer necessary".

- Read Professor Caplan's article in Section 1. Ask the students if they would add or` change ahything.

- Ask the students to compile a list of needs for younger and older children.

WHAT IS DEATH?

2.6

"To live in hearts we leave behind is not to die"

Objectives

Thomas Campbell

To enable students to explore the reality of death.

To stimulate discussion and share different points of view about death.

To prepare students for death in their own families or people close to them.

To explore whether death is really the end.

To examine the role of the media in our attitudes to death.

To be aware of the effects of different types of death, accidental disaster, murder, natural and suicide.

N.B. Because of the sensitive nature of the subject it is important to establish ground rules* at the beginning of this section (* see "Setting the Scene")

INTRODUCING DEATH

Resources

Writing materials.

Method A

1) Ask the group to write the word 'Death' in the middle of a sheet of paper.

2) Invite the students to write down at random (without thinking hard or censoring) all the words that come into their minds when they hear the word 'Death' (Give examples e.g. sorrow, cremation).

3) When the students have finished ask them to circle the words they find most meaningful.

4) Suggest the students write a sentence, short story or poem or make a drawing which explains why these words are important to them.

N.B. This activity could also be undertaken in pairs or in groups.

Method B

(Can be used as an extension of Method A or on its own).

1) Divide the students into small groups with a reporter in each.

2) Allow time for the group to discuss 'What is Death'.

3) Ask each group to decide on a definition of the word 'Death'.

4) Re-form into large group, share the definitions and how arrived at - discuss and clarify.

Extensions

-    Introduce other words to do with loss or use words from the 'Make your own glossary' section

THOUGHTS ABOUT DEATH

Resources

Copies of 'My Thoughts about Death (1) and/or 'My Thoughts about Death (2).

A selection of poetry or prose illustrating* other peoples thoughts about death
(*See 'Creative Writing')
'Oxford Book of Death' and 'Standpoints' - Death'.See 'Additional Resources 3.2'

Method

1) Introduce and hand out activity 'My Thoughts About Death' (1)

2) Ask students to write their statements on a slip of paper then exchange these and read out.

3) Introduce 'My Thoughts About Death' (2).

4) Share in pairs or small groups and/or invite volunteers to share in large groups.

N.B. If only one of these activities is being used adapt the method accordingly.

Extension

- Share other statements from well known people, e.g. "I only know I fear not death if I survive the dying". Sir Thomas Browne. (See Resources above).

- Use 'My Thoughts About Death (2) as a class survey. See 'Life After Death' activity. Remind students this is a sensitive area and select participants carefully.

- Ask the students which types of death are likely to produce the most difficult feelings e.g. guilt and anger.
  see 1.11 and 1.15 and "Feelings Associated with Loss".

MY THOUGHTS ABOUT DEATH (1)

Below are statements some young people have made about 'Death'. Read them carefully and then add your own idea of what 'Death' means to you, in the space underneath -

1) "I wish someone could die, come back to life, and tell us what really does happen."
2) "I don't believe there is a heaven or a hell."
3) "I believe in God because when my little brother died, praying helped a lot."
4) "Bodies wear out, but I don't see how souls can."
5) "I believe we are sent by God and taken back to Him when He likes. We don't own our lives; God does."
6) "I think death is final and it's a terrifying thought: the thought of nothing. So life must be lived to the fullest."
7) "Humans, animals, plants, and all other living things live in different lives, time after time."
8) "There is something, some force, other than my heart, brain, lungs and blood keeping me going."
9) "I think one energy flows through all living things: human beings and nature. Some people think of it as God: the Chinese call it Tao. The name's not important; it's what it is and what it does that matters."
10) "I am a Muslim, so I have to try and follow the rules of Islam as best I can. I believe in a life after death, an eternal heaven and hell, and in God whether He is the God of Christians, Jews, or Hindus."
11) "If you're buried, you rot away to earth. The earth feeds the plants and then something or someone will eat the plants, so your dead body has created an afterlife."

These statements of belief and disbelief made by young people much like yourselves echo the feelings and fears people have had about death in every age.

My Statement about 'Death' is

....

....

....

....

....

....

....

....

....

MY THOUGHTS ABOUT DEATH (2)

"To die must be an awfully big adventure."   **Peter Pan**

1)   Do you ever think about your own death? If so, what feelings do you have about it?

....

....

2)   Have you ever experienced the death of someone close to you? If so, who?

....

3)   The Person's whose death I fear most is?

....

4)   Have you ever attended a funeral? .... Was it for a relative or a friend?   ....

....

5)   Do you believe in a life after death?   Yes .... No ....

Uncertain ....

6)   How much has religion influenced you attitude towards death?
greatly .... significantly .... somewhat ....
very little .... not at all ....

7)   My idea of the ideal age to die is? ....

8)   My idea of the best kind of death is? ....

....

9)   My idea of the worst kind of death is? ....

....

10) Any other thoughts I have about death

....

....

....

....

....

DEATH AND THE MEDIA

Resources

Large sheets of coloured paper or card, glue, scissors, felt pens, selection of newspapers and magazines.

Methods

1) Divide students into small groups and share out resources.

2) Allow 20-30 minutes for students to prepare collages from the articles on 'Death' in the newspapers and magazines.

3) Ask groups to display their collages in turn and share their impressions of how death is portrayed in the media.

Extensions

Students collect their own articles on 'Death' for the following week.

Compare the way the same story to do with 'Death' is portrayed in different newspapers.

Students watch a variety of programmes on T.V. to see how 'Death' is portrayed.

Ask the students to imagine they are reporters. Give them a brief description of a Death, then ask them to write a report on this, as if for a newspaper.

N.B. This activity could be adapted for any form of loss.

Compare the way death & disasters that happen in this country and abroad are reported. e.g. a death in Northern Ireland or a disaster in Bangladesh. Is equal emphasis given, what images are portrayed, what type of vocabulary is used?

Ask the students which types of death get the most cover in the media and why?. Discuss the effects of media coverage on family and friends.

COMING TO TERMS WITH THE REALITY OF DEATH

Resources

Copies of activity Understanding Death (1).

Copies of activity Understanding Death (2).

*And/or excerpt from David Copperfield.

*And/or Grief by Sally Trow.

*see Creative Writing.

Method

1) Introduce and hand out activity 'Understanding Death' (1).

2) Invite volunteers to share their answers.

3) Introduce Understanding Death (2).

4) Again invite volunteers to share their answers.

N.B. For more mature students substitute excerpt from David Copperfield or Grief.

Questions for Students

1) How did the people involved see death?

2) Did they come to terms with death?

3) How would you explain death to someone?

UNDERSTANDING DEATH (1)

Read the following before answering the question below.

As small children we may have learnt to come to terms with a whole range of losses (e.g. changing friends and schools). However, when it came to death, all sorts of problems could have arisen, if adults tried to avoid the subject altogether. As youngsters we may have been aware of dead plants and animals and could have passed butchers and fishmongers. We may also have seen funerals.

Many of our games could have involved death - 'bang you're dead!' - games such as Cowboys and Indians, space ventures, cops and robbers and playing hospitals. Programmes on television could have influenced us as well. Frequently we see death in news, in documentaries, in plays, in films and in cartoons. The problem is for us to sort out the reality from the fantasy - real death from pretend. There is no obvious difference between a reported murder in Northern Ireland and a murder in East Enders.

Therefore when we were young children this could have led to all sorts of misunderstandings. For example, a four year old thought that everyone turned into statues when they died because he'd met Queen Victoria as a statue in Kensington Gardens and was told that she had been dead a long time.

Q. Can you decribe any misunderstandings that you had about death?

....

....

....

....

Q. How would you have liked to have death explained to you?

....

....

....

....

UNDERSTANDING DEATH (2)

Read the following before answering the questions below

A teacher discovers one morning that one of the two frogs she has recently acquired is dead. Before discarding the dead frog she leaves it in a bowl next to the enclosed live one. She knows the children will miss the frog and will ask to see it.

Johnny aged three and a half, comes up to the frog and asks the teacher;

Johnny   Why is the frog here?

Teacher   This frog is dead.

Johnny   Who deaded him?

Teacher   Nobody did anything to him. He died by himself.

Johnny   Why did he die?

Teacher   He jumped out of the mud pan and we couldn't find him; so he had no mud or water and he dried up and died.

Johnny   Is this frog dead?

Teacher   Yes.

Johnny   Put him in water.

Teacher   O.K.

Johnny   Will he bite?

Teacher   No.

Johnny   Why is the frog dead?

Teacher   He dried up and died.

Johnny   Can I put him on the table? Isn't the frog dead?

Teacher   Yes.

Johnny   Can he turn over?

Teacher   The frog is dead so he can't do anything.

Johnny   Give him some food.

Teacher   No, the frog can't eat - he's dead.

Johnny   Why is he dead?

Teacher   He had no water or mud, so he dried up.

Johnny   I'll turn him over.

As he does so, Johnny seems to realise that the frog is unable to move (certainly different from the jumpy live one he had finally made himself touch). But he pokes the dead frog and seems to be watching for a reaction. He asks again, "Is the frog dead?"

. . . .

After almost half an hour of studying the dead frog, Johnny picks it up and brings it to the children at another table and says to them, "See this frog is dead ... See Leoni, this frog is dead because he didn't have any water ..." several of the children asked "Who deaded him?"

1)   What was Johnny's first reaction to the dead frog?

2)   How did the teacher help Johnny to understand about death?

3)   Why do you think Johnny needed to spend nearly half an hour studying the dead frog?

4)   Why did Johnny take the frog over to Leoni and his other friends?

5)   How would you explain about death to a young child?

6)   Why do so many people avoid using the word 'death' when someone has died, and speak of 'passing away', or call 'death' something else instead?

HOW LONG WILL YOU LIVE

Resources

Copies of 'How Long Will You Live'

Method

1) Discuss with students their understanding of 'Life Expectancy'. Read Ecclesiastes Chapter 3 Verses 1 - 8 or a piece of your own choice.

A TIME FOR EVERYTHING

Everything that happens in this world happens at
the time God chooses.
He sets the time for birth and the time for death,
the time for planting and the time for pulling up,
the time for killing and the time for healing,
the time for tearing down and the time for building.
He sets the time for sorrow and the time for joy,
the time for mourning and the time for dancing,
the time for making love and the time for not making Love,
the time for kissing and the time for not kissing.
He sets the time for finding and the time for losing the time for saving and the
time for throwing away,
the time for tearing and the time for mending,
the time for silence and the time for talk.
He sets the time for love and the time for hate the time for war and the time for
peace.

2) Ask the group to brainstorm all the things they can think of that have a limited life span (e.g. animals, different types of machinery, clothes).

3) Hand out Activity and ask students to complete questions 1, 2 and 4.

4) In large group answer question 3.

5) Invite the students to do the questionnaire Parts I and II with their families and older friends as set out in question 5. (Knowledge of students home background is essential before suggesting completion of this part of the activity.)

6) If question 5 is answered, explore their findings.

Were they surprised by the answers?

Were the answers accepted or not by the people interviewed?

Did the findings change their feelings in any way towards those interviewed now that an average life expectancy had been worked out?

EXTENSIONS

Discuss ways people try to lengthen their life expectancy. Why do people do this? e.g. diet and exercise.

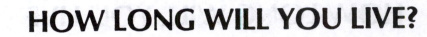

HOW LONG WILL YOU LIVE?

Listed below are some of the conditions and characteristics that can lengthen or shorten your life. The table is based on the Registrar General's figures for England and Wales and the 1972 Statistical Review. Apart from the table, the questionnaire is not of course scientific, but it does indicate some of the factors involved in the life expectancy for the average person. It is however founded on sound *actuarial and medical opinion.

*Look up this word.

PRESENT AGE	MAN	WOMAN
0	63	75
1	70.5	76.5
2	70.5	76.5
3-6	70	77
7-30	71	77
31-39	72	77
40-45	72	78
46-49	73	78
50-52	73	79
53-56	74	79
57-60	75	79
61-62	77	81
66-67	78	82
68-69	79	82
70-71	80	83
72-73	81	84
74-75	82	85

Things to do

1) Work out your average life expectancy from the Table based on the Registrar General's figures.

2) Add or subtract years for your life expectancy according to your answers to the questionnaire in PART 1.

3) Find out what the average age of life expectancy is in the class.

4) Make a list, in order of importance, of those factors which might result in a shorter life.

5) You may be interested in finding out the life expectancy of other members of your family and older friends by using the questionnaires in both PARTS 1 and 2. (Make sure you get honest answers to all your questions!).

Part 1

If you live in South-East or the West of England add 3 years.
If you live in Greater London add 1 year.
If you live in North or East of England, subtract 1 year.
If you live in Scotland, subtract 3 years.

If friends or relations describe you as always calm, add 5 years.
If usually calm add 3 years.
If moderately calm add 1 year.
If usually tense subtract 3 years.
If always tense add 5 years.
If you are given to nervous breakdowns, subtract 6 years.

If you smoke a pipe or cigar occasionally, subtract 2 years.
If you smoke a pipe or cigar regularly, subtract 3 years.
If you smoke under 20 cigarettes a day, subtract 3 years.
If you smoke 20 cigarettes a day, subtract 4 years.
If you smoke up to 40 cigarettes a day, subtract 6 years.
If you smoke over 40 cigarettes a day, subtract 10 years.

If you drink six tots of spirits or its equivalent a day, subtract 5 years.
If you drink half a bottle of spirits or its equivalent a day, subtract 10 years.
If you drink more, subtract 15 years.

If you walk or run four miles a day (or its equivalent), add 3 years.
If you walk or run six miles a day (or its equivalent), add 5 years.
If you never exercise, subtract 5 years.

If you never visit a doctor, subtract 1 year.
If you visit your doctor only for regular check-ups, add 2 years.
If you are often ill, subtract 2 years.
If you are under 40 and have false teeth, subtract 2 years.

Part 2

If you have a professional job, add 2 years.
If you are a civil servant, clerk or secretary add 1 year.
If you have a skilled job, add nothing.
If you have a partly skilled job, subtract 2 years.
If you have an unskilled job, subtract 5 years.

If you are married and under 30 years add 5 years.
If you are married and over 30 years but under 60, add 2 years.
If you are married and over 60 years, add nothing.

If you are over 30 years and up to half a stone overweight,
subtract 2 years.
If you are over 30 years and up to a stone overweight,
subtract 3 years.
If you are over 30 years and up to two stone overweight,
subtract 5 years.
If you are over 30 years and more than two stone overweight,
subtract 6 years.

If you are over 40 years and have false teeth, subtract 2 years.
If you are over 50 years and have your own teeth, add 2 years.

If your father lived to be over 70, add 1 year.
If your father lived to be over 80, add 2 years.
If your father lived to be over 85, add 3 years.
If your mother lived to be over 70, add 1 year.
If your mother lived to be over 80, add 2 years.
If your mother lived to be over 85, add 3 years.

DEATH AND THE FAMILY

Resources

        Copies of 'Death and the Family'
        (See also 'Helping the Bereaved') in Section 2.6
        Articles 'Caught in the Middle' and 'Unhappy Ever After' in Sec. 3.

Method

    1)   Introduce and hand out Activity. 'Death and the Family'.

    2)   Share answers in small and/or large groups.

Extensions

    -     Link this with "Who Helps Me" and 'Resources in the Community' from 'Helping the Bereaved'.

    -     Include divorce using the following figures: and read articles in resources above.

If divorce rates prevailing in the mid 1980's were to continue, then 37% of Marriages are likely to end in the Divorce Court.
On this basis 1 in 5 children will experience divorce of their parents by the age of 16.

                                        (Family Change and Future Policy 1990)

                                         Family Policy Study Centre

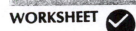

DEATH AND THE FAMILY

Read the following carefully and answer the questions:

Statistics for Britain: (1984 OPCS)

In Britain there are: 3,200,000 widows
                        750,000 widowers
        approx.   180,000 children under 16 who have
                        lost a mother or a father through death.

1 woman in 7 is a widow
1 man in 28 is a widower

1 woman in 2 over age 65 is a widow
1 man in 6 over age 65 is a widower

Every day approximately 500 wives become widows
                        120 husbands become widowers

Of the bereaved children under 16
            approximately 120,000 are widow's children
                        60,000 are widower's children

1) The figures show that there are many more widows than widowers. Why do you think
    this is?

    ....

    ....

2) From the figures shown do the majority of children under 16 lose their fathers or
    mothers?

3) What difficulties do you think a young person could experience if a parent dies?

    ....

    ....

    ....

LIFE AFTER DEATH

Resources

Copy/copies of article 'Heavenly Bodies' (see appendix) and/or information of own choice.
Background reading: see Additional Resources & Educators Booklist - Section 3

*AN INVITATION
TO THOUGHT*

Dead.
To what world do they pass?
To what existence, if any?
To a world of luxury and happiness;
To a world where contentment rules and peace is forever;
To a world we have envisaged;
Upon which we ponder when life is too much for us.
But life, what of it?
It is not something we may take for granted.
It is produced a million-fold each day
But snatched equally quickly
There is no mercy.

> *Life.*
> *We are put on earth.*
> *For what purpose?*
> *To make others happy.*
> *So what are they here for?*
> *Throughout school, we are told to work hard.*
> *And why?*
> *So we can pass exams.*
> *And why?*
> *So we can get a good job and earn money.*
> *With this, we buy materials which will supposedly make our life more*
> *   comfortable.*
> *Whatever the profession, the task is simple:-*
> *To improve human life.*
> *But why bother? They'll all die eventually,*
> *Be it human or natural cause.*
> *The one thing that man can never discover, is the one thing which makes*
> *   everything possible:*
> *Eternal Life.*

A pupil from Dover Girls Grammar School

Method

1) Read the article/poem 'An Invitation to Thought' or information of own choice and then explore the group's understanding of the term 'Life after Death' and the difference between 'Resurrection' and 'Reincarnation'.

2)   Divide the students into groups and ask them to brainstorm the arguments for and against there being 'Life after Death'.

3)   Re-group and make a composite list of answers.

Extensions

-   Find out about the beliefs of 'Life after Death' by different Faiths and Ancient Civilisations e.g. Egypt.

-   Debate or discuss 'Is Death the End or the Beginning of Life'.

-   Discuss beliefs about ghosts and whether this means there is life after death.

-   Explore students knowledge and understanding of 'out-of-the-body' experiences.

-   Discuss the 'Shroud of Turin' and ask the group why they think there is so much interest in it.

-   Carry out a survey of parents/educators/other students to see whether they believe in an after life. Try to find a cross-section of different ages/faiths/backgrounds. Pool and discuss results.

-   Use Mark's story in "Heavenly Bodies" to show how people dften decide to change their lives after a N.D.E. Ask students to write/discuss the changes they would make in a similar situation. On completion ask them why they don't make those changes now.

WORKSHEET ✔

QUESTIONNAIRE ON AFTERLIFE

1a   Do you believe there is a life after death   Yes/No
       (If your answer is no please move on to 2,3 & 4)

1b   If you answered yes to 1a, could you give any reason you have for believing this:

....

....

....

....

....

....

2   What do you think "life after life" may be like:

....

....

....

....

3   Could you describe anything you have read or heard that has influenced your beliefs:

....

....

....

4   Any other comments you would like to make:

....

....

....

....

....

....

Thank you for completing this questionnaire your answers will be kept confidential

HOW CAN WE HELP?   2.7

**"We cannot prevent the birds of sorrow from landing on our shoulder.
We can prevent them from nesting in our hair"**

Old Chinese Proverb

Objectives:

To develop sensitivity to the dying and the bereaved, by exploring our own attitudes and feelings.

To enable the students to identify the factors that need to be considered when supporting the dying and the bereaved.

To explore the resources available to themselves and others at times iof loss and death.

To introduce a variety of relaxation techniques.

N.B. Because of the nature of this subject it is important to establish ground rules at the beginning of this section (see 'Setting the Scene').

Resources

Background reading in Section 1.
Listening skills in Section 2.9.
Articles in Section 3.
Attitudes to death and Dying:

Method A:

1)   Read this extract from Elizabeth Kubler Ross' book 'On Death and Dying' or poem/article of own choice.
Elizabeth Kubler Ross found an eagerness of dying patients to talk about their impending death. They felt relief when they were allowed to unburden themselves and let her know how they felt about dying. Her survey showed:-

> 98% of the people wanted to know they were dying.
>> 60% of doctors did not want to tell them.
>>> 80% of people knew anyway.

2)   Divide the students into four groups with a reporter in each. Ask the groups to brainstorm under the following headings:-

a)   The advantages for the dying person to know that they are dying.
b)   The disadvantages for the dying person to know that they are dying.
c)   The advantages for families or those close to them to know that the person is dying.
d)   The disadvantages for families or those close to them to know that the person is dying.

3)   Group share findings in turn. Discuss and clarify points made and add any additional points.

Extensions:

Discuss why doctors, relatives and loved ones frequently don't want to tell the patients that they are dying.
Discuss 'Helen House' and/or 'My Sunday' and/or 'The Silent Conspiracy'.

Method B:

1) Read 'Death in the First Person' and/or 'Living with Death and/or poem or article of your own choice. This may be read by a volunteer(s).

2) Ask the students what they think people fear most when they are dying. (The three main fears are being on their own, being a burden, or being in pain.)

3) Divide the students into groups and ask them to brainstorm all the aspects of dying about which they would like to have some choice. Give some examples from the following list:-

Would they want to be told?

Would they want their relatives or those close to them to know?

Would they want drugs to be used?
N.B. drugs have 3 main uses: 1) to relieve pain; 2) to alleviate symptoms; 3) to prolong life.

Where would they like to die (Home, Hospital or Hospice)?

Townsend et al (1990) interviewed people expected to die within a year to find out their preference for their final place of care.

In existing circumstances
58% said they would like to die at home
20% in hospitals
20% in hospices
2% elsewhere.

In more favourable circumstances
67% said they would like to die at home
16% in hospitals
15% in a hospice.

4) On completion return to large group and discuss issues raised.

Extensions:

Group develops a list of options for the dying and those close to them, using the answers from the previous activities.

Other types of loss could be explored in a similar way.

Role play situation.

Discuss the difference between emotional, physical and spiritual pain

Many people find it difficult to die because they have unfinished business i.e. someone they have'nt forgiven (could be themselves). Ask students to think of some "unfinished business" they have and invite them to write a letter/poem about it or to the person concerned.

HELPING THE BEREAVED:

Resources:
Reading material in Section 1 & 3
Listening skills in section 2.9.

Copies of Activity (Helping the Bereaved')

Copies of 'Grief' by Sally Trow or 'Lament for Glen' or 'Why Me ?' or 'Kate' or extracts from David Copperfield (see "Creative Writing").
Article I desperately needed to see my son, section 3.
See 'Loss, Grief and Mourning' and 'Stages of grief' in 'Living with Loss'.

Copies of worksheet 'Difficulties in Grieving'.

Method A:

1)   Read poem or prose of your choice. This may be read by a volunteer.

2)   Divide students into groups with a reporter in each.

3)   Give each group one or more statements from the Activity Sheet 'How to Help the Bereaved'. Also share the definition of Bereavement.

4)   Ask the group to imagine they have a friend who is bereaved and say whether these statements are helpful or not for the helper and the bereaved person.

5)   Re-form into large group to share and discuss the answers given.

6)   Summarize answers under the following headings:-

      What bereaved people need most is   ....?

      What bereaved people need least is   ....?

7)   Clarify the   answers using 'Difficulties in Grieving'.

Method B:

1)   Read poem or prose of your choice. This may be read by a volunteer.

2)   Give out the Activity Sheet 'Helping the Bereaved'.

3)   Ask students to complete, imagining that they have a friend who is bereaved.

4)   As 5 and 6 of Method A.

Extensions:

-      Ask the group which of these ideas for helping the bereaved would also be helpful to people experiencing other forms of loss.

-      In small groups ask students to share with others helpful and unhelpful responses they have observed at times of bereavement.

Read "Footprints in the Sand" (Creative Writing) and ask why some people feel God has forsaken them at the saddest times of their life.

Letters of Condolence

Method:

1) What is a letter of condolence? Discuss and clarify with the group.

2) Ask group why these letters are very important and what sort of things should be said in the letter? (Emphasize how important it is for the bereaved to hear good things about the dead person, so that they can remember them with pleasure rather than pain).

3) Ask the students to write a letter of condolence to a person of their choice. This could include someone whose death has been featured in the news or a dead hero/heroine, or an imaginary person.

4) Lady Mountbatten recieved hundreds of letters of sympathy after the terrorist attack on her family in Ireland, when one of her sons was killed. One of the letters included the following old Chinese poem which she still often reads:

He took his candle
And went into another room
I cannot find
But I know he was here
Because of all the happiness
He left behind.

Tell the students this story and ask them what poem they would choose to include in their condolence letter and why.

HELPING THE BEREAVED:

Read the following before answering the questions below.

Bereavement can be described 'as the loss of someone or something that is precious'. The word is most often used in the context of a person but it may include for example the loss of an inanimate object or the ending of a relationship, or a change in a particular situation.

How to help the bereaved:-

If a friend were bereaved I would:-

-        accept their behaviour no matter how odd

-        ignore their loss, pretend it never happened

-        tell them about my own woes

-        let them cry and talk as much as they want to

-        tell them they are luckier than some

-        visit their home

-        give them plenty of sympathy

-        leave them well alone

-        take my cue from them and be myself

-        help them with practical problems

-        tell them about everyone else's misfortunes

-        encourage them to talk about their loss

-        take some burden of everyday chores away

-        tell them they'll get over it eventually

-        provide food and encourage sleep

-        talk about the weather

-        try to make them laugh

-        stick around when I'm needed

-        tell them it could have been worse

-        leave them out of my social circle

-        tell them not to worry or think about it

-        encourage them to go to the doctor for tablets

The above statements   represent the varied responses of people to the bereaved.

1. List five things that would help the bereaved friend.

    a: ....

    b: ....

    c: ....

    d: ....

    e: ....

2. List five things that would not help the friend.

    a: ....

    b: ....

    c: ....

    d: ....

    e: ....

3. From the above answers make your own list of the things you could do to help your bereaved friend.

    ....

    ....

    ....

    ....

    ....

    ....

WORKSHEET ✓

DIFFICULTIES IN GRIEVING

Many people do not pass through the 'stages of grief' without some holdups. Once these have been recognised and worked through the person is able to move forward through the grief process. Listed below are some of the holdups that are common to many bereaved people:-

- opposition to let go - refusal to accept the death
- lack of support - family/friends/community/spiritual
- not prepared to allow themselves to grieve
- marital or family discord
- doubt about the reality of the loss e.g. no body
- violent death or suicide
- mixed feelings towards the deceased
- difficulties in communicating and expressing feelings
- the social or religious customs that demand self-control often results in delayed grief, e.g. some Christian groups emphasise the certain resurrection of the loved one which is to be celebrated with joy and no space is allowed for the natural grief to be expressed
- low self esteem image
- not being allowed or able to attend the funeral (e.g. a child)
- financial problems
- when things have been left unsaid, a visit not made, or any other unfinished business
- dependant family members , allowing no time to grieve
- succession of losses - no time allowed to be able to grieve.

There are three ways commonly used for coping with bereavement (including divorce and other losses) which are not helpful over a long period of time and need to be faced by the bereaved person.

For Young People

1) **Substitution.** The child may want to find a substitute mother or father.

2) **Aggression.** The child may be always fighting, or avoiding School. A variety of discipline problems both inside and outside of school. e.g. drug abuse and general anti-social behaviour.

3) **Helplessness.** This leads to a lack of curiosity and so impairs learning. The child may opt out of life - even become deaf in extreme cases.

For Adults

1) **Substitution.** This might take the form of another marriage or focusing all attention on the children. The problem with a speedy remarriage is that it frequently fails because the grief work from the first marriage has not been done. The problem of the parent focusing all their attention on the children is that the children may feel smothered.

2) **Aggression.** Anger is another way of coping. The anger may be against God, or against the doctor for not giving the right treatment. Sometimes the anger is directed against themselves.

3) **Helplessness.** Another common way of coping is to be 'helpless' and get all the friends and neighbours running around. The problem is that this 'helplessness' has to stop if they are to adjust to their new situation.

WHO HELPS ME

Resources

Copies of 'My Support Group

Method

1) Remind students that loss is something we all share and that asking for support is a sign of maturity and not weakness.

2) Hand out copies of 'My Support Group' and discuss.

3) Ask them to imagine that someone close to them has died and complete the questionnaire accordingly.

4) OPTIONAL: Ask them to share answers with partners of their own choice.

5) In large group ask them for willing volunteer to share.

Extensions

- Ask the students to consider how the people they have chosen might react if they approached them for help.

- Role play approaching one of the people they have chosen.

- Explore other situations of loss.

- Brainstorm what helps/hinders people to ask for support.

MY SUPPORT GROUP

Write in the columns provided the names of the people who could give you the types of support listed in column 'A'.

'A' Types of Support Think of someone who:	Close Friend	At Home	Away from Home
Will let me cry			
Will listen to me and not get bored			
Will not tell me it could have been worse			
Will not encourage me to go to the Doctor for pills.			
Will give me a hug			
Will stay with me when I need them			
Will not ignore my loss and pretend it hasn't happened			
Will not try to cheer me up all the time			
I don't have to pretend with			
Will not betray my confidence			

RESOURCES IN THE COMMUNITY

Resources

Flip paper and pens - copies of list of organizations.

Method

1)   Divide into small groups with a reporter in each.

2)   Allow 5-10 minutes for the groups to list all the places they can think of where they could go for help if someone close to them died.

3)   In the large groups share and check information and make any necessary additions.

4)   Hand out lists of useful organizations.

Extensions

-   The group could visit any of the following:-

>   Libraries
>   Citizens Advice Bureau
>   Community Health Council
>   Community Relations Council
>   Social Services Dept.

    to find the local representatives of the useful organizations and then make their own list of resources.

-   The group could visit or write to one of the places on their list* (remembering to send a S.A.E. if writing).

-   (*see also extended list at end of Pack).

-   The group could find out about resources for a wide range of losses.

-   Speakers could be invited from different religions, a Hospice, C.A.B., D.H.S.S., Undertakers, or local representatives of the groups listed in 'Useful Organizations'.

USEFUL ORGANIZATIONS

AGE CONCERN is developing bereavement counselling in some of its areas, and can give much general support to the elderly. It also has a wide range of fact sheets on practical problems facing the elderly, especially housing.

Age Concern England:

1268 London Road,
London SW16 4EJ,
Telephone: 0181-679 8000.

Age Concern Scotland:

54A Fountainbridge,
Edinburgh, EH2 9PT.
Telephone: 0131 228 5656.

Age Concern Wales:

4th Floor, 1 Cathedral Road,
Cardiff, S. Glamorgan.
Telephone: 01222 371566.

Age Concern N. Ireland:

6 Lower Crescent,
Belfast, BT7 1NR.
Telephone: 01232 245729.

BEARS OF THE WORLD, Audrey Duck, 256 St. Margaret's Rd. Twickenham, Middlesex TW1 1PR. Telephone: 0181-891 5746 (evenings only). Provides Teddies for children who have been traumatized.

BRITISH ORGAN DONOR SOCIETY (BODY). Balsham, Cambridge CB1 6DL. Telephone: 01223 893636

CITIZENS ADVICE C.A.B. is a free general information and advice service available in most large towns. It provides advice and information on practical matters that arise after a death. (A good place to start.)

CRUSE Cruse House, 126 Sheen Road, Richmond Surrey, TW9 1UR, Telephone: 0181-940 4818/9047. There are over 125 branches throughout the country which provide free confidential counselling and other services. National CRUSE also have a wide range of publications and arrange Courses and Conferences.

DEPARTMENT OF HEALTH AND SOCIAL SERVICES Alexander Fleming House, London, SE1, Telephone: 0171-407 5522. The DHSS have branches in all large towns. They can give financial assistance to the bereaved. A wide range of leaflets are available explaining the position regarding benefits.

THE FOUNDATION FOR STUDY OF INFANT DEATHS 15 Belgrave Square, London, SW1X 8PS, Telephone: 0171-235 1721. The Secretary is June Reed. There is a contact network throughout the country to help those bereaved by a cot death, and information is available on research into the circumstances of infant death.

LESBIAN & GAY BEREAVEMENT PROJECT offers help to gay people whose partners have died, especially during the first days and weeks of bereavement. The organisers say it is important to be called in as soon as possible after the death, as there can be problems with relatives and Funeral Directors if the partner is not recognised as the 'chief mourner' or not named as executor of the Will.

LESBIAN & GAY SWITCHBOARD Vaughan Williams Centre, Colindale Hospital, Colindale Ave., London NW9 5AG, Helpline: 0181-455 8894, Office: 0181-200 0511 can put caller in touch with a volunteer of the Lesbian & Gay Bereavement Project.

GINGERBREAD for single parents - Branches all over the country. Headquarters: 35 Wellington Street, London, WC2, Telephone: 071 240 0953.

NATIONAL AIDS HELPLINE. Telephone: 0800 567123

NATIONAL ASSOCIATION FOR WELFARE OF CHILDREN IN HOSPITAL Argyle House, 29-31 Euston Road, London, NW1. Telephone: 071-833 2041.

NATIONAL COUNCIL FOR THE ONE PARENT FAMILY 255 Kentish Town Road, London, NW5 2LX, Telephone: 071-267 1361.

NATIONAL HIV PREVENTION SERVICE, 82-86 Seymour Place. London W1H 5DB. Telephone: 071-724 7993

NATURAL DEATH CENTRE. 20 Herber Rd., London NW2 6AA. Telephone 081-452 6434. Launched in 1991 it's overall aim is to improve the quality of dying (see "The Living Will" in "Euthanasia").

SAMARITANS 17 Uxbridge Road, Slough, Bucks. Telephone 53: 0753 32 713. Provide a 24 hour telephone listening service for people in crises. There are branches in most large town.

SANDS (Stillbirth and Neonatal Death Society) Argyle House, 28 Portland Place, London, W1N 3DF, Telephone: 071-436 5881. A self help group offering understanding and encouragement to parents bereaved by stillbirth.

THE COMPASSIONATE FRIENDS - an international organisation of bereaved parents offering friendship and understanding to other bereaved parents.
Head Office: 6 Denmark Street, Bristol, BS1 5DQ, Telephone: 0272 539639 (Helpline), 0272 665202 (Admin). There is a County Secretary for most Counties, and you could obtain the contact information through the National Secretary at Head Office.

FOUNDATION FOR BLACK BEREAVED FAMILIES 1 Kingston Square, Salters Hill, London, SE19 1DZ, Telephone: 081-761 7228. Help and support for Bereaved Black People of Afro Caribbean origin. Counselling, advice, home visits - attend funerals and financial support.

JEWISH BEREAVEMENT COUNSELLING SERVICE (Greater London only) 1 Cyprus Gardens, London, N3 1SP, Telephone 081-349 0839. Trained Counsellors who will visit as long as necessary.

RELATE (formerly Marriage Guidance), Herbert Gray College, Little Church Street, Rugeley, CV21 3AP. Telephone 0788 573241.

TAKE TIME TO RELAX

**How can Educators help bereaved people
or indeed themselves to relax?**

Relaxation will not cure or change the problems, but it will help us to recognize when our bodies become tense and prevent the build up of lactic acid in our muscles, which creates fatigue. It can also help us to sleep better, lessen pain, avoid dependency on alcohol and drugs, prevent minor headaches and ailments and generally enable us to adapt more easily to our rapidly changing environment and the people we meet.

Here are a few techniques that have been successfully used by myself and others to relieve tension and could be passed on by educators to students or the bereaved:

1) General Relaxation

Sit in a comfortable chair with feet on the floor, slightly apart, bottom well back in the seat and hands loosely in your lap, one on top of the other. Close your eyes. Use a reclining or upright chair; one with arm rests will be more comfortable.

   a) Check right through your body starting with the top of your head.
   b) Feel yourself relaxing each part before you move on to the next. When you feel ready, open your eyes again. Have a good stretch.

2) Breathing

When we are tense we tend to breathe too quickly and shallowly. This exercise encourages us to breathe more deeply, and relaxes our abdominal muscles, where a lot of tension can be held.

   a) Sit well back in the chair, as described in (1).
   b) Put one hand on the upper part of your chest and feel your breathing slow down under it.
   c) Put your other hand on top of your abdomen and feel yourself breathing into this hand.
   d) When read drop both hands gently into your lap.
   e) When you feel ready, open your eyes and have a good stretch.

3) Relief of headaches or migraine - often caused by tension

   a) Follow instructions for relaxing in a chair (see 1).
   b) Place hands loosely in lap one on top of the other.
   c) Picture warmth moving VERY SLOWLY down from your head, across your shoulders, down your arms, into your hands and then to the tips of your fingers and thumbs.
   d) Follow 2e.

   N.B. You may find these exercises difficult at first, BUT DON'T GIVE UP TOO EASILY. Remember it takes many years to build up tension, so it can take equally long to lose it. Relaxation like all skills takes time to learn. Its common to yawn frequently, have stomach rumbles and eyes watering to start with.

4) Acute Stress - emergency technique

  a) STOP.
  b) Breath out, unclench teeth, drop shoulders, unclench fists.
  c) Relax and breathe in slowly.
  d) Move around more slowly.
  e) Lower the voice and speak more slowly.
  f) If possible think about or do something else e.g. go into the garden or another room.

5) Deep Relaxation

I regret there is no room in this article to include instructions for deep relaxation but it can be found in Jane Madders' book and tape* which I strongly recommend.

Best of all, become aware of the things that make you tense and the changes in your body that happen.

Learn to take action to relieve tension before it becomes built in.

Remember, we can't stop things happening to us in our life but we can decide how we let them affect us. Contentment is now always a matter of getting what we want. It is also a matter of wanting what we have.

Jane Madders' cassette tape "Relax" Techniques of Relaxation for Migraine, Fatigue and General Tension, Jane Madders' book "Stress and Relaxation". Both available from The Midlands Migraine Association - Mrs. K. M. Hay, 5 Temple Road, Dorridge, Solihull, West Midlands, B98 8LE. Laura Mitchell's book 'Simple Relaxation' - The Mitchell Method for easing tension. Publisher John Murray.

6) Meditation

Meditation can contribute to mental development, to a clearer sense of identity and spiritual awareness. It can also enable us to quieten busy thoughts and focus our minds. Like all skills it needs practise to succeed. Meditation can include guided visualization (see Creative Activities Sec. 1) or it can be initiated by focusing on an object, e.g. a flower, candle or feeling or a word or "mantra".

7) Silence

Silence allows for thoughts to be stilled, to be open and encourages insight and awareness. It can also deepen relaxation and be followed by asking students to imagine any of the following.

8) Own Special Place

Do relaxation of your own choice, then imagine yourself in a palace where you feel completely relaxed and at peace. It could be walking in the country, on a nice warm beach or in your favorite chair at home. Stay there for a minute or two. Remember there is <u>nothing</u> you have to do, <u>nowhere</u> you have to go and <u>nothing</u> you have to be.

(See books with a **Holistic Approach To Education** in **SECTION 3** for further visualisations)

9) Massage

Simple massage can be a useful aid to relaxation and reduction of stress and tension. Ask the students to work in pairs, with each taking turns to massage and receive (Be aware that some students might find it difficult to work with the opposite sex.)

- Start by asking the one giving the massage to place their hands gently on their partners shoulders so they can get used to their touch.

- At the end of each person's turn, suggest they end with a gentle stroking motion across the shoulders, down the arms to the end of the finger tips.

ACTIVITIES - Demonstrate first on one of the students:

Back Scratch

- Use finger tips and finger nails to give a 'gentle scratch'. Emphasize "no tickling".

Heel of the Hand Rub

- Heels of the hand are used to ease tension and tiredness.

Flat Hand Back Rub

- The same as the previous exercise, but using the flat of hand.

Tickle Back

- Emphasize this is to be slow and gentle and is not meant to make their partner laugh or uncomfortable.

Knuckle Stroking

- The knuckle edges of a clenched fist can be used gently, to run up and down the back, to take away any tension and tiredness.

Side of the Hand Chop-Chop

- The side of the hands are used to give gentle chops up and down the back.

N.B. Any of these methods can also be used with the recipient seated, either on a chair or on the floor, with their partner sitting or kneeling behind.

OTHER MASSAGES

Hand and Arm

- Ask students to work in pairs sitting on the floor, opposite each other. The recipient then gently places their arm on their partner's knee. Suggest they explore their partner's hand or just the thumb, using some of the strokes used on the back.

-These can be extended up the arm to the shoulder.

Foot Massage

- Feet are very sensitive, so the massage should only be undertaken with students who have used the other methods first.

- The giver takes the other person's foot onto their knee, gently squeezing it several times, before following the techniques described for the hand, being careful not to tickle.

Forehead

- This can be done with the giver standing or sitting behind the receiver.

- Place hands gently on the receiver's forehead, so the finger tips touch in the middle. Leave for a moment, to allow partner to get used to the touch. Use gentle, smooth strokes to move outwards to the temples. Repeat several times.

N.B. Students can massage their own hands, feet and forehead.

FOLLOW UP ACTIVITIES

- Ask the students to share their experiences of massage.

- Ask them for suggestions of times when people would enjoy massage.

LISTENING SKILLS

2.8

"If we were supposed to talk more than listen we would have been given two mouths and one ear." (Mark Twain)

Objectives:

To encourage students to recognize there is an 'art' to listening.

To explore factors that contribute and detract from effective listening.

To experience the effects of a variety of different responses as a speaker and a listener.

Resources:

Method A. Flip paper and pens; writing paper.

Method B. A list of suitable topics, e.g. my favourite food or television programme; holidays; journey to work. (Avoid topics that could evoke emotions, i.e. things that make you happy or sad.)

Background Reading. HEC/TACADE 'Working in Groups' (5) Listening Skills. 'Promoting Health – A Practical Guide to Health Education' by Linda Ewles and Ina Simnett, published by John Wiley and Sons.

Method A:

1) Ask the students to think of a time they felt that they were listened to and write down the things that were good about it.

2) Repeat as above, but this time ask them to think of a time that they didn't feel listened to and write down the possible reasons for this.

3) Share findings in small and/or large groups. Discuss and clarify points made and any additional points.

4) Ask groups to come up with a definition of listening, e.g. a child once defined listening as 'wanting to hear'.

Method B:

1) Ask the group to divide into pairs around the room, sitting opposite each other.

2) Explain that you are going to give them a number of simple exercises to experience very simple points about listening.

3) Ask the partners to choose to be 'A' speaker and 'B' listener. Explain that each will have a turn as speaker and listener.

(Choose a different topic for each exercise and ask the students to change roles after two minutes. At the end of each session ask the pairs to share how they felt with each other. Finish with feedback from the whole group.)

KEYS TO GOOD LISTENING

By Karen Stott and Dick Littlewood of 'Link' Hillingdon

Warmth and Caring – being concerned, accepting, friendly.

Empathy – trying to understand how it feels to be in someone else's shoes and showing that you want to understand.

Non-judgemental Acceptance – not being shocked or judging someone. Accepting the person and their feelings.

Respect – allowing someone the dignity of having the right to feel any emotion and the free choice to choose any action.

Genuineness – being real, not just someone 'playing' a role.

Limit your own Talking – you can't talk and listen at the same time.

Clarifying – if you don't understand something, or feel you may have missed a point, clear it up by asking a relevant question.

Summarising – periodically check back with the person that you have heard them correctly by summarising the main points of what has been said. You may wish to encourage them to do the summary.

Questions – always use open-ended questions, i.e. questions which cannot be answered by just 'yes' or 'no'. Be careful not to interrogate.

Don't interrupt – a pause, even a long pause, doesn't mean the person has finished saying everything they want to say.

Turn off Your Own Words – personal fears, worries, problems not connected with the person easily distract from what they are saying.

Listen for Feelings – don't just concentrate on the facts as these are often less important than the feelings.

Don't Assume or Jump to Conclusions – don't complete sentences for the person either verbally or in your mind.

Listen for Overtones – you can learn a great deal from the way the person says things and what they do not say.

Concentrate/Attention – focus your mind on what the person is saying. Practice shutting out distractions.

THE COMMUNICATION CAKE

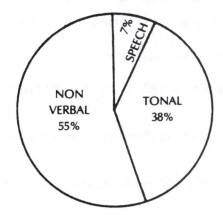

"A Handbook of Communication Skills" GOOM HELM 1986

Unhelpful Behaviour:

- Displaying boredom, impatience or hostility.

- Being condescending or patronising.

- Devaluing:
  a) By minimising (e.g. 'Lots of people have that problem').
  b) By disbelieving (e.g. 'I don't think you really feel that').

- Jumping to premature identification of the problem.

- Passing judgement.

- Distracting body gestures (e.g. fiddling with your pen, keys etc. Looking at your watch).

- Filling in a silence too quickly. Listening is more than saying 'yes' and 'no' in the right places. People need space to come to terms with their feeling.

- Asking too many questions, when the person is trying to think something out. (A good check is whether you are asking the questions because they are necessary to achieve your counselling aims, or because you are curious.)

- Interrupting. There is an 'art' to listening between the lines to pick up what is really being said.

- Using jargon.

SELF ESTEEM AND SELF IMAGE 2.9

"Every second we live is a new and unique moment of the universe, a moment that never was before and never will be again. And what do we teach our children in school? We teach them that two and two make four and that Paris is the capital of France. We should say to each of them, "Do you know what you are? You are a marvel. You are unique. In the millions of years that have passed, there has never been another child like you."

Pablo Casals

OBJECTIVES

- To encourage students to respect and value who they are and what they do.
- To combat the low self-esteem and self-image that can occur at times of loss, and usually reflects childhood experiences (see below).
- To develop skills to improve self-esteem and self-image.

N.B. Bereaved people with low self-esteem often find it very difficult to ask for or receive support.

RESOURCES

See 'Book List' and 'Additional Resources' -
- '100 Ways to Enhance Self Esteem in the Classroom'
- 'Let's Co-operate'.

Materials and Resources for different activities.

"CHILDREN LEARN WHAT THEY LIVE

IF
a child lives with criticism, she learns to condemn.
IF
a child lives with hostility, he learns to fight.
IF
a child lives with ridicule, she learns to be shy.
IF
a child lives with shame, he learns to feel guilt.
IF
a child lives with tolerance, she learns to be patient.
IF
a child lives with encouragement, he learns confidence.
IF
a child lives with praise, she learns to be appreciated.
IF
a child lives with fairness, he learns justice.
IF
a child lives with security, she learns to have faith.
IF
a child lives with approval, he learns to like himself.
IF
a child lives with acceptance and friendship, he or she learns to find love in the world."

Scottish Health Education Group

SELF-ESTEEM

Self-esteem is how you value yourself. When your self-esteem is high you feel confident. You trust your judgement and you know what you are capable of. You respect yourself for what you do and who you are.

When you lack self-esteem you feel weak and helpless. You are uncertain of the value of anything you do. You don't trust yourself or other people's reassurances. You are unsure of who you are. This is a common experience which may result in difficulty in making satisfactory relationships.

A student that has grown up feeling loved and secure is more likely to have a high sense of self-esteem. They will have grown up with a true sense of who they are. They will have learnt to trust the reactions they receive from the outside world. They feel secure.

Many students grow up without a sense of who they are. They may have to struggle to be what someone else wants. They may have been given confusing messages about what they should and should not do; maybe never praised for achievement nor given helpful criticism.

SELF-IMAGE

Self-image has two sides - the ideal self (the person I would like to be) and the actual self (the way I see myself). The ideal self is an image put together by identifying with models such as parents, friends, pop-stars or people we admire or wish to emulate. Television and other media are particularly powerful in presenting "ideals" and stereotypes to us. We tend to 'measure' the perceived "self" against this ideal.

Students need a clear idea of their own identity, a feeling of being a person distinct from others - separate and unique. The main components of self-image are:

- The "Outer" Me - physique and body image
- The "Inner" Me - feelings, emotions likes/dislikes
- The perception of self as a learner
- The roles the student is called upon to play.

N.B. Bereaved people with low self-esteem.

CIRCLE WORK

It is often a good idea to get the group to sit in a circle when sharing. This enables everyone to have eye contact, and can help create an atmosphere of trust, empathy and tolerance.

SELF-APPRECIATION

Builds self-awareness, self-acceptance.
- Ask the students to write down a list of things that they can do . . . say 8-10. Get them to start with "I can . . .". It often helps to give examples of things that you can do. Ask the students to read them out to a partner or group.

- The next stage is slightly harder and can be done as a separate session or it can follow on from the last.

- Ask them to finish these sentences :

"One thing I like about myself is . . ."

"One thing others like about me is . . ."

- You may well need to give examples, e.g. I'm kind, I'm a good sport, I always tell the truth.

'THE PRIDE WHEEL'

Builds confidence and a sense of self-worth.
Discuss with the group how difficult it can be to say:
- "I am proud that I . . .',

Ask them to think about the following:

- Things you have done for parents.
- Things you have done for a friend.
- Your work.
- How you spend your free time.
- Your religious beliefs.
- Something you've bought recently.
- Habits that you have.
- Something that you do often.
- Something you have shared.
- Something that you have tried hard for.

N.B. They may not be able to do them all.

- Ask them to draw a circle with spokes, get them to write the sentence. "I am proud that I..." on each spoke, and complete it.

- The centre can be decorated, and a border put around the edge; this would make a Mandala for each.

- The work can be displayed/discussed/shared.

- It could be extended into poetry/story writing/journals (see Creative Activities in Sec. 1.)

'REVIEW'

Builds self-evaluation and self-appreciation.

- At the end of each day/week/term ask the students to share their successes, and what they have learned.

- This can be done verbally or as a written piece. (See also Planning & Evaluation in Sec. 1.)

KILLER STATEMENTS AND GESTURES

Builds self-awareness and acceptance of feelings, honest and direct relationships, empathy with others.

ACTIVITIES

Everybody begins by sitting in a circle.

Questions To Ask:

- Have you ever worked hard at something you felt was not understood or appreciated?

- What was it? (Give time for responses).

- What was said or done that made you feel your effort was appreciated? (Again allow time for responses).

- Have you ever wanted to share things, ideas, feelings, something you've written or made, but were afraid to do so?

- Were you afraid people might put you or it down?

- What kind of things might they say?

Introducing 'Killer Statements and Gestures'.

- All of us have many feelings, thoughts, and creative behaviour, that are 'killed off' by other people's put-down comments and physical gestures, e.g.:

- "We don't have time for that now."

- "Only babies cry."

- "That's a stupid idea."

- "You know that's impossible."

- "Are you serious/loony/dumb?"

- "Only boys/girls do that."

Ask the students to keep a record of all the 'killer statements' they hear to bring to the next session.

Questions To Ask:

- What do 'killer statements' protect you from? How do they help you?

- Are there things that you would really like to say but are afraid, so you say a 'killer statement' instead?

APPRECIATIONS AND RESENTMENTS

This following activity can be very powerful. It helps towards creating a harmonious and healthy group atmosphere, particularly when groups are spending significant amounts of time together, e.g. a class, a staff, a family. There are always some unexpressed communications among those who are frequently together, e.g. children and adults. Some of it will be positive and some negative. What is unspoken remains 'in the air', and influences the relationships in the group. This activity supports the previous ones above by encouraging honest and direct communication.

It shows students that it is acceptable to let our feelings and needs be known, but that it doesn't mean we get what we want every time.

- It's essential to sit in a circle and to have eye contact.

- The students are asked to express appreciations to each other.

- They need to say the person's name, and to look at them, then say the appreciation, e.g. "Peter, I really appreciate your kindness." "Jane, thank you for helping me today, and looking after me when I fell over."

- The other student doesn't reply except perhaps to say 'thank you'.

- The person getting the appreciation just receives and takes it in - very difficult for some people to do this.

The next stage is to move into 'Resentments' and 'Requests':-

- Sit as for the previous exercise and state the resentment, e.g.:
  "Sharon, I don't like it when you take my pens without asking me."
  "Paul, it upsets me when you laugh at me"
  "Jill, I really wish you would stop day dreaming. It makes me really angry."

- The receiver, as before, doesn't reply, but sits and listens, and hears/accepts, as best they can.

This activity clears the air and deals with a lot of minor squabbles. It increases caring and empathy, and creates a togetherness.

A HOPI INDIAN RITUAL

Builds a positive environment, inter-personal relationships.

Ask each student to bring from home an object which is important to them, or if possible they are taken outside to find something from nature which has the same meaning.

- The group sit in a circle with the object, and close their eyes for a few moments to be silent.
- They sense everyone else in the group and make silent contact with them.

- They open their eyes, and anyone can start the 'ritual'.

- Ask the first person to take their object into the middle of the circle, turning round so that everyone sees. This is done in SILENCE.

- Then ask the student to tell the class what the object is, and why it is important to them.

- Then put the object in the centre of the circle and return to their place.

- This continues until everyone has done it, and created a sculpture of objects.

- When that is complete, allow a moment of silent looking at the sculpture they have create, and which is a symbol of the group.

N.B. If a student forgets their object they can describe what they would have brought and its importance.

A MATTER OF LIFE AND DEATH -2.10
Controversial Issues

EUTHANASIA

HIV/AIDS

ALLOCATING RESOURCES

DRUGS

ABORTION

CAPITAL PUNISHMENT

SUICIDE

'Thou shalt not kill'. The Sixth Commandment (Exodus 20 v 13). One of the common features of a developing civilisation has been the religious concept that life is 'sacred'. That is, 'set apart' or 'holy'. Life was seen as something to be protected and respected. Jews and Christians, together with Muslims, have argued that they have been made 'in the image of God' and therefore humankind was seen to be unique from the rest of God's creation.

Today, we take this concept for granted. The idea of human life being sacred and unique is reflected at the heart of British Law. However, with the enormous advances in medicine, and a rapidly changing social environment, there have been many demands for changes in our laws with far reaching consequences for our society.

Objectives:

- To help students to understand the complexities of the law regarding the sanctity of life.

- To recognize the underlying principles and common factors involved in death and the law.

- To give students an insight into the problems of allocating limited resources which can affect life and death.

- To enable students to understand why some people use drugs at times of bereavement.

- To increase awareness.

ABORTION

Resources:

- Copies of Activity Sheet 'Abortion'.
- Flip Chart.

Method:

1) Ask the students to clarify the meaning of the word 'abortion'.

2) Hand out copies of the activity sheet 'Abortion'.

3) Get the students in pairs to share their answers. Then, using the flip chart with the large group, list down their main arguments for and against abortion. Discuss and clarify using the check list below:-

Some of the arguments for legalized abortion:
- Women should have the right to do what they like with their bodies.
- Abortion should be allowed in the case of rape or where the life of the mother is in danger.
- Unwanted children should not be brought into this world.
- It will stop back street abortion.

Some of the arguments against legalized abortion:
- The unborn child is not part of the mother but a separate human being.
- The unborn child has a right to life - sanctity of life (religious argument).
- Only 2% of abortions today are for cases of rape or where the mother's life is in danger. Most abortions are for selfish reasons.
- The long-term psychological effects it may have on the mother or father.
- Sterility in the young girl.

4) Have a debate with the large group, either on 'Do you think that any rights should be given to the foetus?' or another question of your choice.

Extensions:

- Invite the students to write for more information from both 'The National Abortion Campaign' and 'The Society for the Protection of the Unborn Child'.

ABORTION

Read the following carefully and answer the questions

Abortion Figures:

- In 1989 there were 183,974 abortions in England and Wales. Only two of these were carried out in emergency to save the life of the mother.
- There are over 600 abortions each day in Britain, one abortion every three minutes.

- Over three million abortions have taken place since the 1967 Abortion Act.

    (Although the numbers of abortions continues to rise, the number of under 20's now have the fastest declining abortion rate as more of them are keeping their babies.)

No Easy Choice:

For women who find themselves with an unwanted pregnancy there are three main options. First, she may have the child and keep it. Secondly, she may choose to have the child and then have it adopted. Thirdly, she may choose to have an abortion. This is no easy choice for a woman to make as people do have very strong emotional feelings about abortion. Very often her choice comes under pressure from others around her who sometimes want to impose their own will on her. How will her partner, family, friends, doctor, and others react when they hear of her decision! If she keeps the baby that could be wrong in some people's eyes and if she aborts the baby that could be wrong as well.

The 1967 Abortion Act had four main points:-

1) Abortion was permitted if the pregnant woman's life was endangered by continuing her pregnancy.

2) Abortion was to be allowed if the pregnancy was to endanger the mental or physical health of the woman.

3) If the continuance of the pregnancy would risk the mental or physical health of any of the woman's existing children (social clause).

4) Abortion was to be permitted if there was a strong risk that the child was to be born handicapped or have mental or physical abnormalities.

Abortions in Britain are now only allowed until the 24th week of pregnancy, since the 1990 'Human Fertilization Embryology Act', except for 2 or 4 above when abortion can take place up to the moment of birth.

There are groups that campaign for and against abortion and identify strongly with people's 'rights'.

National Abortion Campaign:

'The National Abortion Campaign believes that women must have the right to choose whether or not to have children. This choice is only possible if they have the right to birth control of all kinds. If this right is restricted, either by lack of free, safe, dependable contraceptives, by forced sterilization as a condition for getting an abortion or by legal and medical restrictions on abortion, then women do not have the 'right to choose'.

170

'Under the present law women have no automatic right to an abortion: they have to have the permission of two doctors.

They want a new law:

-   where women have the right to choose with no legal or medical restrictions.

-   that legalizes all safe methods of abortion acceptable to women.

-   which gives the women the right to be told about methods of abortion, so that they can choose. Many people do not realize there are several methods of abortion.

-   where women do not have to agree to be sterilized in order to obtain an abortion.

-   which doesn't discriminate against young people. Abortion and contraception laws should cover all women including young persons (those under 16 years). It should not be necessary to get parents' permission.

(Quoted from the National Abortion Campaign 'Declaration of a Woman's Right to Choose'.)

The Society for the Protection of the Unborn Child:

'In 1989 183,974 lives were taken by abortion in England and Wales. Nearly 93,626 of these took place between 9 - 12 weeks gestation - so-called 'early' abortions. At nine weeks after conception the baby can make a fist and grasp an object stroking the palm of their hand. The baby is able to squint and swallow and may even get hiccups. The baby's heart begins to beat only 24 days after conception. At conception a new human life begins - the colour of hair and eyes, gifts and talents are all established at this point.'

'Pro-abortionists proclaim abortion as a "woman's right" but they do not want women to be told the facts about the methods of abortion, the humanity of the unborn baby and the physical and psychological effects of abortion on the mother. Physical scars may leave the woman unable to bear another child (up to 10% according to Sir John Peel, the Queen's former gynaecologist) and increasing evidence shows that the emotional scars on women - unable to come to terms with the loss of their babies' lives - may last a lifetime.'

'The Society for the Protection of Unborn Children is working to save the lives of unborn children by means of education and political change.'

(Quoted from John Smeaton, Secretary S.P.U.C.)

Religious Teaching:

The traditional Christian teachings have always stood against abortion on the grounds that 'all life is sacred' and that it is a gift from God that is not to be destroyed. The Roman Catholic Church stands against all abortion whereas the Church of England and Free Churches do accept abortion in situations where the mother's life is at risk, or where the child may be born severely handicapped, or after rape. No Christian would want to see abortion used as a means of birth-control. Christians would also stress that a more responsible attitude to sexual relations would prevent many of the unwanted pregnancies.

In Judaism and Islam, like Christianity, there is a concern about abortion denying the sanctity of life. However, liberals do advocate limited abortion.

Many people are concerned about abortion because they see it as the 'slippery slope' for humanity. Once we accept abortion on demand, then why not euthanasia and the killing of the handicapped?

171

1)   List some of the arguments for abortion.

2)   List some of the arguments against abortion.

3)   When would you consider that life begins! Give reasons.

4)   Do you think the father should have any say or not in determining whether the child should be aborted?

CAPITAL PUNISHMENT

Resources:

Copies of Activity - Capital Punishment.

Method:

1) Discuss and clarify the group understanding of the term 'Capital Punishment' and hand out activity sheets.

2) Share answers in pairs of small groups and/or volunteers in the large group.

3) Clarify answers and add any arguments from the following check list that have not been included:-

Check list of some of the main arguments for capital punishment:

1) The death penalty is necessary: it is one way to make criminals so scared that they will not murder.

2) Once a murderer, always a murderer. A person must not be given the chance to murder again . Society must be protected.

3) The Bible says 'an eye for an eye, tooth for tooth' (Exodus 21 v 24) Whoever hits a man and kills him is to be put to death' (Exodus 21 v 12) The Old Testament takes up the concept of limited revenge.

4) Families and the general public want to see revenge for murder.

5) Hanging would deter violent crimes which are on the increase and give greater protection to the police.

Check list of some of the main arguments against capital punishment:

1) To hang a man in cold blood is worse than murder.

2) The death penalty does not act as a deterrent to violent crime or terrorism.

3) There is always the risk of killing someone who may be innocent.

4) It is a violent form of punishment which denies the religious teaching of the 'sanctity of life'.

5) All too often the public feel sympathy for the murderer because of the publicity and forget the victim.

6) Life imprisonment is a much tougher sentence for people as it gives them time to think about the crime they have committed.

7) People can change and reform their lives. They go on to be good and useful citizens.

8) To execute the murderer does not bring back the victim.

Extensions:

- The main arguments for and against capital punishment could be brainstormed and discussed in groups.

- The student could debate 'This group believes in the reinstatement of capital punishment for the act of ....'
  (own choice e.g. terrorism)

CAPITAL PUNISHMENT

Read the following before answering the questions below:-

Hanging was abolished by Parliament in 1965. Capital punishment in the British Isles had dated from A.D.450. During this time it had been abolished by William I and reinstated by Henry I. Between 1830 and 1955, the most convicted murderers hanged in a year was 27 in 1903. In 1956, there were no hangings in England, Wales or Scotland. Since then the highest number of hangings was five in 1964.

With the rise in violent crime and terrorism there have been many demands for the death penalty to be re-established. The last time that hanging was debated in Parliament was on 1st April 1987. It would seem that the public are more in favour of hanging than the Parliamentarians. A survey in one London newspaper showed that out of the people interviewed 24 to 1 were in favour of hanging. The M.P.s voted against capital punishment by a majority of 112. If Parliament had voted for its reinstatement they would have had to decide whether or not to replace hanging with an alternative form of execution such as the electric chair.

1) What are the main arguments for capital punishment?

....

....

....

....

....

2) What are the main arguments against capital punishment?

....

....

....

....

....

3) Why do you think many people argue that the death sentence should be re-introduced for certain crimes?

....

....

....

....

....

DRUGS

DRUG USE AND LOSS

Psycho active drugs (drugs that affect our feelings) have been used throughout history. Drug use has been mainly social; but also to 'deal' with strong emotions.

Today anti-depressants and/or tranquillisers are often prescribed for people suffering from loss or bereavement. Also some people may self-medicate with alcohol or illegal drugs. Unfortunately these drugs generally only delay the grieving process by putting us out of touch with our grief.

In the short term they may help us cope; in the long term it may lead to dependency as attempts at stopping bring the return of feelings that have not been dealt with and withdrawal can also bring a sense of loss.

RESOURCES: Flip Chart paper
Pens
Information on types of drugs/drug use

METHOD:

1.   Brainstorm names of drugs - try and include legal and illegal drugs.
i.e. Tea, coffee, nicotine, alcohol, glue, heroin, cannabis, amphetamines, LSD.

2.   Split into small groups and list reasons why people may use drugs.
e.g. Fun, cure illness, peer group pressure, low self esteem, depression, to dull the pain of loss e.g. suicide, divorce, abuse, difficult relationships.
Feedback to main group.

3.   Explain types of drug use.

Triangle of drug use

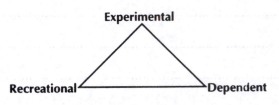

Discuss meanings of recreational, experimental and dependent
i.e.:

Experimental	-	trying first drink; how old were you?; who gave it to you?
Recreational	-	Smoking cannabis at a party; with other people; not every day.
Dependent	-	Using alone; everyday; cannot manage without it; no choice.

Definition of Terms:-

Physical Addiction	-	A substance that causes physical withdrawal symptoms when use is stopped after a period of regular use.

Psychological Dependence	-	A substance that is depended upon to deal with psychological symptoms, i.e. depression, anxiety, loneliness.

Although only some drugs are physically addictive, i .e. Heroin, we can become psychologically dependent on just about anything, i.e. chocolate. This can be particularly noticeable with psycho-active drugs, i.e. drugs that affect our feelings, such as nicotine, cocaine. It is our reliance on a substance to 'deal' or mask our feelings that may make stopping difficult, rather than the substance/drug's addictive properties.

4. Feelings Exercise

a. Brainstorm words for feelings i.e. happy, bad, embarrassed.

b. Sit group in circle, leave one chair empty next to the educator. Ask each member of the group to pick one pleasant feeling and one unpleasant feeling and think of the situation when it occurred, i.e. 'I was angry when my tape player broke last week'.

When this is done, get each participant in turn to sit in the empty seat where the leader will ask about the bad and good feeling. Everyone in the group should participate by listening and speaking in their turn.

IMPORTANT Always ask for the bad feeling first and make sure the good feeling is a good feeling.

The purpose of the exercise is to help people recognise different feelings and to talk about them. It can be useful to focus on whether it was easy or hard to talk in front of a group, how it felt, whether the group were supportive, etc. The link to drug use is that we may become dependent on drugs to hide our feelings if we are unable to identify them or talk about them, i.e. the widespread use of alcohol.

Extensions:

a. Get 5 large sheets of paper and write agree; disagree; strongly agree; strongly disagree; disagree; not sure; on the sheets. Place the 'not sure' sheet in the middle of the room and the other 4 in each corner.

b. Make statements such as "Its OK to take anti-depressants to deal with grief", and ask participants to stand by the word(s) that are closest to their beliefs. Repeat but use comfort eating, alcohol, or tranquillisers, instead of anti-depressants and compare answers.

c. Ask each small group why they have chosen their particular stance
or
get the different groups to talk to each other and see if they can convince others to move.

EUTHANASIA

Resources:

- Copies of Activity Sheet 'Euthanasia'.

- Copies of the articles 'My Sunday' and 'The Silent Conspiracy'.

(See Appendix 3.1)

Method:

1) Discuss what the group understands by 'Euthanasia' see below.

2) Hand out copies of 'Euthanasia' Activity Sheets.

3) Share and discuss the answers volunteered by the group bringing out the complexities of the issues raised by euthanasia.

Extensions:

- First read the articles 'My Sunday' and/or 'The Silent Conspiracy'.

- Then discuss the ways in which the introduction of Hospices in recent years have largely eliminated the need for euthanasia. British Medical Association say 95% of pain can be eliminated, although Hospices are still in short supply, and there can still be unpleasant symptoms that can't be controlled, e.g. breathlessness.

- In what ways are Hospices different from ordinary hospitals?

- Watch, read or discuss extracts from Tom Stoppard's play, 'Whose Life is it Anyway?' (the story of a man who was a quadriplegic and wanted to die).

- Discuss why we put animals to sleep when the law forbids us to do the same for human beings. Find out more about the Natural Death Society.

- How does AIDS affect our outlook on euthanasia?

- Use a values continuum or debate issues, e.g. 'If you switch off the life support machine, it's murder?'

Voluntary Euthanasia is when a dying person asks a doctor/relative or friend to speed up the death process.

Enforced Euthanasia is the term used when the State or some other group decide certain people are unfit to live, e.g. Nazi Germany.

Mercy Killing is when there is a direct intention to end the life of a dying person. The motive is generally one of compassion.

Passive Euthanasia means shortening the inevitable death process by not giving drugs or using a life support machine, e.g. when someone is brain dead or very old and has pneumonia (pneumonia was once known as "the old man's friend".

Controversial issues might include:-

- Do we have the right to say when we want to die?

- When should the decision to die be take..
  - a) because the person is a burden to society?
  - b) because they are in unbearable pain?
  - c) because they are a trouble to friends and relatives?
  - d) because they no longer have a meaningful life?

- Who has the right to decide when someone should die? The patients themselves, the medical staff or the relatives? How could the " Living Will" below help this decision.

- When is someone really dead? When their heart has stopped beating or when their brain has stopped functioning properly?

Living Will

Published by The Natural Death Centre
20 Heber Road, London NW2 6AA
(tel 081 208 2853, fax 081 452 6434)

This Living Will (also known as an 'Advance Directive') has been adapted by the Natural Death Centre from those put out by the Terence Higgins Trust, V. E. S. and others. The British Medical Association approve of Living Wills (see over). You would be well advised however to discuss your Living Will (and to lodge a copy) with your GP (it might be best to change doctor if necessary, in order to find one who is sympathetic to the Living Will concept) and with your relatives. If you go into hospital, you can show it to your doctors there and have a copy put in your notes. You should also update the form every five years, even if just to sign and have witnessed the statement (below right) to the effect that it still represents your wishes. Strike out any parts which you do not wish to apply to your case - or write your own version entirely. If you appoint representatives (below) these should be people you trust absolutely, especially if they would benefit financially from your death. Keep the Living Will summary (below right) in your wallet.

TO MY FAMILY, MY PHYSICIAN AND ALL OTHER PERSONS CONCERNED. THIS DIRECTIVE is made by me at a time when I am of sound mind and after careful consideration.

I wish to be fully informed about any illness I may have, about treatment alternatives and likely outcomes.

I DECLARE that if at any time the following circumstances exist, namely:

(1) I suffer from one or more of the conditions mentioned in the schedule below; and

(2) I have become unable to participate effectively in decisions about my medical care; and

(3) two independent physicians (one a consultant) are of the opinion that I am unlikely to recover from illness or impairment involving severe distress or incapacity for rational existence,

THEN AND IN THOSE CIRCUMSTANCES my directions are as follows:

(1) that I am not to be subjected to any medical intervention or treatment aimed at prolonging or sustaining my life;

(2) that any distressing symptoms (including any caused by lack of food) are to be fully controlled by appropriate analgesic or other treatment, even though that treatment may shorten my life.

(3) that I am not to be force fed (although I wish to be given water to drink).

(4) that I wish to be allowed to spend my last days at home if at all possible.

I consent to anything proposed to be done or omitted in compliance with the directions expressed above and absolve my medical attendants from any civil liability arising out of such acts or omission.

I wish to be as conscious as my circumstances permit (allowing for adequate pain control) as death approaches. I ask my medical attendants to bear this statement in mind when considering what my intentions would be in any uncertain situation.

I RESERVE the right to revoke this DIRECTIVE at any time, but unless I do so it should be taken to represent my continuing directions.

SCHEDULE

A Advanced disseminated malignant disease.

B Severe immune deficiency.

C Advanced degenerative disease of the nervous system.

D Severe and lasting brain damage due to injury, stroke, disease or other cause.

E Senile or pre-senile dementia, whether Alzheimer's, multi-infarct or other.

F Any other condition of comparable gravity.

Living Will summary to photocopy and carry around with your credit cards

> **LIVING WILL:** I have made a Living Will stating, inter alia, that, if terminally ill, I do not wish to have my life prolonged by medical interventions. This Living Will is lodged with Dr...
> Tel...and with my
> proxy ....
> Tel..

EUTHANASIA

Read the following before answering the questions below:-

Euthanasia literally means 'an easy or good death'. The word is used when people are allowed to die with dignity, quickly and easily, rather than suffering a long and painful death.

Doctors have always had the dilemma that they are meant to preserve life and not destroy it. Medical advances can mean that people are kept alive for longer. Much valuable research has been done with the terminally ill encouraged by the Hospice movement. Drugs can now be administered to control and ease most of the pain. Dame Cecily Saunders, founder of the Hospice Movement has suggested 'Euthanasia should be unnecessary, and is an admission of defeat'.

The law is quite clear. It is illegal to help someone to die or kill them at their own request. There are people who 'think this law should be changed for humanitarian reasons. Despite the House of Lords has twice turned down legalizing euthanasia since 1969. The Voluntary Euthanasia Society was formed in 1935 (once called EXIT) and has always campaigned for the right of people to choose to die with dignity when there is little or no hope of a cure and (or) they are in great pain. In the Netherlands, approximately 75% of doctors practise euthanasia.

One of the main arguments against voluntary euthanasia has been the fear that it could lead to abuse in the future with such vulnerable groups as the handicapped, and the mentally ill. Although in a survey carried out by the National Opinion Poll in 1989, 75% of the respondents were in favour - similar figures have been recorded in many countries throughout the world.

The religious arguments against euthanasia centre around the teaching of the sanctity of life. However, although voluntary euthanasia is not accepted generally, some people feel that God would not want people to suffer and so releasing them from pain is seen as a loving act and not selfish - it is the pathway into the next life.

1) What do we mean by 'dying with dignity'?

....

....

....

2) List the main arguments for euthanasia.

....

....

....

3) List the main arguments against euthanasia.

....

....

....

HIV and AIDS

Objective

To raise awareness of the emotional and social implications of being HIV+ with a particular focus on the possible perceptions of loss.

Resources

Sets of cards with the various case studies on them. See below
The five discussion questions worksheet.
Articles in Section 3.
Information about where people faced with these situations would receive support in your community.

Method

The case studies can be used as a basis for individual written work/group discussion.

1)   Hand out the case studies to individuals or groups and ask them to answer the questions overleaf.

2)   Invite individuals to feed back responses to whole group.

Extensions

- Students could be asked to draw a circle and put the name of the person inside it and then to imagine who else would possibly be effected by this situation and to place these imaginary characters in smaller circles around the person with comments on how these people might feel or questions they may have. These notes can then be used to discuss how one person's HIV status can have important implications for the wider circle of friends and family. This will require students to imagine possible circumstances and family/social settings.

This activity should enable the educator to show the range of positive and negative responses which have been witnessed when people have shared the fact that they are HIV+ with people around them. It is important to stress that it is the person themself who should decide who to tell about their HIV status and not anyone else. The activity should highlight the varied possibilities and the potential advantages and disadvantages of sharing personal information of this nature.

- Read or ask one of the group to read "PEOPLE DO APPRECIATE AND REACT WELL TO HONESTY" (at end of this section) and discuss.

CASE OUTLINES :

SIMON

Simon is fifteen and he is HIV positive. He was infected with HIV by receiving factor 8 for haemophilia in 1984. This is a treatment which contains contributions from the blood donations from many donors. Simon suffers from a severe form of haemophilia and he has to avoid any form of physical contact sports, although he would love to play rugby. His parents are very supportive but he sometimes sees his mum crying.

TINA

Tina shared a needle once when she was at a party, she thought she would be safe as it was her boyfriend she was sharing with. Unfortunately he didn't know that he was already HIV+ so all his reassurance was in vain. Tina only had one sexual partner, Dave this boyfriend, so when she was late for her period she knew who the father would be. On discovering several months later that she was HIV+ she decided to have the baby adopted. She was not able to face the responsibilities of parenthood at this time when she had so many things to sort out for herself. She told her boss about her situation and in a matter of a few weeks she was told she was no longer required. She did not have the energy to fight the case on the grounds of unfair dismissal.

DEREK

Derek is in his mid thirties and he knows he was infected with HIV in 1983 although he is not too sure when or how it happened. He knows he had unprotected sex on several occasions during his twenties, although he would not describe himself as promiscuous. At the time he found out his wife had just been diagnosed HIV+ having received infected blood at a transfusion. He did not think the doctor should have told his wife as it did not look likely that she would pull through. The doctor had insisted that Derek be tested immediately 'just in case' and Derek felt that he had no choice but to comply. A week after the funeral Derek received a letter informing him that he and Sheila, his wife had been accepted as adoptive parents. Life can be so ironic at times!

EDUCATOR'S NOTES

IS IMPORTANT TO AVOID THE NOTION OF INNOCENT AND GUILTY "VICTIMS" AND TO FOCUS UPON THE NEEDS OF ALL PEOPLE WHO ARE INFECTED WITH HIV.

When staff are preparing to teach this part of the curriculum it is helpful to focus upon the feelings and attitudes that this issue raises and to ensure that attention is given to students' fears.

The other aspect which should receive time is the skills development necessary to ensure that information can be applied. This will involve helping young people to discuss sexual health, developing their ability to resist pressure, and be clear about the complexity of the sexual decision making process.

HIV and AIDS - Background Information

HIV is used to describe the virus which can lead to AIDS. This virus effects humans and can result in a breakdown in the body's natural defence system. The letters stand for:

H Human

I Immune Deficiency

V Virus

A Acquired

I Immune

D Deficiency

S Syndrome

HIV is acquired this means that it is passed on in specific ways. It is now established that HIV is passed on through blood,semen and vaginal fluid. These body fluids have to pass from an infected person into the circulating blood stream of another person and the most common ways that this happens are:

*   sexual intercourse (vaginal/anal)

*   blood to blood contact (sharing needles/syringes, unscreened blood/blood products in some countries. An infected mother may also infect her child at birth.)

*   There is a 12-30% chance that an infected woman could pass HIV on to her unborn child. Children born HIV antibody positive have to be tested at 18 months to determine if the result indicates that they are actually infected, an earlier result may only be showing that the child has the mother's antibodies. Infection can occur before, during or immediately after birth.

It is important for people to have the right information upon which to make choices and to hold attitudes and values which will reduce the risks of infection to themselves and others. PREVENTION of further HIV infection and SUPPORT to those who are already infected are both important ways to minimise the impact of HIV on our lives.

HIV infection can be asymptomatic and people may remain well for several years before showing any signs of infection. At the moment it appears that over a ten year period 50% of those infected would go on to have AIDS and 80% would have some form of related illness. After infection it can take the body three months to develop sufficient antibodies for an antibody test to show up positive. IT IS IMPORTANT FOR PEOPLE TO REALISE THAT ONCE A PERSON IS INFECTED WITH THE VIRUS THEY CAN INFECT THEIR SEXUAL PARTNER(S).

STAGES OF HIV INFECTION

HIV INFECTION   possibly a short flu like illness

for a few days

SILENT/ASYMPTOMATIC INFECTION   No symptoms

Averages 10 years

AIDS RELATED CONDITION   Mild symptoms eg. swollen glands skin disorders,tiredness

Can last several years

AIDS   Severe symptoms eg skin cancer, pneumonia

2-5 years

AIDS is not one disease it is a condition marked by various symptoms/infections like extreme weight loss, muscle wasting and dementia. Some of the opportunistic infections can be managed and treated by drugs but often these can have various side effects and these may require further medication to deal with the toxic effects of the drugs.

There is a move towards describing all of these as HIV infection or disease rather than differentiate between the stages of HIV/ARC/AIDS.

HIV can affect people differently and for many it is the stigma and prejudices which are harder to deal with than the actual physical infections.

TEACHING POINTS

* Avoid referring to "risk groups' this can give people a false sense of security. It is what people do which is important.

* Distinguish between HIV infection and AIDS and avoid terms suchas AIDS test.

* Refer to "people living with the virus" rather than "victims"or "sufferers".

* Focus on skills development to encourage prevention and support rather than medical facts or statistics.

'PEOPLE DO APPRECIATE AND REACT WELL TO HONESTY'

Brian explains how he told his work colleagues that he had Aids.

A Message From Brian Planning Department

Dear Friends,

I apologise for not being able to think of a better way of bringing you this news. The news being the fact that I have Aids. I thought it best to tell you through this note rather than have you hear it on the Grapevine. Most of you will realise that I have contracted Aids from infected blood concentrates used to treat my Haemophilia. It is a sad reflection of the state of our so-called "civilised" society that I have felt the need to explain how I contracted the disease.

I do not know exactly how long ago I became HIV positive (when the virus is simply carried in your system without displaying any of the full blown Aids symptoms.) I was told around the end of 1985. I did not take the news as seriously as I should have, being told that there was a good chance that I wouldn't actually develop Aids. I was formally diagnosed in January this year when I contracted the particular type of Pneumonia that is one of the infections associated with and used to diagnose Aids.

I have not informed you before, largely on medical advice. Two years ago there was considerably more prejudice and ignorance about Aids. I also didn't want you to behave any differently towards me. I have decided to tell you now, not because I anticipate being poorly again in the immediate future, but I simply don't like living with this secret or having to make up excuses for the occasional medical check up. I also feel that you now know enough about Aids to realise that I am not a risk to your health. To put it bluntly, unless I was to rape or abuse you or we engage in a blood brother/sister ceremony or you are a secret vampire, there is no danger!

I am sure many thoughts have flashed through your minds whilst reading this: 'What the hell is he still doing at work!! "How do you cope with such a situation?"

184

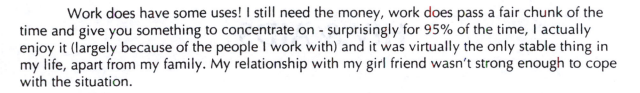

Work does have some uses! I still need the money, work does pass a fair chunk of the time and give you something to concentrate on - surprisingly for 95% of the time, I actually enjoy it (largely because of the people I work with) and it was virtually the only stable thing in my life, apart from my family. My relationship with my girl friend wasn't strong enough to cope with the situation.

Coping? Being a Haemophiliac has helped enormously. I am used to hospitals, being laid up, etc. I am not worried about or frightened about what might happen and feel an inner calm.

I realise that the chances of a cure being found for me are slim. But if you believe that death is not the end, one can carry on living and living well with Aids. It makes you think about what is really important in life and its nice to be able to live in the present.

Please feel free to approach me and discuss any aspect of Aids or my medication - I won't bite you! (Sorry.)

Please try and carry on being just as you are.

BRIAN

Brian writes:- 'Re-action to my note was fantastic. Several people I hardly knew wrote to me and shook my hand, I was promised kisses under the mistletoe etc. I have not been aware of one bad reaction or of anybody avoiding contact with me. I am sure this one action has added months to my life."

Brian's Letter is published by permission of The Haemophilia Society and first appeared in their Members Bulletin in 1989.

**Reproduced with permission from leaflet by Lantern Trust,
72, Honey Lane, Waltham Abbey,
Essex. EN9 3BS.**

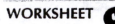

HIV & AIDS

Read the case study that has been given to you and answer the following questions.

1   What losses has this person had to come to terms with?

....
....
....
....
....
....

2   What might they feel angry or guilty about?

....
....
....
....
....
....

3   Who could they contact for help and support in your area?

....
....
....

4   Why is HIV/AIDS such an emotive & controversial subject?

....
....
....
....
....
....

SUICIDE

Read the following carefully and answer the questions:-

Disturbing Figures:-

- About 5,000 people commit suicide in the United Kingdom in a year.

- Someone commits suicide in the U.K. every 2 hours.

- At least 200,000 people attempt suicide in a year.

- Someone attempts suicide every two and a half minutes.

- 750 per 100,000 in the 15-19 age group try suicide - more than twice as many as ten years ago.

- Suicide attempts are increasing faster for young people than any other age group.

- Actual suicides are increasing for young people.

- Suicide is the third most important cause of death for young people.

- Someone who has attempted suicide is 1,000 times more likely to try again than someone who has not.

Why Do People Commit Suicide?

From these figures we discover that 5,000 people commit suicide in each year in the U.K. and many more attempted suicide. The reasons why people commit suicide vary greatly but for many life seems unbearable or pointless. This might be the result of loneliness caused by bereavement or a broken relationship, such as a marriage, failure at work, redundancy, unemployment, inadequate housing, stress or depression. It is important to note that most people who commit suicide are not mentally ill.

Suicide and the Law:

Until 1961 it was against the law to commit or attempt suicide. Even as late as the 1950's people were occasionally given prison sentences for attempting suicide. In the Middle Ages all the person's possessions were confiscated by the Crown. It is still illegal to help someone else commit suicide (see Euthanasia).

Suicide and the Church:

It is only in this century that suicides have been buried in churchyards with a full burial service. Christians have always seen suicide as wrong because it goes against the Sixth Commandment, 'Thou Shalt Not Kill'. Strictly speaking, even today, the Church of England does not give a full burial for people of sound mind who have killed themselves, but this is largely ignored. The Roman Catholic Church teaches that suicide is a mortal sin. The Qur'an also condemns suicide as a sin, comparing it to murder - life is seen to be God-given.

As the Church of England had control over burial grounds until the last century suicides could not be buried in them. As late as 1882 they were buried at cross-roads with a stake driven through the body. The stake was used to prevent the ghost of the person from escaping. Cross-roads were chosen because should a spirit rise from the body it would be confused about the direction to go. Also the cross-roads made the shape of a cross, making a good symbolic alternative to a churchyard.

The Samaritans:

The Samaritans were started by Chad Varah, an Anglican Priest, in 1953. Today there are over 185 Samaritan branches throughout Britain and Ireland. It is run by volunteers who offer a 24 hour service to take emergency telephone calls. They are kept extremely busy. Over 400,000 people call the Samaritans for the first time each year. There are also branches around the world in 23 other countries, all linked to each other through membership of Befrienders International. The volunteer's main task is to listen to the person and befriend them. The line literally becomes a life-line. All the information given is treated as confidential and the caller does not have to give a name. This confidentiality is the reason why so many people use the Samaritans.

Samaritans have also recognised that they have a role to play on occasions when people have been subjected to traumatic events. Thus they have been involved in the aftermath of most of the major disasters that have occurred in the last few years: Kegworth, Lockerbie, Zeebrugge and many others. Experience has shown that after such tragic events, Samaritan empathy can be helpful to the relatives and friends of the victims, to those awaiting news and to members of the public services. Asked by a TV interviewer what she most needed after the Clapham rail crash, one of the nurses involved in the treatment of the injured said, "Someone to talk to." Often in such circumstances Samaritans find that, as well as disclosures of current anguish, they encounter deep-rooted sorrows. At Lockerbie, Samaritan volunteers listened not only to the horrendous experiences of those who had to scour the moors for human remains, but also to the stored-up memories of earlier traumas, such as the Falklands War.

1)   Why do you think the law regarding suicides was changed in 1961?

2)   Why are the telephone volunteers called 'Samaritans'?

3)   Why do people ring the Samaritans?

4)   How do you think they help their callers?

5)   Why do you think so many teenagers try to commit suicide?

6)   Why do you think Samaritans have developed their work to include crisis intervention with groups.

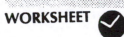

THE SAMARITANS: TWO CASE STUDIES

These stories are made up because the Samaritans never tell outsiders about the lives of those who call. However, they are typical and will help you understand how the Samaritans work.

Prepared by a volunteer, Hilary, of the Central London Samaritan Centre and of the special branch that works at pop festivals.

Peter

Peter's home life had been unhappy as long as he could remember. When his father wasn't shouting at him, he was shouting at his mother, who always seemed to be in tears. Peter had just shut himself off from it all, like living in a tiny room with the door closed. Somehow he'd survived, and then one day when his father had hit him, he'd just run away, and hitched a lift down to London. He didn't stop to think what he'd do once he got there, he just knew he had to get away from the violence and anger. Once in London some of the problems hit him - no job, nowhere to live, but worst of all, no friends. He found a hostel, but the other guys there seemed so different from him, and anyway he didn't trust them - he'd never trusted anyone, let alone loved anyone or been loved. Everything seemed black and whenever he passed a chemist's he thought of stealing some pills to swallow. But then a poster on the wall caught his eye. The Samaritans. Well there was nothing to lose. It was hard to start talking at first - he wasn't used to talking about himself, and then he was a little worried they might contact his parents. But the volunteer, Anne, assured him that no one would know he'd called. Peter was surprised to find that here was someone who really listened, who could share his feelings, who didn't criticise him or tell him what to do. Slowly he began to realise that one doesn't have to be lonely, that there are people who care, although it would take a long time to learn to trust people.

Linda

Linda had always been a little shy, but when she met Martin at the Club, and he invited her to go to hear the band playing down at the Queens Head it had opened a new chapter in her life. Martin made her feel so special, and he'd come round two or three evenings a week. But then last night he'd phoned and said he wouldn't be round, and he sounded kind of distant. Then today at school her friend had told her she'd seen Martin walking down the High Street with his arm round Angie. Linda felt as if someone had knocked her down - life just didn't seem worth living any more, and the thought of having to go home, where her parents would just be sitting staring at the television was just too much. She wandered down the high street miserably, and then remembered the sign she'd seen in the telephone kiosk.

"Suicide? Despair? Samaritans care". Maybe someone there would understand how she felt. She went into the kiosk and dialled the number. Ten minutes later she was sitting in the centre, telling Rosie, the volunteer everything that had happened. It was such a relief to tell someone how she felt.

HOW WOULD YOU CHOOSE?

Resources

Copies of the Activity   'How Would You Choose?'

Method

1)   Introduce the activity and hand out the sheets.

2)   Ask the students to make their own individual choice of the two people who should receive the machine.

3)   Divide the students into small groups with a reporter.

4)   Ask each group to discuss their individual choices and come up with a joint decision.

5)   Get reporters to feed back decisions made.

Extensions

Ask groups to share:-

a)   On what basis did you decide who would receive the machine.

b)   How would you feel if you had to make the decision for 'real'?

c)   What pressure is put on the officials who have to make the decisions?

How did the groups come to an agreement -

a)   What happened first?

b)   What feelings were shown?

c)   What feelings were not shown?

Alternative

a)   Nothing happened until ....

b)   I thought ....

c)   The others seemed to ....

d)   In the end we ....

190

HOW WOULD YOU CHOOSE?

DECISION MAKING (CHANGES BROUGHT ABOUT BY MEDICAL SCIENCE)

All the following have Kidney disease. Only two machines are available to enable two of them to survive.

What factors will you consider to help you arrive at your decision which of the two will receive the machines (give your reasons).

PATIENT 1.   LYNN: She is 34 years old. She has 4 children between the ages of 7 months and 8 years. Lives in a pleasant house by the river. Her husband recently had a heart attack (mild).

PATIENT 2.   TOZO: She is 18 years old. A Sociology student at London University. The daughter of a Japanese Diplomat who has a vast private income and who has contributed heavily to medical research in the UK. She is unmarried but is the girlfriend of a Japanese Cabinet Minister's son. She has recently been the subject of a nationwide T.V. documentary on the newly liberated Japanese woman.

PATIENT 3.   ROY: He is 41 years old and born in Central Africa. He is heavily involved in his church and in voluntary work with the unemployed in South East London. He is married with 11 children aged between 6 to 19 years.

PATIENT 4.   RAYMOND: He is 28 years old and unmarried. He has been out of the Army for 2 years and spent three spells of duty in N. Ireland. He has been unsettled since returning to civilian life and is at present drinking heavily. He is unemployed but does a lot of voluntary work with disadvantaged young people. He is also studying for a degree with the Open University.

PATIENT 5.   CHRISTOPHER: Christopher is a man of 38 years who has been divorced for 6 years. He is a medical research Scientist and is recognised as a world authority on AIDS. He has twice spent time in a psychiatric ward suffering from manic depression. He is living with another member of the research team, James.

PATIENT 6.   DOROTHY: Dorothy is 62 years old and lives alone, she is widowed, in a Council flat in Harrow. She has 7 cats to whom she is devoted and is known locally as slightly eccentric in her ways, especially in respect to the hundreds of wild birds she encourages into her garden and feeds throughout the Winter. There have been complaints to the Council about her from near neighbours.

LAST RITES   2.11

Objectives:

- To help the students to know what to do when someone dies.

- To explore the different types of funerals that are available.

- To examine the different customs and rituals surrounding death.

- To encourage the students to think positively about their death.

What To Do When Someone Dies

Resources:

- 'What To Do When Someone Dies' (see book list).

- 'What To Do After A Death' (D.H.S.S. free).

- Activity Sheets 'What To Do When Someone Dies'.

Method:

1) Discuss what the students think should be done when someone dies.

2) Give out copies of the Activity Sheet 'What To Do When   Someone Dies'.

3) Clarify the parts played by:-

> Family
>
> Doctor
>
> Hospital
>
> Police
>
> Coroner
>
> Undertaker
>
> Registrar
>
> Minister of Religion
>
> Others

Extensions:

- Invite or visit an undertaker, a minister of religion or others in the above list, to answer questions about their part played when someone dies.

- Hand out copies of the D.H.S.S. booklet 'What to do after a death'. Tell students to imagine that someone has died and.to use the booklet to make a check list of the things they would need to do.

192

What To Do When Someone Dies

CHART 1

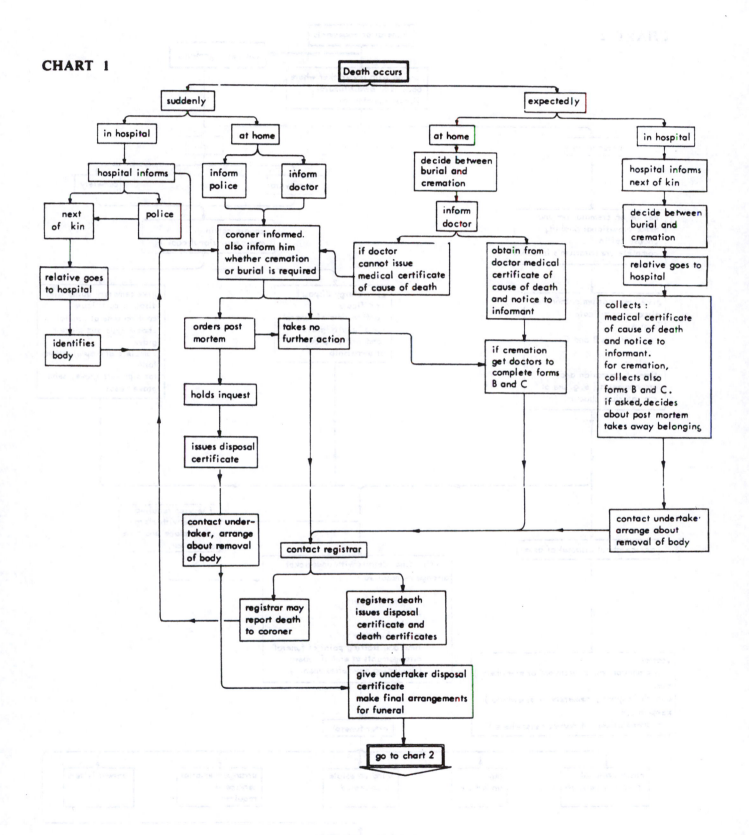

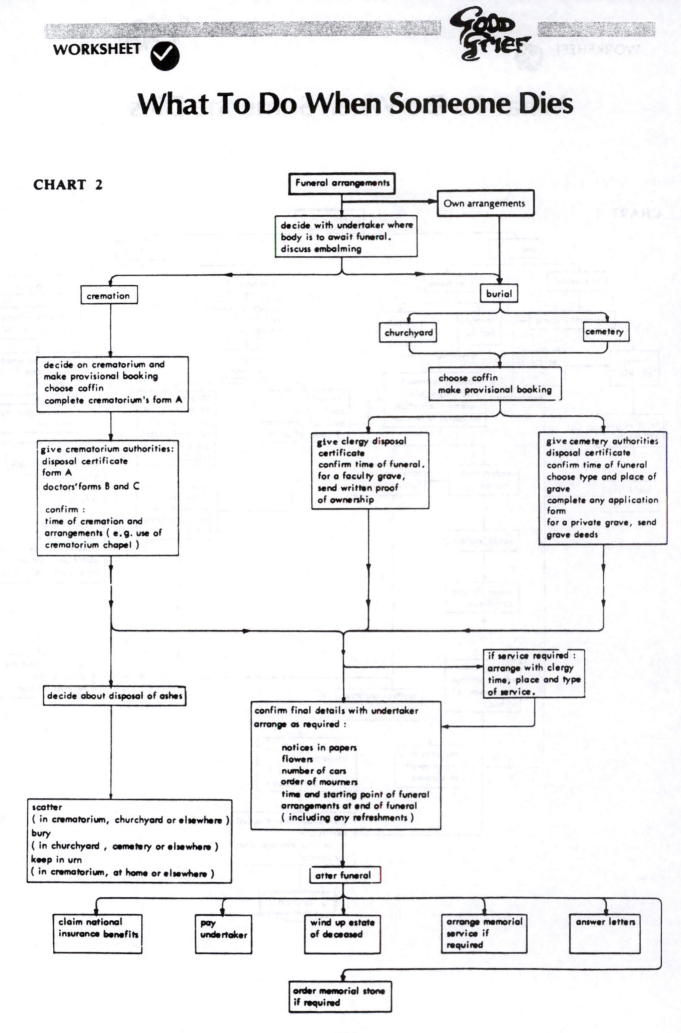

What To Do When Someone Dies

CHART 2

Funeral arrangements

Own arrangements

decide with undertaker where
body is to await funeral.
discuss embalming

cremation

burial

churchyard

cemetery

decide on crematorium and
make provisional booking
choose coffin
complete crematorium's form A

choose coffin
make provisional booking

give crematorium authorities:
disposal certificate
form A
doctors' forms B and C

confirm :
time of cremation and
arrangements (e.g. use of
crematorium chapel)

give clergy disposal
certificate
confirm time of funeral.
for a faculty grave,
send written proof
of ownership

give cemetery authorities
disposal certificate
confirm time of funeral
choose type and place of
grave
complete any application
form
for a private grave, send
grave deeds

if service required :
arrange with clergy
time, place and type
of service.

decide about disposal of ashes

confirm final details with undertaker
arrange as required :

notices in papers
flowers
number of cars
order of mourners
time and starting point of funeral
arrangements at end of funeral
(including any refreshments)

scatter
(in crematorium, churchyard or elsewhere)
bury
(in churchyard , cemetery or elsewhere)
keep in urn
(in crematorium, at home or elsewhere)

after funeral

claim national
insurance benefits

pay
undertaker

wind up estate
of deceased

arrange memorial
service if
required

answer letters

order memorial stone
if required

194

WHY DO WE HAVE FUNERALS?

Resources:

- Copies of activity sheet 'Why do we have funerals?'
  Useful Addresses and Article Cremation, Burial & Memorials ... in Sec. 3.

- Flip chart and pens.

Method:

1) Divide the students into small groups and brainstorm the reasons why we have funerals.

2) Give out copies of the activity sheet 'Why do we have funerals?'

N.B. The statistics for widows etc. given in the section 'What is death'.

3) Ask the students to share their answers in pairs or in small groups. Then, using the flip chart, ask them to make up a list of the customs surrounding death in their community that they have seen or heard about.

4) Discuss how these customs might help the bereaved.

Extensions:

- Using newspapers etc. look at the funeral arrangements of a V.I.P. (e.g. film stars) to see how the wider public were included or excluded at the funeral.

- Ask the students to design a memorial or choose or compose a piece of music to play at a funeral. (You might like to send for information first [see Resources above]).

- Writing/art or verse could also be used - see Creative Activities in Sec. 2.

- Ask the students to describe the sort of funeral they would like for themselves. It could include a choice of readings / music / venue. Cremation / burial, religious / non religious and who they would like to attend.

WHY DO WE HAVE FUNERALS?

Read the following and answer the questions.

a.   The funeral gives a structure to secure the reverent disposal of the body.

This greatly helps to keep the emotions under control and reduces the anxiety of the bereaved.

Customs and outward forms of observance vary greatly from place to place. What they do give is a framework for the bereaved to express their grief and sorrow in a way that is recognized and accepted by the wider community. (This is an important early stage of the grief process).

Examples of such Customs:

-       Do the family prepare the body for the funeral?

-       Is the body brought back to the family house?

-       Is it expected that the relatives will kiss the deceased?

-       Does the family wear black, white or any other colour?

-       Do the women attend the funeral or not?

-       What sort of feast or wake is held after the funeral?

-       Are the children forbidden or encouraged to attend the funeral?

-       Are all the curtains drawn in the house as a sign of mourning?

-       For how long is the accepted time of mourning?

Make a list of the customs surrounding death that you have heard about or are practised around where you live.

....

....

....

....

....

....

b. **The funeral makes real the death for society.**

-   It is a public recognition of what has happened.

    -The more important the individual is in our society the more people will wish to share in the funeral act itself.

-   Where people are well-known families often prefer to have a private funeral which is followed later by a 'memorial' service for all the friends and associates of the deceased.

-   With the more important public figures society itself takes over most of the funeral arrangements from the family, e.g. The Royal Family; leading politicians.

i) Why is it that the more public a person's life has become the more the public are involved with that person's funeral?

    ....

    ....

ii What is the purpose of a memorial service?

    ....

    ....

c. **The funeral symbolizes the change in status of those in the family.**

-   The wife becomes the widow.

-   The husband becomes the widower.

-   The child becomes part of a one parent family or an orphan.

Why does society need to formalize the change of status of the bereaved by calling the wife a 'widow' etc?

WHY DO WE HAVE FUNERALS?

Resources:

- Copies of activity sheet 'Why do we have funerals?'
  Useful Addresses and Article Cremation, Burial & Memorials ... in Sec. 3.

- Flip chart and pens.

Method:

1) Divide the students into small groups and brainstorm the reasons why we have funerals.

2) Give out copies of the activity sheet 'Why do we have funerals?'

N.B. The statistics for widows etc. given in the section 'What is death'.

3) Ask the students to share their answers in pairs or in small groups. Then, using the flip chart, ask them to make up a list of the customs surrounding death in their community that they have seen or heard about.

4) Discuss how these customs might help the bereaved.

Extensions:

- Using newspapers etc. look at the funeral arrangements of a V.I.P. (e.g. film stars) to see how the wider public were included or excluded at the funeral.

- Ask the students to design a memorial or choose or compose a piece of music to play at a funeral. (You might like to send for information first [see Resources above]).

- Writing/art or verse could also be used - see Creative Activities in Sec. 2.

- Ask the students to describe the sort of funeral they would like for themselves. It could include choice of readings/music/venue, Cremation/Burial, Religious/Non-religious and who they would like to attend.

DISPOSAL OF THE BODY

Read the following.

Burial or Cremation?

Until recently in Britain the tradition was to bury the dead. However, today, the majority of British people choose cremation. (In 1986 68% chose cremation). The first crematoria were opened in England in the 1880's and there are now 223 crematoria throughout Britain. There are religious groupings who object to cremation. Orthodox Jews and Muslims will not be cremated. Although Roman Catholics have been allowed to be cremated since changes made in Rome in 1963 many of them still prefer to be buried. In other countries, such as India, the tradition has been to cremate the dead.

Burial:

Advantages:

-   Family tradition (family grave).
-   Graves can be visited and cared for after the funeral which can give much comfort to the bereaved.
-   A headstone can be erected.
-   More personal.

Disadvantages:

-   More expensive.
-   Burials can be more distressing for a family.
-   Some graveyards look unkempt, cold and miserable.
-   It can be difficult to get the elderly relatives and friends to the graveside.
-   Bad weather can make the funeral difficult for those attending.
-   Family and friends can be distressed years later when the grave becomes overgrown - perhaps because the relatives are elderly or live some distance from the grave.

Cremation:

Advantages:

- Cheaper.
- More pleasant and comfortable surroundings which are not dependent on the weather.
- Easier for the family and friends to participate in the service or ceremony.
- Easier for the clergy, or whoever is leading the funeral, to be heard and to give an eulogy.
- More hygienic.
- Saves land.
- The ashes can be buried or scattered sometime later.

Disadvantages:

- Many people psychologically dislike the committal proceedings when the coffin slides away on rollers or a curtain falls across the front of the coffin. The coffin has disappeared but it is not a true commital to fire. The earth is cast on to the coffin in a burial.

- Many people find later that they would have preferred the chance to visit a grave with a headstone. Plaques on a wall, buried or scattered ashes, or a rose-bush don't seem adequate in themselves.
- The funerals can feel staged or rushed as the time is limited in the cremation chapels - one funeral every half hour is quite normal. This can make it feel more impersonal.

At funerals most officiating Ministers will welcome participation by the family in the service (obviously arranged in advance), e.g. a favourite reading or poem of the deceased might be read by a member of the family, or maybe they give the eulogy, or play and sing a special piece of music.

'If words do not come naturally to them other means of expression might. Why not encourage people to kiss the coffin, or put a candle by it, or stick a label on it - or anything else to serve as active tokens of their grief, no matter how vulgar or unorthodox?'
(Christopher Martin)

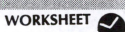

ARRANGING YOUR OWN FUNERAL

"I'd like to buy a coffin."

"You mean, you'd like me to arrange a funeral?"

"No, I'd like to buy a coffin - 5'5" and as plain as possible."

"You don't want me to arrange the funeral?"

"NO, I want to do it myself."

"Well - I suppose it's all right."

"Oh yes - I know it is - I've done it before."

Death has been taken away from us - it is big business and even in the medical and nursing professions death is shied away from, decisions are taken from us and many people find it hard to talk about or accept death.

This changed dramatically for me when a close friend in his early thirties died of cancer. He and his wife took many decisions together, that he should die at home, that a few people close to him should do as much for him as was possible - this continued after he died. His wife decided that we should do the funeral too and with the help of an outstanding and sympathetic GP this was arranged for the same day. We bought a coffin, did the minimum of preparation to his body, and took the coffin ourselves to the local Crematorium in the back of an estate car. I felt privileged to have been part of this; it made a bond between the four of us who helped and I believe that knowing that we personally did everything we could, has made it easier to grieve.

This certainly was the feeling after arranging my mother's funeral a few months later. The previous experience made it possible for me to carry out her funeral. I knew much more what was possible; but also what changes I could make in the arrangements. My mother and I discussed much of what should be done before she died. For many people, the physical action of placing a loved person in the coffin and closing the lid is inconceivable but there are usually others, perhaps friends and/or relations who could and would like to help. Also many people think that there is a lot to be done in the preparation of the body - in fact, usually very little needs to be done and there is usually someone, perhaps a District Nurse, who could do the simpler things which in some circumstances might need to be done. In cases such as removal of a pacemaker, the services of an experienced person might be necessary but this is an exception rather than the norm.

In olden days death was much more part of life and the elaborate and expensive funerals we have today were unknown. There has been much interest shown in our experiences and people involved in the care of the dying have been positive in their reactions. A sister (Community) from a hospice feels that most problems are surmountable, e.g. in hot weather perhaps the body could be placed in the north facing room with fans or wounds could be dressed with waterproof plaster.

It used to be done - why not now?

Death, dying and the sort of funeral/burial one has is much more a matter of choice than most people think. For some, the greatest way of showing their love, respect and grief is to have the ritual of an arranged funeral and that is right for them, but for others perhaps the knowledge that one can do it extremely simply, personally and cheaply may be of benefit. It also may be of interest to people of other religions who would prefer to carry out their own funerals (whether burial or cremation) according to their customs or beliefs.

Jane Warman

RITUALS AND CUSTOMS

Resources:

- Copies of the activity Sheets:-

    'Rituals and Customs'
    'A Non-Religious Funeral Service'
    'Religious & Cultural aspects of Dying & Bereavement' (see section 3)

Method:

1) Ask the students what they understand by the word 'ritual' and why it plays a central place at funerals.

2) Hand out copies of the Activity Sheet 'Rituals and Customs'.

3) Divide the students into pairs or small groups and/or the large group, ask them to share their answers.

Extensions:

- Hand out copies of the activity sheet 'A Non-Religious Funeral' and ask the students in pairs to list the ritual which is common to those found in religious funeral rites. Then ask the students to compare their answers in the large group.

    Dividing the students into small groups ask them to draw out how the Jewish funeral rites reflect the 'stages of grief'.

RITUALS AND CUSTOMS

Read the following carefully and answer the questions.

The rituals and customs surrounding a funeral reflect the beliefs of the deceased and the society in which they live.

The major world religions give hope - that death is not seen as final but rather as a stage in the journey of life. People are naturally afraid of death and the way they will die, death itself and about what sort of life, if any, there is after death. The religious beliefs incorporated into the services give the bereaved hope and reassurance and helps them to grieve and to look forward.

Ever since the beginnings of religious beliefs people have paid great attention to the burial of the dead. This was seen to be a preparation of the departed for the next life.

For example, tribal people are frightened of the dead because they believe the power of the dead spirit can bring bad luck. The dead depend on the living to perform the death ceremony correctly so that they may rest peacefully. The living depend on the dead to link the family with the spiritual power which the ancestors possess. To ensure that this happens, the dead are buried with great care.

Examples of Funerals

1)   A Funeral of the Toraja people of Indonesia:-

For many, the death of a person is an unhappy time not only because they may be losing someone who has been close to them but also because they may be unsure of what comes after death. This uncertainty can often cause fear. Tribal people, too, are frightened of the dead because the power of the dead spirit can bring bad luck. For this reason the dead are buried with great care; a word or action out of place during the ceremony could result in the dead person bringing bad luck. The dead depend on the living to perform the death ceremony correctly so that they may rest peacefully. The living depend on the dead to link the family with the spiritual power which the ancestors possess. When the ceremony is performed correctly both the living and the dead are much happier.

If you were to visit a funeral ceremony of the Toraja people of Indonesia, you might think you have come upon a carnival rather than a funeral. The people who gather for the funeral are in very high spirits and they appear far from sad. Processions of people arrive at the funeral field with buffalo ready to be sacrificed in honour of the dead person. A large pavilion is built from bamboo and everyone awaits the procession which brings the body to the funeral. The dead must be given a good send off. The dead person is about to become an ancestor. The coffin containing the dead person is brought onto the field. In a special ceremony the bamboo pavilion is burnt and buffalo sacrificed. The Torajas believe that the pavilion and the buffalo will go ahead of the dead spirit and be there in the spirit world to await its arrival. The body is taken to the grave site where it is to be buried. A wooden statue is made and placed in a sacred place alongside other statues. The ceremony is complete and the dead person takes its place among the ancestors.

2)   A Hindu Funeral:-

-       The funeral ceremony aims to set free the atman (soul) for another incarnation.

-       There are readings from the Holy Sanskrit Books and prayers are said.

-       Sacred objects and significant symbols such as rice and gold are placed beside the body.

204

Exercises in Listening

Choose topics most appropriate to the age, ability and experience of the group and the time available. It is better to use only one or two exercises and leave plenty of time for discussion than to try to cover all of them.

Exercise 1: Both students talk at once.
Debrief: We need to have dealt with our own problems and get plenty of listening for ourselves if we are really going to listen to others. All too often we are waiting for a turn to 'put our spoke in' and speak.

Exercise 2: One student speaks and the other ignores them.
Debrief: The importance of non-verbal feedback. See the diagram 'The Communication Cake'. Bad feelings when not listened to properly can stop us asking again.

Exercise 3: One student speaks and the other listens without speaking (non-verbal).
Debrief: Compare with exercise 2 and refer to worksheet 'Unhelpful Behaviour'.

Exercise 4: Both students have their eyes closed or sit/stand back to back.
Debrief: As in Exercise 2 above.

Exercise 5: The Students have an ordinary conversation with a topic of their own choice.
Debrief: Conversation is comfortable but it will not clarify problems. Conversation is useful at the beginning of a meeting to enable the speaker to feel at ease and at the end to bring the person back to the present gently if they have been upset.

Exercise 6: Discuss the following worksheets 'Keys to Good Listening' and 'Unhelpful Behaviour'. Then ask students to share something that is on their mind.
Debrief: Discuss what has been learnt from the exercises.

Extensions:

As emotions may be evoked, these activities are suggested for advanced students under supervision.

- Put the students into groups of three, speaker, listener and observer. The speaker talks about a real or an imaginary problem. Afterwards each member of the group gives their feedback of what was most/least helpful. Speaker first, then listener and finally observer. Repeat the exercise swapping the different roles.

- As above but try these different approaches:-
a) Listening in silence.
b) Offering solutions all of the time.
c) Encouraging the speaker to explore his/her feelings and different aspects of the problem.

- Place the students in pairs to share experiences of tears and anger and explore how these feelings might interfere with listening to others.

- Again in pairs ask the students to share experiences of loss and bereavement and how these could prevent us listening to and helping others.

Debrief:

- The eldest son, or closest male relative, has the duty to ignite the funeral pyre (obviously this is not permitted in British Crematoria).

- The eldest son collects the ashes which are scattered in the nearest river.

Cremation is normal but if friends of the deceased are sure that he has obtained Moksha (escape from reincarnation) he need not be cremated. Instead the deceased is buried in a seated position of meditation.

3) A Jewish Funeral:-

'Within the Jewish religion burial rather than cremation is usual. Burial takes place as speedily as possible - as official mourning cannot take place until after the burial. Direct family members (i.e. children, brothers and sisters) of the deceased are the only ones who are involved officially. This means that directly after the funeral, where prayers and an eulogy are offered by the Minister, the men of the family say 'Kaddish' - mourning prayer. Those in mourning sit on low chairs for seven days. Prayers are said within the home every evening and early morning prayers are said daily in the Synagogue. The family are visited daily and at any time of the day and for evening prayers visitors make a special effort to be with the family.

"After seven days mourning are over, under religious law one is instructed to get on with living. For a whole year the men of the family pray (special mourning prayers) every morning and evening. At the end of a year a memorial stone is consecrated at the grave - where a 'final service' is held. It is at this time that we are told by our Rabbi that the days of mourning are over.

4) A Christian Funeral:-

Christians choose either burial or cremation. During the funeral service the Minister:-

- commends the departed to God's care

- proclaims the belief in life after death seen in the resurrection of Jesus Christ

- reminds those attending the funeral of the certainty of their own coming death and judgement before God.

In the past Christians have sought burial rather than cremation because of the belief in the literal resurrection of the dead at the second coming of Jesus.

5) An Islam Funeral:-

- Muslims believe in resurrection and a Day of Judgment.
Each personality is judged according to their deeds. The faithful entering paradise which is portrayed as a celestial garden of delights with cool streams and rivers of milk and honey. In contrast the unfaithful are thrown into hell - a fiery place where they are given scalding water to drink and bitter fruit to eat.

- Muslims are not cremated because of their belief in a physical resurrection of the body.

- If possible the burial takes place the day after the death has occurred or else at the first opportunity.

- During the funeral service a prayer is said asking for God's forgiveness for the deceased.

205

- The body is buried with the head facing Mecca, the holy city of Islam.

- No extreme forms of mourning are permitted. Instead the reading of the Qur'an is encouraged. The period of mourning usually lasts from one week to three months.

6)   A Sikh Funeral:-

The Sikhs believe in reincarnation and therefore do not see death as final, but as part of the cycle of life and rebirth until the final achievement of unity with God.

The body is bought home where it is washed and dressed.
Then the coffin is left open for a short time so that the family and all the relatives can see the dead person for the last time.

The body is then taken to the crematorium. After the cremation the friends and relatives usually return to the Gurdwara for a short service with prayers and hymns.

In the days following the death the whole family is in mourning. Relatives and close friends will come to keep the family company and comfort them.

Women may wear white after the death as a sign of mourning.

A NON-RELIGIOUS FUNERAL SERVICE

People who have little or no faith may choose to have a non-religious service.

The Humanist Society helps many people arrange funerals and will lead them if requested.

Extract from a letter by David J. Williams - British Humanist Association ....

❝ As far as funerals are concerned, we see the ceremony and the whole process of mourning as of considerable help to family and friends in adjusting to the fact that someone near and dear to them has died. It is healthy to mark this change in circumstances by public ceremony as long as it does not become extravagantly morbid.

We are not in favour of great pomp or displays of wealthy ostentation at funerals. The officiant is there to help the mourners have their own ceremony with words and music to meet their expectations. We are very happy to assist friends or members of the family to conduct the ceremony themselves, although most people don't have the courage to take it on.

As far as attitude to death is concerned, the Humanist accepts that death is the natural end of all of us. We do not believe in any tangible survival beyond death. It is an evident truth that you can't be dead: you can only be alive. Being is synonymous with living.

The Humanist funeral ceremony - or memorial meeting - is therefore not being held to help the departed soul on its way to the beyond. We don't think in terms of souls and we don't believe in the beyond. The ceremony is to help the living.

Humanist funerals need not be terribly sad. If somebody has had a good life and is remembered with affection, there is no great cause for grief. The music can be cheerful and respectful at the same time. The words that are spoken might even cause the mourners to laugh. There is a proper place for a certain degree of ritual and the point of committal is to be marked with due respect.

Finally, the occasion of the funeral allows us - society as a whole - to remind those of us still living that life is good thing and we had better do something useful with it while we can. Some families ask for a non-religious funeral because it avoids awkward clashes of different religious faiths in a multi-cultural society. A Humanist funeral is not anti-religious: it celebrates
the Human values we all share and cherish❞.

....

a. What are the common factors of all the funerals?

b. Why do you think the Toraja people are not sad at their funerals?

c. Look at the funeral service or ceremony of one major world faith and show how that service reflects their beliefs.

d. Why is it that many families choose to have a religious funeral service when they are not practising believers?

TRIBUTES TO THE DECEASED

Resources:

- Activity Sheets:-

    'Humorous Epitaphs'
    'A Summary of Your Life'
    'Your Own Personal Coat of Arms'

Information from organisations that specialise in Memorials (see Useful Addresses (Sec.3))

Article in Sec (3) Cremation, Burial and Memorials: The Options and Choices.

Method:

1) Clarify with the students what is meant by the word 'tribute' and why people want to make them to the deceased.

    Check list:-

    - the mourners want to share in the memories and achievements of the deceased.
    - usually an eulogy is given at a funeral.
    - many well known figures have a memorial service.
    - an epitaph or plaque maybe left in their memory.
    - public figures usually have an obituary published in the newspapers.

2) From the newspapers give out examples of recent obituaries.

3) Hand out copies of the Activity Sheet 'Humorous Epitaphs'.

4) Brainstorm the students to draw out the sort of things they would like to be remembered for.

5) Hand out copies of the Activity Sheet 'A Summary of Your Life'.

6) Get the students in pairs to share their epitaphs and eulogies. Then ask for volunteers to share these with the whole group. Draw out the common features of their epitaphs and eulogies. e.g. They were good and what they had done.

Extensions:

- Hand out copies of the Activity Sheet 'Your Own Personal Coat of Arms'. Close by asking volunteers to share their own 'Coats of Arms'.

- Ask students to design a memorial or choose or compose a piece of music to play at a funeral (use e.g. of TV programme where dying person chose own funeral service and asked for song "Memories" to be played.)
- Ask students to write a letter/essay or poem or draw a picture.

N.B. You might like to send for information first (see resources above).

HUMOROUS EPITAPHS

Read these through carefully:-

For a Mr Box
Here lies one Box within another.
The one of wood was very good.
We cannot say so much for t'other.

Miss Arabella
Here rests in silent clay.
Miss Arabella Young,
Who on the 21st May,
Began to hold her tongue.

The Tired Woman
Here lies a poor woman who always was tired;
She lived in a house where help was not hired.
Her last words on earth were, "Dear friends, I am going
Where washing ain't done, nor sweeping nor sewing;
But everything there is exact to my wishes.
For where they don't eat there's no washing of dishes.
I'll be where loud anthems will always be ringing,
But having no voice, I'll be clear of the singing.
Don't mourn for me now, don't, mourn for me never -
I'm going to do nothing for ever and ever".

For a Favourite Dog
Thou who passest on the path, if haply thou dost mark this monument, laugh not I pray thee,
though it is a dog's grave; tears fell for me and the dust was heaped above me by a master's
hands who likewise engraved these words on my tomb.

Most of us have little idea of how we will be remembered and certainly we will have no
chance to comment and challenge what is written or said about us. All of us, deep down, do
care what our loved ones think about us.

Have you ever thought about how you will be remembered?

What you do with your life is an outward expression of the real you. The things you spend
your time doing and the way you relate to those around you reflect your interests and
beliefs.

Here lies Les
Gone for sure
Shot to death
By a 44....
No Les.
No more.

A SUMMARY OF YOUR LIFE:

Read the extract below and answer the questions:-

Violet Szabo, who was shot for her work with the French Resistance in World War II, wrote these words:-

The life that I have is all that I have,
And the life that I have is yours.
The love that I have,
Of the life that I have,
Is yours and yours and yours.
A sleep I shall have,
A rest I shall have,
Yet death will be but a pause,
For the peace of my years in
the long green grass,
will be yours and yours and yours.

****

1) Write a short epitaph that summarises your life which you would like to go on your own gravestone or plaque.

2) Write your own eulogy to include the following:-

   a. Strong points in your personality.

   b. Aspects of your personality that could have improved or developed with time.

   c. Deeds that you have accomplished or would like to have done.

   d. Things you would have done differently and why?

   e. How you could have made your life more positive?

   f. Things you will be remembered for.

   g. Things you would like to be remembered for.

   h. Any other points you would like to include.

YOUR OWN PERSONAL COAT OF ARMS

Read the following instructions and complete your own coat of arms:-

Your personal Coat of Arms is divided up into four main sections together with a place for your motto.

Complete your Coat of Arms as follows:-

1)   In the top left hand corner draw, or briefly describe, how you see the past in your life.

2)   In the top right hand corner draw, or briefly describe, how you see the future in your life.

3)   In the bottom left hand corner draw, or briefly describe, whoever or whatever is closest to you.

4)   In the bottom right hand corner draw, or describe briefly, how you see death.

5)   Write in your own motto.

6)   Working in pairs compare your shields and see what they may be saying about you.

Your Own Personal Coat of Arms

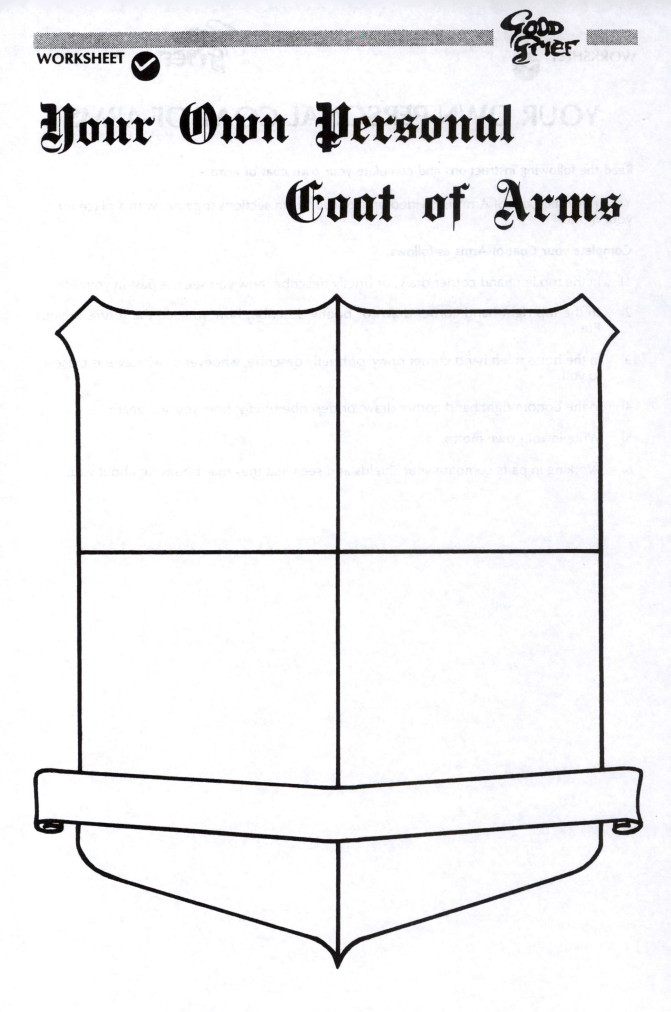

Section 3

Appendices

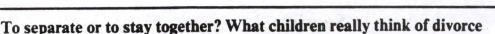
3.1   To separate or to stay together? What children really think of divorce

Tomorrow a children's television programme will tackle the subject of divorce. Will it make uncomfortable viewing for parents? **Sally Brompton** investigates

Abbi was five when her world fell apart. "My mum ... went upstairs and packed her bag, she put her coat on ... she opened the door and she said, 'I'm going away for a few days.' And then I said, 'Why are you going away for a few days?' and then she didn't answer and walked away. Then I started crying and I thought I'd never see her again."

Five years on, Abbi can look back calmly at that terrible moment when her whole life crumbled. At the time, however, convinced that she was somehow to blame for the break-up of her parents' marriage, she retreated into a cocoon of guilt and confusion.

As Britain's divorce figures soar, more and more children suffer the psychological backlash of broken marriages. Enmeshed in their own unhappiness, it is perhaps understandable that the adults unwittingly overlook — or cannot cope with — the profound effects their actions may have upon their children.

Two million youngsters are currently affected by divorce and another 160,000 join them each year. One child in five will watch parents split up before he or she is 16. These are the forgotten casualties of a conflict commonly cloaked in mysteries and half truths. But even quite small children often appreciate more about the situation than their parents realize.

"The instinct of the adults is to conceal the truth, whereas children are almost psychically aware of atmosphere," says Charlotte Black, director of tomorrow's children's television documentary, *Unhappy Families* (BBC2, 5.05pm), which studies the children of divorce.

The programme explores the effects of divorce on six children aged between 10 and 14 from a mixture of backgrounds in the Avon area. Anxious not to exploit the children or cause additional trauma within the family, Black selected youngsters who seemed able to look back on the experience objectively.

In the words of 13-year-old Sarah: "Before our parents actually split up, I used to think that if they did I'd never get through it. But now I've realized that if you persevere, you can."

The children in the documentary tell their own stories, providing a revealing insight into their individual reactions. "I used to think it was all my fault," admits 11-year-old Debbie, who was four when her parents separated. "I used to think that they were rowing because of me and that if I wasn't there it wouldn't happen ..."

When his father left home, Demian, now 12, became aggressive towards his younger brother. "I used to thump him and cry and break things ... he used to make Lego models and I used to stamp on them, kick them about the room ... I used to think that everybody else has got a dad and I haven't and I don't deserve one."

Philip Darley, a social services training officer in the Bristol area, believes that

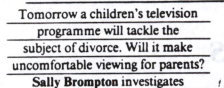

ABBI, 10, WHOSE MOTHER PACKED HER BAGS AND WALKED OUT FIVE YEARS AGO ...

'I started crying and I thought I'd never see her again'

Unhappy ever after?

"children vary in their reactions according to how they have experienced their parents' marriage. If their needs were being really well met in the first place, they will have a lot of internal strength to cope with the divorce."

"Another factor is their age. Quite young children find it very hard to believe that the problem isn't of their making. It is important to reassure them that it isn't." While adolescents, according to counsellor Lynda Osborne, resent the fact that "just when they want their parents to be the wallpaper, they suddenly come off the wall and create problems of their own".

Because children often find it difficult to accept that they are not alone in their predicament, they tend to be reluctant to talk about it. Darley, who runs "Surviving Divorce" courses for both parents and children, has found that the main reaction of the children is relief — "at being able to talk to other children in the same boat and share ideas about how to cope.

"One of the saddest things is that a lot of children don't know what is going on, and they know they don't know. I've had three children tell me, 'My mum says my dad is living at the office', and each of them knew that dads don't live in offices. They knew they weren't being told the truth but somehow they couldn't demand it."

So few divorcing parents know how to respond to their children's needs that a small, independent organization called People Projects has produced leaflets* for both parents and children explaining how to cope with divorce. Parents are advised to tell their children the truth from the start and to emphasize that

though they no longer love each other, this in no way affects their feelings for the child. Practical arrangements and continuity are very important to children who want to know how their day-to-day lives are going to be affected. Their opinions should be asked about custody and access arrangements but they

should never be expected to take sides or choose between their parents.

Children are warned that their parents may be very upset and may not understand how they can love their other parent.

"They are all obvious things but in some ways it is the most obvious things that need saying," says Mary Travis, a former marriage and relationship counsellor who formed People Projects and produced the leaflets.

In the television documentary, 11-year-old Liam believes that children should be given an explanation as to why their parents are separating so that "it won't come as a big, big shock". It came as a shock to Sarah and her younger brother, David, despite the fact that they had noticed that their parents "didn't seem to be getting on like they used to ... just little things like dad didn't kiss mum when he came in from work". When their parents eventually told them that they were splitting up, "it was a shock because we didn't want to know, in a way."

The parents, who were not present during the filming, were amazed at how mature and articulate their children were about their experiences. "They were surprised at the power of the conclusions and feelings their children had

come to, that they knew quite definitely who they wanted to live with and that, in many cases, the adults hadn't realized what they were going through," says Charlotte Black. She found that the children all had "a forced independence of emotions and had learned self-reliance early on" as a result of their emotional upheaval.

It was the children's decision to take part in the programme. "I think that most of the parents would have preferred to let sleeping dogs lie but because they felt it was the children's right to talk they let them do it," Black says.

She is hoping that parents will watch the documentary — as well as their children — in order to gain a clearer insight into the ways that youngsters react. It will not necessarily make the adults feel that they should never get divorced, but it will bring home to them the need to consider their children, whose views are often more circumspect than their parents realize.

In Debbie's words: "I don't think divorce is bad ... it can be a good thing because it can stop the parents from being upset and sometimes the child can be happy as well."

*Available through The Children's Society, Edward Rudolf House, Margery Street, London WC1X 0JL. Send 50p and a large SAE for the two leaflets

SARAH, 13, AND HER BROTHER, DAVID ...

'Dad didn't kiss mum when he came home'

CAUGHT IN THE MIDDLE

Finding that increasing numbers of children from broken homes are being referred to school psychological services, Kathleen Cox and Martin Desforge have made a special study of their difficulties and of the way teachers can avoid making things worse.

The final straw for many families is the failure of the annual vacation to live up to the promise of the holiday brochures. With the end of the summer holidays many children whose parents have recently separated will be returning to school.

Obviously children cannot learn efficiently if they are thinking of personal problems rather than classroom-based lessons. But does the school, its practices and curriculum also inadvertently add to the pupils' distress?

Schools, like children, find themselves caught in the middle of a situation not of their making but which they cannot ignore. There are few clear expectations and guidelines for either and limited experience to call upon to decide what to do. Teachers, parents and pupils are equally unsure what to expect of the school.

Some teachers regard themselves simply as educators. They feel they have been trained specially for this task and resent being asked to act as social workers even though they recognise that anxieties caused by parental separation and divorce may make pupils less receptive to teaching.

Some parents think their separation is a private matter and are reluctant to tell teachers of the home crisis. They may fear the teacher will be prejudiced against divorced parents and their children and often wish to keep such a personal matter private. Others, hoping for a reconciliation, do not wish to inform the school of what they hope will be temporary disruptions.

Some pupils habitually prefer their home life to have nothing to do with school. They like to separate their two lives, to leave their family concerns at home and their academic life in school whether or not there are problems in either place. These children resent what they see as prying teachers who may appear over-anxious to help.

However, with one in five children experiencing divorce before their sixteenth birthday and an unknown number affected by parental separation, schools can no longer ignore such events.

About two-thirds of children will show marked changes in school behaviour following parental separation. Common changes are a deterioration in work standards, restlessness, lack of concentration and a big increase in day dreaming. About one-fifth of these children exhibit sadness in school.

The changes often disrupt friendship patterns, with friends understanding even less than the pupils themselves and avoiding contact. The period of disturbance can last up to two years or more.

With a disturbed home life pupils can be lacking basic physical requirements such as sleep or regular meals. Under these circumstances the most basic requests from schools are difficult to meet and can be an additional burden to a pupil trying to maintain an interest in school. Homework, for example, may be impossible to complete if out of school facilities no longer exist.

Schools are in a unique position to help as all children are obliged to attend. The familiarity of school routine can in itself provide comfort and security to a child without any special efforts on the part of the school. Predictable routines can afford safety and stability at a time when home and family are undergoing change.

Schools and teachers contrast with clinics and counsellors in that they are not problem focused and can help by their mere normality. They can respond flexibly in a child-centred approach which allows children to talk when they wish to rather than when they have to in response to a clinic appointment. A sensitive teacher, by allowing children to express worries and fears in a calm atmosphere can certainly help them to re-establish their own sense of place and purpose in a changing situation.

Through routine daily contact pupils and teachers develop a relationship and trust which is available to help with personal problems. For this teachers need only basic counselling skills to encourage pupils to share their problems.

Many children whose parents separate have never had the opportunity to discuss their situation with anyone and say they would liked to have been able to talk with a neutral adult. Attentive listening can help resolve difficulties by allowing children time and space to define problems in their own way.

Some parents turn naturally to school to help them too. At the outset of such a parental interview it is essential to try to establish whether it is the parents' or the pupil's problems which are under discussion and to draw a clear distinction between the two.

Most teachers wisely choose not to involve themselves in parental difficulties directly and one way of helping parents in this situation is to know and suggest alternative sources of help: marriage guidance counselling; the DHSS, a solicitor or the Citizen's Advice Bureau for more practical problems, the Samaritans if the parent needs a sympathetic listener.

Parents and teachers should try to establish together what can be done to help the child who is their joint concern. It may become apparent that the school could complement existing parenting if the quality of parenting provided from home is temporarily diminished.

Extra attention may be required from a teacher who is prepared to hear children's news when their parents are too busy dealing with the essentials of living to give sufficient attention. Support of a more tangible nature is required to provide the materials the school requires for its curriculum, such as in home economics or PE.

The school's procedures should ensure that the facts about a pupil's life are recorded and updated as necessary and are accessible. Twenty-nine out of 30 parents in one survey in 1984 had informed the headteacher, but this did not mean that those who taught the child were aware of the situation.

Parents no longer living together but still maintaining an active role in child care may require separate copies of letters and reports. Offering this service rather than waiting to be asked is a positive way of helping both parents who may be too embarrassed to make such a request.

The school needs to know the basic arrangement of custody, care and control and access. This means that legal terms and their practical implications must be understood.

For the post-divorce family, schools can be one of the places where separated parents can work together for the well-being of their children. Parental cooperation following separation can be a valuable way to help the children to recover from the trauma of the split. Most parents are concerned about the education their children receive and school can be one neutral place to meet and discuss unemotively a topic of mutual concern, namely their children's education.

Until recently most school organizations assumed that their pupils were being brought up in a traditional nuclear family where father was the major breadwinner and out of the house during the day and mother was responsible for the daily lives of the children.

The practice of sending one letter to the child's home automatically addressed to Mr and Mrs all state clearly the assumptions on which the school is operating.

Failure to conform to the school's expectations with regard to family patterns affects the 200,000 or so children per year whose parents separate or divorce. The re-assessment of school practices and the innovation of others to take account of different situations accepts that not all children are brought up in stereotyped families.

The assumptions about family life are also reflected in the specific content of some subjects although not apparently directly relevant to the subject. In modern languages the vehicle for conversation is often the nuclear family in its stereotyped form.

In history, comments on the significance of certain marriages and their political implications reflect views on marriage today. In craft children may be encouraged to make things for homes and people which do not actually exist; a most obvious example being mother's or father's day cards. Christmas celebrations with the emphasis on the perfect family is stressful as parents and children privately compare their own situation with the ideal.

Personal and social education is now on the timetable in most schools in some form with a recent HMI report recommending it should be as much as one-sixth of the syllabus of a school. Although it does not yet enjoy the status of other subjects on the timetable, it is important both as a preparation for life after school and also may help pupils to see their own lives in a different perspective.

Another school practice which could help these children is the availability of books where separation and divorce occur. Including such books in the library accepts the occurrence and enables pupils to read, in relative privacy, books they may need. Friends may also gain a deeper understanding of their predicament which those directly involved are unable to express.

Schools should recognise that pupils' emotional and social development may be impeded as well as their academic work. Some will regress to an earlier stage of development and become more immature, while others do not regress but become fixed and cease to progress emotionally.

Friendship patterns can become disturbed as a consequence of changing lifestyles, and valuable peer support is lost in these ways. Pupils' social development might therefore need more active help from the school in order to overcome impediments to normal social maturation.

Teachers know the range of behaviour to expect in a certain age group and knowledge of children allow them to be aware of changes in individual behaviour. Teachers can assess reaction to stress and should consider referral to an outside agency if this reaction differs greatly from what is expected.

Initially, however, by knowing a significant number of children will be in this position, by expecting prolonged reaction and by being sensitive to the assumptions about the family which the school makes, teachers can go a long way to help

Kathleen Cox and Martin Desforges work for Sheffield's School Psychological Service.

215

Fear stifles Aids message

by Clare Dean

Schools are failing to spread warnings on the risks of Aids to pupils because of fears of prosecution under the law governing the teaching of homosexuality, it was claimed this week.

School governing bodies are erring on the side of caution because of Section 28 of the Local Government Act, which makes it illegal for local authorities to promote homosexuality, according to Veronica Payne, HIV/Aids training and development officer of the faculty of education at Bristol Polytechnic. "People are self censoring rather than getting involved. No one has been prosecuted under that legislation."

Although the Act applies to local authorities, school governors who have responsibility for sex education are worried by the prospect of prosecution.

Fears about governor responsibilities for Aids education were raised at a conference on HIV/Aids and young people last week. Ms Payne, who spoke at the conference, organised by the Society of Public Health and Youth Support, said governors "tend to be cautious about what they should include in sex education, because they don't want to be seen to be promoting homosexuality."

She said it was crucial that the risks of HIV, pregnancy and sexually transmitted diseases are explained to young people in schools.

"Concerns about falling foul of that particular piece of legislation must be balanced against the importance of providing young people with the information they need."

The responsibility for sex education was given to school governors in the 1986 Education Act. It says they should ensure that sex education is presented in the context of moral considerations and the values of family life.

Felicity Taylor, of the Independent Institute for School and College Governors, admitted that Aids education was a problem for governors.

"It certainly comes as a shock to some governors when they see some of the material. I am not critical of the material but if you are going to talk about this you have to be pretty frank, you can't be mealy-mouthed," she said.

TES March 8 1991

TES August 30 1991

Why Aids campaigns fail

Health education campaigns which highlight the links between promiscuity and Aids are likely to fail, research into the attitudes of young people has revealed.

Those most at risk from the disease are least likely to identify themselves as vulnerable, Dr Dominic Abrams of Kent University told the British Association.

He interviewed 1,000 youngsters in Dundee where there is a high incidence of intravenous drug misuse, following recent research by the Health Education Authority (HEA) which found that 25 per cent of young people did not always use a condom during sexual intercourse.

The conclusions of Dr Abrams' research are even more alarming than those of the HEA, and he called for a campaign aimed at changing behaviour and forcing the most vulnerable to recognise the risks.

"A combination of national and local media coverage and work with small groups of young people in schools and youth clubs would seem to be a sensible strategy," he said.

"We were struck by an enormous disparity between judgments young people made about the risks to themselves compared with the likelihood that others would become infected," he said. A substantial minority believed they were unlikely to be infected in the next five years. Yet they believed almost half their peer group would become infected.

They had the erroneous belief that they were somehow different and had what Dr Abrams termed Aids-invulnerability. Although the overestimation of survival could be psychologically healthy to cancer victims, "Aids-invulnerability could prove catastrophic," he said.

A cause of complacency was the extent to which individuals overestimated the number of partners others had compared with themselves. "These young people thought that, on average, their peers, and especially men, would have had between three to six times as many partners as themselves."

Another factor was the belief that their partners were safe, too. More than 60 per cent said they would trust their partners to tell them the truth about past sexual encounters and only 14 per cent thought that anyone they had a sexual relationship with was likely to have the Aids virus.

Asked if they would only have sex with someone they knew well, 70 per cent agreed and 14 per cent disagreed.

Asked whether they would carry a condom if they thought they might have sex with someone new, 51 per cent agreed and 18 per cent disagreed.

When asked if they would use a condom if they had sex with a new partner, 79 per cent said yes, and 5 per cent said no.

"The findings reveal a small (5 to 18 per cent) but important minority of young people who seem prepared to take risks with HIV infection," Dr Abrams said.

The behaviour of this small group showed further causes for concern.

Those who said they would have casual sex had significantly more partners than those who said they would not.

"However, and most important from our point of view, those who had most partners of all were the ones who mistakenly believed that the majority of people shared their own view that casual sex was OK," he said.

The 18 per cent who said they would not carry a condom if they thought they were going to have sex with someone new were among the most ignorant, being less likely that the rest to believe that HIV infection can lead to Aids.

"Recent campaigns had stressed the HEA figure that 25 per cent of young people were not using condoms. This strategy is backfiring.

Our research demonstrates that those who are most likely to engage in risky practices falsely believe that the majority do the same as themselves.

That is, they believe there are social norms that validate and justify their actions.

"Campaigns which emphasise the possible promiscuity of one's partners, or which highlight the fact that some people do not use condoms with new partners, may inadvertently reinforce these false perceptions that irresponsible sexual practices are widespread."

Dr Abrams concluded: "We know that young people tend to see themselves as relatively restrained and limited in terms of the number of partners they have.

They may therefore assume that statistics about the spread of Aids only apply to others because – as implied by the campaigns – it is others who are changing partners so often.

This then may exaggerate their sense of Aids-invulnerability."

216

Harsh transition to a new way of death

Illustration: Martin Loxton

Rufus Reade tells the story of Mui, a refugee whose feelings of dislocation were compounded by her husband's sudden death and an alien culture's bewildering way of dealing with bereavement and the rituals that surround it.

An adult experiences the world in terms of his position in relation to it. As father, as worker, as attender at the temple, as member of a culture with its own code, language and custom. Within this framework he has purpose and is seen as having a social identity. He may be known in different spheres as different things: as family man at home, as religious man at his place of worship, as a worker in his factory.

For the refugee, all these externalities are suddenly removed. He has left that which is most familiar, often leaves not knowing where he heads, and upon arrival finds that all is strange. If the refugee moves into a new and unfamiliar cultural zone, he is equipped with social skills that are often deemed inappropriate or strange.

Since a refugee's experience is to be dislocated from the external elements of identity, further crisis has the additional effect of traumatising, without there being any of the customary ritual, nor the sense of self which would guide the refugee through the event to some sort of sanity beyond it.

Mui came from a Chinese family in Vietnam. The wife of a carpenter she escaped with her husband and children by boat and after nine months in a camp in Hong Kong came to Britain, where she spent eight months in a refugee centre before being settled into a large council house. At the centre she had learned the rudiments of British life and a little English. Resettlement brought a house, neighbours, enormous distance from fellow Vietnamese, an unemployed husband, children who were quickly outdistancing her in their English language skills, the non-availability of customary foods, no local knowledge, a strange and bitter climate, peculiar gifts of money and goods from a social security system that bewildered her, the symbols of the rich — their TVs and cassette players, and a complete cultural ineptness that made her feel clumsy and her actions inappropriate.

Sense of loss

A refugee must grieve for everything once known and now a memory still half believed in, still half sought after. In this process of grief the refugee moves through the sense of loss, to guilt, then to anger at the deprivation. There may follow a loss of patterns of conduct with social/psychological disorganisation. Hopefully, a reconciliation with the change will come. But some refugees remain fixed in the sense of loss, continuing to crave for what was once their familiar daily world.

So grieving, the refugee must also learn the new skills of her adopted society: an adult feeling like a child in this process of learning. Making mistakes and finding progress slow. That sense of identity so totally removed and washed away can now begin to grow. But in any culture there are keys to identity, without which there can be no full identity.

Shared identity

In the refugee's home society, where unemployment may be uncommon, to work and be a father, to work and be a mother, to reap and thank the Gods, all help stabilise the sense of identity in the individual. In the West, each facet of life is often separate from the other. Who you are has one meaning at your place of work and another meaning in your home. The refugee in Britain may only have his family around him, with only their language, their food and their religion common to them. They share a private and restricted knowledge of who they are. Without the language of their neighbours and an occupation, they cannot have a wider sense of shared identity.

The problems of being a refugee are faced in several ways: the refugee may elect to fight, by learning the new language and looking for work. Those who learn the language soonest are those most likely to survive and succeed. Many turn inwards because they find the struggle too great. Others appear to outsiders as grasping, demanding excessively, remembering injustices long after the event and becoming jealous of apparent discrepancies in the treatment of their peers.

The refugee who experiences a lost motherland must move through the processes of grieving before going on to grasping an understanding of the adopting country. The issue, however, that tests the refugee's identity and resurrects the internal conflict between the old world and the new is the unexpected trauma, the sudden loss, the upheaval once again when all had begun to settle.

One morning Mui woke; she had been in her new house seven weeks. She warmed the baby's milk and checked that the older children were dressed and ready for school. Her husband complained he felt cold and asked to be left at peace in bed. Within 35 minutes he had died of viral pneumonia. Feeling she should have been able to save him by prompter action, she was filled with remorse and tried to throw herself from the window. She knew the procedure in Vietnam of how she should have dealt with his symptoms; she had failed to act appropriately and he had died.

Death in the West is a province for specialists. Death is at first a medical matter — most people die in hospital. Once the cause of death is known, the body becomes the object of the undertaker's art. Vocabulary changes and words are used to convey respect for the loved one, avoiding the trauma of the plainer language of death. The ritual and procedure of the burial reflect an alliance between the undertaker and the church. The body travels unaccompanied by the family in a hearse, the coffin is carried closed and is kept horizontal. The grave is dug in alignment with all the other graves to econmise the land use, and there are paid men to dig and fill the grave. Beyond this, there is a world of coroners, death certificates, death grants, wills, probate, widow's pensions and changed status for the surviving family.

Imagery of death

Through this separate, self-contained culture Mui had to pass. And pass in grief with her own Sino-Vietnamese construction of reality. For the British the imagery of death is symbolised by men with dark coats in black limousines accompanied by solemn organ music. The Chinese use white for death and mourning and the funeral procedure is directed to both help the dead man's spirit and to protect those still living from the ill omen of the funeral. Since one man's customs may be another man's blasphemy, those who have to deal with this rite of passage may find themselves horrified with what appears to be the insensitivity of the other culture.

Mui wanted to prepare the body for burial. She wanted personally to dress him in his finest clothes, but because the body was with the coroner and had been so cut up by the post mortem, the refugee workers made the "professional" decision to deny her this right. Mui wanted the body buried near her living relatives in Britain. It proved cheaper to fly the coffin than use British Rail. Before the flight, however, she had taken the children to see her husband's body in the undertaker's funeral parlour. The visit entailed a religious ceremony with rice and chicken, as well the placing of a coin in the dead man's mouth. The spirit is helped on its way with money at various stages, but when rigor mortis has set in, a dead man's mouth will not open. The family were finally ushered out while the undertakers (seen as men with special powers) forced the dead man's jaw open, placed the coin in then allowed the family to return. Prayers, jos sticks and spiritual power, the family believed, saw the issue satisfactorily resolved.

Because the body had to travel by plane there was some doubt whether the spirit would lose contact with it. The spirit was expected to return seven days after death to visit the body in the family home, but with the corpse far removed and the family home empty there was concern that the spirit might wander aimlessly. Accordingly, after the air journey, the family went to see the body at the new undertaker's chapel of rest. The money was still in place. As before, the dead man's wife and children covered their heads in white cloth and this time Mui's brothers took photographs: there were photos of the family grouped round the reopened coffin and close-ups of the dead man's face. Another brother wandered round with three lighted jos sticks and lit the candles in the chapel.

In a sense, the conflict between cultures had been accommodated to mutual satisfaction. Difficulties arose when Mui's brothers refused her permission to stay in either of their adjacent flats. The wife of one of the brothers was pregnant. A birth could easily be tainted by the ill omen of the death, since those associated with the death transmit bad fortune. That ruled out one flat. The other brother and his wife explained that from the day they moved into their flat they had worshipped the god of hearth and that they were not prepared to consider disloyalty to this god by either leaving or introducing into the flat such an inauspicious person as Mui.

Buddhist blessing

Mui had travelled 400 miles that day to stay with her brothers. The British refugee workers gasped at their insensitivity. A weeping widow kept from the solace of her family; five small children waiting in a cold dark van crowded with their possessions. For an hour and a half they waited. The issue was reluctantly resolved when one brother agreed to empty his flat upon the understanding that remaining furniture would be purified by the blessing of a Buddhist monk in seven weeks. Mui seemed to understand, recognising a construction of reality that bewildered those who could only perceive callousness.

In grief there is a retreat into the internal familiar world, a partial reflection of the very world the refugee has lost. It is the new adopted country that begins to appear callous and unappreciative of the needs of the dead man. Funeral customs comfort those left alive. They are also procedures to aid the dead person. Prayers, consecrated ground, proper conduct: but whatever their assistance to the souls of the dead, they provide a ritual allowing the dead to become "forever gone".

Special divination is commonly involv   in choosing the grave site and Mui's eld mother wanted the grave to be dug pointing south. The cemetery superintendent pointed to the alignment of the other p' on the hillside and said it could only   south east. In vain the family pleaded and then they wandered off to survey th cemetery. Some land laid aside consecrated for Roman Catholics was better choice, the elderly mother said. The superintendent said that o unconsecrated ground was available. family was evidently worried that the man's soul and body would not get the full benefit of a proper final rest. The g should not remain unmarked, but to th consternation the vast amount this buria was costing would not include gravestone. Was the superintendent cer that the site of the grave would not becom lost? He replied that wooden crosses an concrete headstones were not allowed, the family could make their gravestone, so long as they used marble o Portland stone.

Culture betrayed

Perhaps it is common to most culture that a man is not "dead" until he is bur We cannot know whether the compror here achieved has laid the dead man's sou and his widow's mind to rest. A key rite o passage improperly done, and the ref can turn neither to the sanctuary of the mother culture which feels so betrayed no can she find comfort in this new strange of procedures. She remains dislocated.

The refugee worker must operate in thi possibly unsatisfactory dialogue betwee cultures much of the time. The refug understanding of language and behavio often lacks the finer interpretation of th silent inner world of practice and custe Interpreters have to cope with the gross of the translation, the clums transliteration that attempts to satisfy on or other party, but seldom both.

Still dislocated

Mui, as an adult refugee, h internalised the funeral practices of Sino-Vietnamese culture. The experience o flight from Vietnam and rese lement i Britain witnessed the loss of mo t of external expressions of her sense identity. Now with her husband dead sh must also make the step from wife t widow. She must grieve for her husb when her grief for her homeland was n completed. And amidst this persona trauma a vital rite of passage spoiled ' unhappy compromise. Mui rem dislocated, and will perhaps never settle a a widow in the way that, as a wife, sh might have succeeded.

Rufus Reade is currently working for the Save the Children Fund, helping to resettle Vietnamese refugees in Scotland.

RELIGIOUS & CULTURAL ASPECTS OF DYING & BEREAVEMENT

Guidelines for those offering support to people experiencing loss on the importance of an appropriate religious ritual.

The dying person is faced with the necessity of letting go of family, friends, job, lifestyle and ultimately of life itself. In many ways it is not only the family who may commence their grieving before the death occurs, since the dying person is also grieving for the impending loss of his or her own life.

It is, I believe, important that people are able to grieve in their own way. Those who seek to offer care and support at such a time need to build a relationship which takes into account the other person's expectations and cultural patterns of behaviour in times of sickness, death and bereavement. To achieve this we need to be attentive to: the **assumptions** we may hold about how people should behave; the **value** to the other person of what is lost or about to be lost; create for the other person a **safe space** so that they may express some of the fears and anxieties they may have; be attentive to the **quality of the time** as much as the length of time that we give to the other person.

by Peter Speck

Peter Speck is Chaplain at the Royal Free Hospital, London.

As a hospital chaplain within the Christian tradition I find that supporting the bereaved ideally begins prior to the death of the person and is often related to a threefold pastoral aim:

1. To Reconcile

People frequently need help to re-establish broken relationships between man and God, man and man, and sometimes with themselves through the assurance of forgiveness. This is a common source of spiritual pain and anxiety for patient and family.

2. To Sustain

The ministry of word and sacrament in the Christian Church (and the equivalent religious ministry in other faiths) is important if we are to be able to endure and transcend what is happening to mind and body and make sense of the experience. This requires a willingness to share pain and **be with/stay with** distressed people i.e to create safe space without imposing religious ideas on to others. The dying may need to be given permission to let go. In this way the individual may be enabled to grow and attain true health/salvation. Although it may seem a contradiction in terms, for some people this growth may be achieved through their dying and death.

3. To Guide

Many people will rightly look to the religious leader, and others who practise their faith, for guidance both in what they should do and in their understanding of God, and the afterlife. However, not all believers will be equally strict adherents of that faith and so we cannot assume that they will all require the same form of ministry.

The letting go and the search for meaning with the establishment of a new role/identity are an important aspect of grief in any culture. An appropriate ritual can facilitate this process in that it may act as a **Rite of Passage.** This term seems to have been used initially by Arnold van Gennep who described three stages—**Separation: Transition: Incorporation.** Thus within the Christian tradition many of the rituals that one may perform can help the grief process (though not replace it) provided they are performed in a personal and relevant way.

1. Scripture Reading and Prayer

The dying may wish to hear familiar passages in a particular version. It is important to remember that we minister to their needs not our own. In respect of prayer it is important to pray with, not over, the patient—whether conscious or not.

2. Baptism

Usually performed at the request of parents for terminally ill children. However, this act of initiation may also be requested by adults in which case it may be combined with Confirmation.

3. Reconciliation and the Sacrament of Penance

The desire to "put things right" may require a formal act of confession and absolution as an important part of letting go of the past.

4. Holy Communion

The last receiving of holy communion (the Body and Blood of Christ received in the forms of bread and wine) is known as "viaticum" or the provision for the journey. The manner of receiving may need to vary according to the circumstances and may be accompanied by anointing with oil and the laying on of hands. It is important for there to be a good liaison between the hospital staff/GP/clergy/family.

5. Marriage

Contrary to the ease of hospital marriage as depicted on films and TV it can, in fact, only be performed by Archbishop's Licence or Registrar General's licence in extremis. A doctor must certify that the person is unable to be moved to a place licensed for weddings now or in the foreseeable future, and has a limited life expectancy.

6. Commendatory Prayers

For the Christian, prayers at the time of death should express confidence in Christ and his saving work, and commend the dying to God's mercy and love. It can have the effect of giving permission to die, although one should check what the dying person's needs are and that we have understood what they require. Other major religions will also have similar affirmations of faith at such a time.

7. Last Offices

Each culture has its own rituals for preparing the dead for burial and disposing of the dead. Intercultural factors are best dealt with by asking the next of kin for any do's and don'ts. In the case of the Jewish and Muslim community, for example, one should have no direct contact with the deceased, nor should the body be washed since this has to be done ritually. If in doubt, ask. Some relatives may wish to take part and assist. Some will wish to see the body and to have prayers at this time. Viewing the body and saying farewell properly can be very important in initiating the subsequent grief work. It is important that people have sufficient time with the deceased to say their goodbyes in the way they wish to. Cultural factors are important and we cannot assume all Christians will react in the same way. For instance an African lady danced around her husband's death bed because she reverted to her former cultural patterns of behaving. It was important not to stop her but allow it to continue until the 'keening' began.

8. The Funeral

This is also very important, whether it is religious or secular. If it is well conducted it can greatly facilitate the grief process. If not it can be a source of great bitterness. In the absence of a body to bury (lost at sea or donated to anatomy) a memorial service can help to give a focus to the grief. For example, after the Korean plane disaster relatives carried jars of sea water to the memorial service. They had no body to touch or to cremate, and so they carried some of the water in which the body had been lost. As Buddhists they mourned the lost of the body as much as the person since they were unable to pray for the release of the spirit of the deceased through cremation. They were expressing a deep religious and spiritual need.

SEPARATION

This is the first requirement of a rite of passage. Most of the major religions have evolved rituals which should facilitate the separation of the bereaved from the person who had died. Within these rituals it is important that the deceased is pronounced dead and enable people (children as well as adults) to let go of the body. Requests for post mortem or organ donation may distress relatives if separation is not yet possible because the reality of the death has not been acknowledged. Similarly the thought of cremation is not acceptable to some bereaved people since it represents a very speedy and final separation from the physical body. Certain religions, however, favour cremation because it speedily enables the soul of the deceased to separate from the body and enter new life or the new incarnation (e.g. Hinduism, Buddhism).

TRANSITION

Transition is the next part of the rite of passage. This is an in-between time when Mrs. Jones, wife of . . . becomes Mrs. Jones, widow of . . . The transition may be seen in relation to the deceased and the bereaved. In respect of the deceased, transition is often related to the anxiety expressed by many bereaved people as to where the dead person has gone to, and whether they may still be influential e.g. the feeling that "one should not speak ill of the dead" is often related to fears of reprisal.

For the bereaved the transition phase of the rite of passage is the time when the past is left behind and the future has not yet begun.

One's point of reference has gone and time seem to stand still as an endeavour is made to discover and accept a new identity and status. There can be much uncertainty and confusion as one looks to friends and family for help and support in adjusting to a new status as "widow, orphan, single person". The funeral ritual and associated events are a vital part of this because the funeral has the capability of encapsulating the full process of separation, transition and incorporation and thus enabling the bereaved to move forward in their grief. It does not do the grief work for them, but it can act as a catalyst. The extent to which the ritual achieves this aim of stimulating grief work is dependant upon several factors: what is done before the funeral service, the attendance and support of the family and friends, the individual character of the bereaved, and the level of actual involvement of those attending.

The presence and support of family and friends, both at the funeral and subsequently at the house, is something appreciated by the bereaved even if the motives for coming may be suspect in some instances. If the bereaved are to be aided in moving from old to new status they need to feel that other key people also acknowledge this change and are not going to accelerate them through the transition. In most major religions the funeral rite offers a way of saying "goodbye" and is a key event in the total rite of passage. Those attending are recognised as mourners and thus are given permission to grieve.

INCORPORATION

This third part of the rite of passage aids the re-entry into the community of those who have been branded or stigmatised by death. In that the funeral encapsulates the entire rite of passage, in miniature, then such re-entry can be symbolised by the return to the house by the family and friends after the funeral. People usually return to the house for an act of group sharing. It is a time for offering support to the next of kin, for reminiscence, renewing old acquaintances and perhaps for settling old scores! Traditionally there is a meal and drinks. A great deal of emotion is expressed as laughter or tears and discussion of the future. Such gatherings are more common in the North of the country and in Ireland than in the South (especially in the form of the 'Wake' which can sometimes become a riotous party).

Active support for the bereaved may not continue for very long. The family may need to return home to various parts of the country, the neighbours need to return to the needs of work and their own families. People also become tired of hearing what "a marvellous husband Harry was". Sometimes, of course, it is the bereaved who withdraw from the community.

If the bereaved go away to stay with relatives immediately after the funeral, or move house, this may delay or complicate incorporation. By going away at this stage the community does not have the same easy opportunity to visit. When the bereaved return home weeks later the community has returned to its normal activities and the opportunity and stimulus has been lost for visiting and support. This may then lead to a heightening of the isolation that the bereaved may already experience.

Full incorporation of the bereaved back into the community is parallel to the final phase of grief work. We are therefore thinking in terms of a period of time nearer to eighteen months than the two or three months that people usually allow. Attempts to hurry the process are often an expression of our anxiety and embarrassment in the face of grief. A difficulty that faces many people in our society is the lack of a structure within which to do their grief work, and which would mark off the end of grief—as exists within the Jewish community.

In the absence of a structure the bereaved will look to various key people in the community for guidance as to whether certain actions are deemed acceptable or unacceptable and when grief may be officially 'ended' in the sense that it is all right to socialise. A young widow who wished to remarry sought the approval of the local community in case she should be censured later for marrying "before her first was cold in t'grave".

People may, therefore, turn to the G.P. or local clergy for "permission" to stop grieving, especially around the anniversary. Continued visiting and the support offered by organisations such as Cruse, Still-birth & Perinatal Death Association, and the Compassionate Friends (for bereaved parents) can all assist incorporation. They may also be able to identify when people are using their religious faith in a stoical way, such that they deny any grief feelings: e.g. "I believe in God and an after-life. Therefore, I should be happy that my husband is with God So I shall smile and show the world how Christians face bereavement. If I cry and grieve that will indicate a lack of faith". It is not a case of letting God down but of being fully human, as exemplified by Jesus' distress at the death of Lazarus. Often the clergyman is seen as someone who will support the mourner in such a stoical stance. The clergyman may therefore have the difficult job of challenging this way of coping with loss.

CONCLUSION

Religion and culture can offer tremendous support and comfort to people in sorrow, provided it is a mature belief and a supportive and relevant ritual. We cannot know all the intricacies of another faith and not all adherents will be equally strict in their practice. However, if we can attend to our own assumptions about other people and give full value to what they wish to do, plus the space in which to do it, we will be able to facilitate their grieving—and learn much ourselves.

Bereavement Care 1985, Volume 4, No. 3.

Cremation, Burial and Memorials: The Options and Choices of Bereaved People

by

Frances Clegg, BSc, MPhil, PhD, ABPsS

Senior Clinical Psychologist, The National Hospital,
Maida Vale, London

EDITOR'S COMMENT

I remain as puzzled as I always have been by memorials. I suspect their main value is to reassure the bereaved of the dead person's importance. Death brings home the transience of life yet I do not want to think of my father-in-law as no more important than a blade of grass. So I am glad to know that there is a stone in Micheldean Church which is carved with his initials. This was his church and his name remains in much the same way that children carve their names on their school desks for fear of becoming anonymous. Memorials are not directed at the family (who will not forget) but at the rest of us (who will forget very soon if not reminded).

The bereaved need to create something very physical to fill the physical gap left by a dead person. A memorial is more than a kind of memo. It is a physical symbol of an internal object, an outward and visible sign of a being who cannot be any more, a foot stamped into the naked concrete of eternity.

I wax lyrical, but it is very hard to write intelligently about anything as preposterous as a memorial. How can a squared block of stone with a name on it represent a person? In this paper Francis Clegg reports the ordinary answers which she obtained to this extraordinary question and to the equally extraordinary question—how do you dispose of the dead body of a person you love?

Dr. Colin Murray Parkes, MD, FRCPsych

During 1987, Cruse branch leaders were asked whether local members might help with a research project into decisions made during bereavement. Sixty-two branches expressed an interest, and over the next few months 132 people from all over Britain completed questionnaires and sent them to me. The members who helped in this way were 120 women (of whom 110 were widows), and 12 men (of whom 10 were widowers).

I am grateful to all these bereaved people for participating, and for being prepared to disclose information which in some cases was clearly quite painful for them.

Choice of burial or cremation

The main topic of the research was the decisions which bereaved people have to make, and perhaps the most fundamental one concerns the choice of burial or cremation. Sixty-eight per cent of the respondents said that cremation had been chosen, and this corresponds very closely to the propro-tion of cremations carried out currently in this country as a whole.

Regardless of whether burial or cremation was chosen, for half of the respondents this choice was the dead person's wish. Many couples had discussed the topic prior to the death, and so had arrived at a joint decision. The ownership of a family grave or the existence of a family tradition of burial seemed to be the main factor in a decision for burial with many people, whilst only one or two respondents mentioned religious reasons as a basis for this choice.

Regrets

Fortunately, 90 per cent of the respondents had no regrets about the choice of burial or cremation. However, six widows had some regrets following cremation, and another six widows described somewhat stronger feelings of regret following burial. These regrets occurred from within a few months of bereavement to as late as 20 years later. They concerned such things as the actual choice of burial or cremation, not knowing where someone's ashes lie, having no grave to visit, or being unable to visit the cemetery or crematorium grounds because of the distance involved.

The research has shown that for bereaved people, regrets can occur at varying time periods following a loss, and that their nature can change with the passage of tim For instance one lady says that she has no regrets about cremation now, but a few years ago deep' regretted not having a grave t. tend. It is clear that for some elderly people it may be quite a blessing in later years not to hav to travel far to visit a grave, or worry about its upkeep. The air of neglect in some large and unkemr cemeteries, and in some cases actual fear of visiting them, were mentioned by some respondents as good reasons for preferring crem tion. No one in the survey criticiseu crematorium grounds for being un-tidy, and indeed several peopl' spoke highly of some Gardens Remembrance as being pleasant and comforting places.

The Desire for a Memorial

The next major area of interest on the questionnaire concernr memorialisation. Fourteen per ce. of all the respondents were de-finitely against having a memorial and a further nine per cent we either initially against the idea u. uncertain, but went on to obtain some form of memorial. There w no difference between the choi of burial or cremation and sub-sequent wishes for a memorial, and this finding contrasts with t results of similar surveys in whic. memorials were more popular after burial than cremation.

Whilst a headstone was the mc common choice of memorial follow ing burial, a much greater variet, of memorials was mentioned ' cremation. An entry in the Book Remembrance was most frequently cited (and probably the surve under-estimates the popularity this form of memorialisation, fu many people do not even think of as a form of memorial), with her stone, rose, shrub, donatic plaque, and seat also being mentioned several times each. Many respondents listed two, three and sometimes four chosen memorials. Sadly, for a few people, the preferred memorial could not be obtained for financial reasons. However, on the whole, wishes seem to have been satisfied.

Many reasons were given for wanting a memorial, and on average each person suggested either two or three. The most frequently named reasons were commemoration; the bereaved person's wish; having a point of contact; and as a help in grief. Respect and "for the benefit of future generations" were also mentioned a few times.

Memorials as a help in grief

Respondents were asked to say whether the chosen memorial had helped them—"No, not at all", "Not much", "Yes", or "Yes, a great deal". To simplify the data analysis, these four categories were collapsed into two, which then described whether a person thought the memorial had or had not been helpful. "No, not at all" and "not much" were combined into one category whilst "yes" and "yes, a great deal" made up the other category. Excluding those people who were unable to have the memorial of their choice, the results indicated that 79 per cent had felt helped by having their chosen memorial.

Is there a particular type of memorial which people find the most helpful? For this question, the results of this survey confirmed the findings of previous work. It is clear that no single type of memorial (e.g. a rose-bush or a headstone) carries outstanding therapeutic qualities. However, it seems that the perceived helpfulness of a particular memorial is related to its connection with the dead person. By this, I mean that if a memorial has been chosen to reflect some special aspect or memory of the deceased, then it is likely to be more comforting than one which has no connection with them other than marking the spot where the remains lie. Thus a rose-bush in a crematorium may be a very special and helpful memorial for someone who loved plants and gardens or else it may be a rather meaningless plant among hundreds of others. Similarly, an expensive headstone may simply mark the grave, or else it may be a most powerul and poignant link with the dead person, perhaps because of a specially worded inscription or symbol.

It is of considerable concern to me that in their efforts to keep cemetery maintenance costs to a minimum, many Local Authorities in the United Kingdom now greatly restrict the choice of permitted headstones. Indeed, in some lawn cemeteries, a traditional headstone may not be allowed at all. Misunderstandings about the restrictions on headstones are another cause for subsequent regret, and ideally this matter should be considered when a plot is being purchased, rather than after the burial or committal of ashes has taken place.

The results showed that satisfaction and help from a memorial are not particularly linked to cost. In other words, spending a lot of money on an expensive type of memorial is not going to guarantee that it is helpful. For instance many people felt greatly helped by memorials which cost them very little or nothing, for instance collecting donations which are then given to a chosen charity.

The decision not to have any tangible memorial, or no memorial near where the body or ashes are placed, can be successful but is probably more likely to succeed when it is the result of previous discussion and positive convictions. One aspect which seems to be commonly overlooked is that if the main mourner makes the decision not to have a large funeral, not to have flowers, or not to have a memorial, then he or she may also be denying many friends, relatives and acquaintances a chance to grieve and say goodbye. During my research I have been struck by how powerful and positive an effect the presence and support of many others can be. More than one person has said that she felt tremendously comforted by the big turnout for her husband's funeral, and that she benefited from this public statement of how much her husband was loved and valued by so many people. One widow, who was initially against having a memorial, was encouraged to do so by the number of people who expressed a desire for one. Not only was she surprised by how many people wished to pay respects to her husband, but also by the fact that she herself felt helped by the chosen memorial.

Memorials and memories

Many people believe that memories are the only true form of memorialisation, and they firmly believe that their memories of the dead person are sufficient. For them, the lack of a tangible memorial may pose no problems, and in this survey none of the people in this category spoke of regretting this decision. However, every person is different, and the majority of respondents felt that some link with the dead person in the form of a memorial was helpful. Many people described how, with the passage of time, the importance of this physical link gradually diminished and was gradually replaced by by memories. Perhaps, therefore, for most of us a memorial provides us with a temporary link with the deceased person during the extremely painful "letting go" period. Particularly during these early months and years it fulfils many possible functions: marking an exact spot, providing a tangible link, creating a focus for grief, making a public statement, providing a permanent record, and allowing the bereaved person to continue to have a role with the deceased, in that the memorial may need tending. With the passage of time, a memorial's psychological value diminishes somewhat, and ultimately many bereaved people are content to have memories of their loved one as the main memorial.

Helen House

Helen House is a small hospice which gives day-to-day love and care to gravely ill children and supports their families. The idea of Helen House started in 1980 and thanks to the wonderful generosity of thousands of people building began in 1981. Helen House opened in 1982, the first of its kind in the world. It relies entirely on voluntary contributions.

Why is it called Helen House?

Helen was a bright, lively, happy child, two and a half years old. In 1978 she suddenly became very ill. She had to have an emergency operation to remove a brain tumour. Although the tumour was successfully removed, Helen's brain suffered severe, irreversible damage. Now she remains totally helpless, unable to speak, sit up, or control her movements. She seems to be partly aware of her surroundings but it is impossible to know how much she understands. Shortly after the operation, Mother Frances, who is the Superior General of the Anglican Society of All Saints and is also a Registered Sick Children's Nurse met Helen and her parents and a close friendship developed. She visited Helen frequently during her six months' stay in hospital. After Helen returned home, Mother Frances looked after her from time to time at All Saints Convent in order to give her parents a short break. Helen House grew out of this friendship with Helen and her family.

Families who have a very sick child usually want to look after their child at home once hospital no longer seems appropriate. But the strain and the loneliness can be very great. Helen House is small and homely, a place where children and their families can come to stay from time to time – just as most of us have a holiday occasionally or go to stay with friends for the weekend. Friendship, support and practical skills are what we offer.

Who is Helen House for?

Most of the children who come to Helen House have chronic, life-threatening illnesses of one kind of another.* They live at home with their families and visit us every now and then for a short stay. Families are welcome to come too – parents, brothers and sisters, occasionally grandparents; we have even welcomed a dog, a terrapin and a pet terantula! Sometimes though the family will take the opportunity, while their child is cared for in Helen House, to have a holiday or do things at home which they could not normally do. The frequency of visits varies according to the individual needs of each family and we try, to the best of our ability, to meet these needs sensitively.

A few children come to Helen House at the end of their lives. Our aim is to provide a loving, supportive environment for them and their families, ensuring that pain and other unpleasant symptoms, which can cause acute distress and anxiety, are controlled or prevented.

We welcome children of any race or belief and of any age from birth to sixteen.

Illnesses such as muscular dystrophy, Batten's disease, mucopolysaccharidoses, malignant disease and many others.

We are sometimes able to continue to care for children after they have reached sixteen but we cannot normally take anyone for the first time beyond this age. There is no defined catchment area and children from many parts of the United Kingdom and the Channel Islands come to Helen House. We make no charge. We do not provide long-term care and would not attempt to look after those who would benefit more from treatment in an acute hospital ward. We cannot normally look after children with an illness or handicap which is not life-threatening.

What is Helen House like?

Helen House can take eight children at any one time and each child has his or her own bedroom. Parents may choose to sleep in the same room as their child, or alternatively, there is family accommodation with two double bedrooms, a sitting-room, kitchen and bathroom, providing comfort and complete privacy.

The living rooms are designed to be as homely as possible. A jacuzzi provides therapy and relaxation and fun for the grown-ups as well as the children. Outside, the garden of Helen House gives the feel of being in the country and is in constant use in fine weather. Just around the corner are busy little shops and all the activity of local town life and a little further away the beauty of the City and University of Oxford.

The routine is like that of any family and tends to vary depending on who is staying. Families who stay can choose to take an active part in looking after their children or they can leave this to the team.

Who works in Helen House?

Helen House is run by people whose common qualification is their love and concern for children. They include trained nurses, teachers, a nursery nurse, social worker, physiotherapist, a chaplin, and others, some of whom are parents themselves. A local Practitioner is the medical officer. An administrator, a secretary, two sisters from All Saints Convent and a few volunteers complete the team. Everyone shares the household chores as well as the care of the children and families, and no one wears uniform. If a child's home is near enough to Helen House, the doctor or other professionals who care for him or her at home are welcome to continue to be involved at Helen House.

What does Helen House try to do?

Our aim is quite simple – to offer friendship and practical help to very sick children and their families. We try to be sensitive to their individual needs, enabling the child and family to achieve the best possible quality of life for them. If and when the time comes for a child to die we try to ensure that this happens with dignity, the child surrounded by the people he or she knows and loves best, whether at home or in Helen House. The friendship and support does not end there but continues for as many months or years as the family wishes.

Helen House relies entirely on voluntary donations.

You can become a Friend of Helen House by making a minimum contribution of £5 a year, or a Friend for Life by giving £50. As such you will receive our newsletter twice a year.

Correspondence should be addressed to:-
HELEN HOUSE
37 Leopold Street
OXFORD OX4 1QT
Telephone (0865)728251

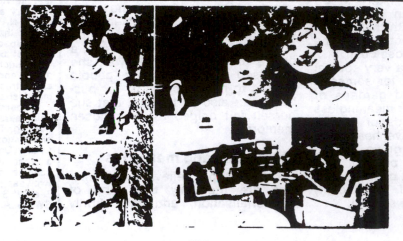

MY SUNDAY

LIZ GAMLEN
HOSPICE NURSE

6We've been married a year and have a small flat in Forest Hill, about two miles from St Christopher's. The alarm goes at 6.22 – that seems much later than getting up at 6.15! I creep around, making a cup of tea, trying not to wake Laurence who has early starts other mornings – he's at the Church Army Training College in Blackheath. After dressing, reading and praying, I'm off on my cycle by 7.15. It takes about 15 minutes, which gives me time to change at the hospice and be on duty by 7.45.

I'm staff nurse on a ward of 14 men, most of whom have some form of cancer. There are five or six of us on duty, some trained nurses, some auxiliaries. I walk through the ward and peep in the bays, especially if someone's been quite ill the previous day. I'm looking to see if everyone's there.

If I'm in charge I'll go to the office and get a report from the night nurse. Not much may have happened. Night duty is less eventful than in a general hospital where there are emergency admissions.

At 8.00 we have prayers on the ward. Everyone has a prayer card on their locker. There's a brief prayer, a verse from the Bible, maybe a promise about God's faithfulness or love; a final prayer and the grace. We can have tough competition from TV AM! The men have their headphones. It's not policy to thrust our faith upon them. Some haven't been to church since they were at school or in the army, but they like to say the Lord's Prayer.

At 9.00 there's the first drug round. Others will be at 1pm, 5pm and 9pm. Each takes up to an hour. Those who are well enough will be up and dressed, others will have been helped into more comfortable positions. Because most men are in their ordinary clothes it's unlike a general hospital. Women seem to stay in their nighties more readily than men remain in their pyjamas. If someone's lost his hair he may be wearing a hat.

Helping the family

The average stay's about 13 days, but while some come in for a few

For the first in a new series on how Christians spend their Sundays we visit St Christopher's Hospice in Sydenham, South London, which was founded by Cicely Saunders.

Polly Toynbee wrote in *The Guardian:* 'If some Victorian illustrator were to romanticise

days, or even hours, others might be with us for months. A few will return home having been in to give the family a break. A handful are discharged to receive home treatment under our own clinic.

After someone has been admitted

her life, just as Florence Nightingale became the Lady of the Lamp, Dame Cicely Saunders might appear as the Angel of Death. Easing our passing, delivering us from pain, casting out fear, comforting the bereaved.' Liz Gamlen has been a nurse at the hospice for two years.

the family is encouraged as far as possible to remain involved in his care. We want the family to draw closer together, to discover their strengths. Broken relationships, past disagreements and lack of communication are the greatest source of mental anguish in the one who is dying, and in his family. Sometimes tense family situations are resolved in the Hospice.

On Sunday mornings it's chapel – Anglican Church tradition. On some Sundays there are free church services, largely unstructured, with choruses and maybe testimony. If there isn't a communion service the chaplain will take the sacrament to the wards.

When we've finished the drugs we scamper round helping any who want to go to chapel. If necessary, the beds can be wheeled through the doors, put in the lift, and taken to the chapel. I'm never totally comfortable attending if I'm on duty, wondering what's happening on the ward. Visitors come and go freely during the day from eight to eight, except on Mondays. Relatives need one day off, especially a husband or wife who's been travelling daily. They remain all night if someone's really ill.

Some patients have no visitors, but there's a lot of chumminess on a men's ward – we're all in this together, mate! The ages vary from the twenties to the nineties, but there's a lot in their forties and fifties.

On Sundays we're all more relaxed, with no formal doctor's rounds. It's great just being with the patients, talking, listening, laughing.

Talking about death

If someone has died in the night others may want to talk about it. Not all. A few will pass off any mention with a casual comment like, 'It's not raining outside, is it?'

When people talk about their own death the questions are usually about when and how. The when is difficult, the how is easier. We usually explain that they'll gradually become weaker and drowsier, more susceptible to a chest infection. They can understand this, having seen it happen. It's rare to have a sudden death as you do in a general hospital.

Patients have lunch at 12.00. Because it's a small ward we can often vary the menu, giving what a patient wants, within reason. A wife may worry that her husband isn't having his regular roast beef but really it doesn't matter what he eats – it's for pleasure now, not to keep going.

I have lunch at 12.15, normally sandwiches I've brought, in the coffee lounge downstairs, and am back on the ward at 1.00 to let the morning shift go to lunch. The late shift comes on then.

Another drug round. The doctor leaves instructions so the dosage can be adjusted. Some men take a nap, others sit in the day room with their visitors, or in the summer go into the lovely gardens. There are more children around on Sundays, it's when the family comes. The Hospice places great emphasis on their needs. Towards the end when a patient becomes more drowsy we spend lots of time talking to the relatives.

Comforting the dying

It's so absorbing, so demanding, there's hardly time to think of life outside, even of Laurence. The really ill need intensive nursing, including turning every two hours. If there's no one else we sit with them. If someone has always been a loner we wonder whether we're intruding, whether he wants to die as he's lived. Instead of holding his hand we may simply sit there.

I instinctively find myself praying simple, basic prayers if symptoms are hard to control, if a patient won't settle or is obviously in anguish, whether it's physical or something deeper. 'Lord, please may this one work,' I pray as I give the extra dosage the doctor's prescribed.

It would be hard to survive without a faith, but I only became a Christian three years ago. I'd been to Sunday school and confirmation classes to please my mother, but when the vicar asked whether I was going to take the wide or the narrow path I said 'the wide'! I came to Christ through a friend who was going into the Salvation Army.

As a nurse it seemed strange that people made so much fuss about bringing babies into the world, having specially trained midwives and maternity hospitals, and did so little for someone when the time came for them to go out of it. St Christopher's shows how we can deal with distress and death, how the medical profession mustn't abandon a patient who is beyond cure.

Nursing here provides opportunity for Christian witness, but not more than in a general hospital. If I'm in a bad way with God I'm not much use whatever the situation. I learned a lot from one patient who was a Christian, and I think I helped him too. Even those who believe can find dying difficult – saying goodbye to all they've known, wondering what will happen here when they're no longer around.

Questions about heaven

We show our faith by loving, caring, easing pain, being with them. When someone asks about heaven I explain what the Bible says. It's the place, I say, where none of the effects of evil will be present. God is just and will always do what is right. Some believe in life after death, and I can talk comfortably to them about heaven and hell; others think death is the end. I don't rush in. I wait until specifically asked.

Often a man will demand where is God's love as he looks around the ward. 'God does love you,' I'll respond, and they'll listen if I've built up a relationship. Some become special friends, but we have to learn to love without taking each death as a personal loss. We're sometimes more upset for the relatives, but the whole Hospice tries to help them.

At 4.00 I'm off home. Laurence will have been to the morning service at St Mildred's, where he plays the guitar, and will have cooked a meal for us. It's a late lunch for him, early supper for me. In the evening we go to church. We've quite a mixed congregation but not as mixed as it should be considering the neighbourhood.

I'm really tired when we get home. It's hard to fit into one day all the working and all the relaxing, but we pray together for our family and friends, for the Church Army and St Christopher's, unless I fall asleep first!

LIVING WITH DEATH

The silent conspiracy

THERE IS A POWERFUL DESIRE TO PROTECT EACH OTHER FROM PAIN, WHICH CAN MAKE IT UNBEARABLY HARD TO TELL SOMEONE YOU LOVE THAT THEY ARE DYING. BY DENISE WINN.

It is now a few years since my mother died from cancer of the oesophagus. Caring for someone much loved and dying is painful enough but the added burden for my sister and myself was that we were never able to share with her the truth: she chose, we think, not to know she was dying.

Dr Elisabeth Kübler-Ross, who is dedicated to counselling the dying and their bereaved, says that people know when they are dying. We expected that a time would come when we and our mother would acknowledge her impending death, share her fears—and ours—and consolidate all that we had felt for each other. As we were prepared for that, for the dignity of acknowledgement, we were all the more unprepared for its opposite, the collusion in recovery and the unsaid truths. For the acknowledgement was our choice, not hers, although where those choices begin and end I still don't know.

The surgeon told us at the outset that prognosis was very poor indeed. The most he could do was insert a tube so that she could swallow and hope that she would "slip away" (alas, not the case),

probably within weeks. "Will you tell her?" we said. He replied, "I will if she asks. Most people only ask what they want to know." Our mother didn't ask. She had always been an intuitive person, and she didn't hide from truth. Yet she didn't ask.

In hospital she talked of recovery. The "growth" which the surgeon later mentioned to her became changed in her own mind to something else. "My gullet was twisted," she firmly told friends. "So they had to put in a tube." We didn't correct her. Almost imperceptibly, the collusion had already started.

The operation was not a success. Threatened rejection of the tube brought its own additional problems which we agreed—or, perhaps, even suggested—were just temporary, to be expected. In not telling the truth, because we had not yet been asked, we felt forced into telling lies, worse, offering false hope.

My sister and brother-in-law and I had already prepared a room in their house, painting it in a way she would like. "It's only till you are ready to manage on your own again," we said. We didn't believe that the pretence would go on. We waited—partly in fear and partly desperate for relief—in hope of the moment when, clear to us all that she was daily deteriorating, we could share the terrible knowledge we reluctantly held.

But it didn't happen. She spoke in the early days of the need to keep her strength up. Even when the pain started

and the blood came, she didn't swerve in her seeming conviction that this was a part, albeit perplexing, of the recovery process. Research shows that people who deny their cancer have a higher remission rate than those who accept it and resign themselves to death. Our mother had always been a fighter. Who were we to remove those shreds of hope? But who were we to foster illusions if there would come a time when we were inadvertently forcing *her* to collude with us?

We found ourselves looking for signs that it was she, not we, who was directing this particular tragic scenario. I heard her tell my young nephew that it was all right now, nanny was getting better. When her mind began to wander, she told me perhaps she needed to spend more time talking, not sleeping, as that had to be the reason for her dazed behaviour; the morphine concoction, given at increasingly shorter intervals to anticipate the pain, was never anything other than "medicine".

We agonised, too, over signs that might have been invitations to the truth and which we, caught up now in our unwilling fabrications, might at last have been too frightened to respond to. To tell or not to tell became, in its delay, so momentous an event in itself that we felt we should all be there when it happened, both to share the responsibility and also not to deny the others a moment so intensely intimate and fearsome. I still wonder if in the end we forced ▶

227

LIVING WITH DEATH

◄ her to suppress, and face alone, her own fears of dying, unable to broach them because somehow the pantomime had developed a momentum of its own; or if she felt we were the ones who were frightened of discussing it; or that acknowledging *our* pain was as upsetting to her as acknowledging her own imminent death.

But, worse, I wonder if there was a last lucid moment on her last night when she wanted to reach out, to acknowledge and accept, but she no longer had the strength to call out to us. In the end, although we were there holding her, she was beyond reach and we didn't say goodbye. And even now, a few years later, when the pain of seeing our mother suffer is fading, the pain of depriving her—and of being deprived ourselves—of that last, most intimate-ever sharing, is still as hard to bear.

I have since read the section on dying in the *Macmillan Guide to Family Health* by Dr Tony Smith (£19.95), which confirmed my fears and feelings: "Always let a person with a terminal illness decide the timing and extent of any discussion of death. If no questions are asked, knowledge should not be forced on the dying patient. This does not mean you should hold out false hope of recovery. Someone who is misled in this way will be unable to understand why he or she is growing weaker instead of stronger, and if he or she suspects the truth, will be denied the opportunity to discuss fears and seek reassurance. Uncertainty often gives rise to greater fears than certainty does."

> "Our mother was always a great fighter. Who were we to remove those few shreds of hope?"

But this was so hard to fit to circumstances when the signals we received were so conflicting and confusing; we didn't know when to say what for the best.

Maybe it is easier for a dying person to talk to a caring outsider like a doctor, who can break down the barriers erected in the family by the mutual desire to protect each other from pain. A hospice doctor I spoke to said that a patient "often broaches the subject with an outsider, especially if it is a professional person involved with caring in some way. You can sense how much someone wants to know and the dying person will let you know when you've said enough.

"We believe that everything has to be honest, but it is not vital that someone should express the knowledge that they are dying. Sometimes we know they know and they know we know but nothing is ever said."

Not all doctors or nurses are themselves comfortable talking about death. But there are hospice doctors and Macmillan nurses, specially trained in care for the dying, who will visit people at home. Cancer Relief Macmillan Fund, Anchor House, 15-19 Britten St, London SW3 3TY. Tel: 01-351 7811.

For my part, I do believe people know when they are dying and I shall never underestimate again the skill it may take for all involved to know when and how to voice it. ◨

Denise Winn is the author of a new book, The Hospice Way.

Reprinted by kind permission of the publishers from SEARCH, Winter, 1990;4, 5-7   JOSEPH ROWNTREE FOUNDATION

THE GRIEF THAT DOES NOT SPEAK

MAUREEN OSWIN

The emotional needs of people with mental handicap who suffer bereavement can too easily be neglected. Their broken hearts are not problems requiring treatment. But providing comfort can be difficult: it needs time, honesty and training.

John Longworth

An art therapist working in a long-stay mental handicap hospital became concerned when one of the residents attending her class seemed very depressed. He then suddenly said he was worried because his parents, who usually came each Sunday, had not visited him for several weeks. The therapist went up to his ward but could not find anyone on the staff to give her any information, so she looked in his case notes for any clues to explain why his parents' visits had ceased.

She discovered that his father had died. This meant that his frail mother, who was unable to use public transport, could no longer visit him.

Nobody had told the young man what had happened. All that was recorded in his case notes was the bare fact that of his father's death.

No recommendation was made that anything should be done about breaking the news of the death to him, let alone helping him with his bereavement or arranging that he ▷

John Longworth

should be in contact with his mother. Nobody had made a deliberate decision not to tell him: but everyone on the staff had somehow assumed that he knew, that somebody had told him. In that impersonal institution, the bereaved resident as a sensitive, worried son had been quietly forgotten.

THIRTY year old Miss A. had very severe learning difficulties and additional physical disabilities. She had always lived at home. She could not walk or speak. She needed help with all ordinary tasks such as dressing, eating, washing, going to the lavatory. Her father had died when she was in her twenties but her mother had continued to care for her on her own. Once a week Miss A went to a local day centre, and on other outings when her mother and a neighbour pushed her round the park or to the supermarket in her wheel-chair.

When her very robust mother suddenly died, Miss A lost everything - not only her mother and her mother's loving care, but every vestige of family life and routine and the security of her home and the neighbourhood where she had lived all her life. The same day that her mother died the social services department arranged that Miss A should go into the care of a mental handicap hospital. She was lifted, washed and fed and clothed by strangers who knew nothing about her or her previous life. She was unable to ask questions because she could not speak. Without any speech it was almost impossible for her to relate to

the strangers who were now caring for her, especially when she was also grief-stricken for her mother.

For many months Miss A pined and grieved. The kindly staff worried about her wan condition and deterioration: "We feel so helpless when people as handicapped as her come into hospital after a parent dies; we don't know them, they don't know us, and they must feel so unhappy."

AFTER Mrs Z was widowed, the doctor advised: "don't tell your son". She had enough problems. "He might make more problems for you, and anyway he won't understand". Acting on his advice Mrs Z kept the death of her husband a secret for several months and merely told her mentally handicapped son that father had 'gone away'. It was a dreadful strain for her, grieving for her husband and at the same time having to keep the death a secret from her adult son who was sharing the same house.

When she did finally tell him, she discovered that he had known for some weeks, and felt very resentful that she had not talked about it to him before. He had somehow found out from things he had overheard at his day centre. The doctor's advice to his mother had set the widow and her son apart at a time when they had both needed to be emotionally close and supporting each other.

Why did he give such crazy advice? Was it because he did not know any people with learning difficulties and had a stereotyped

image of them as being disruptive and troublesome, and not having any emotional needs? It is sometimes said by thoughtless professionals working in the health services that "people with mental handicaps don't have the same feelings as other people."

THE majority of professionals are not callous or insensitive; so how do these things happen? Perhaps, in the grey area of emotions and grief, with the double taboo of death and a learning difficulty, it is very easy for bereaved people to be lost in a muddle of misconceptions and a panic of reorganising their lives - so their needs as grieving people are quite forgotten.

People with learning difficulties have a right to grieve; they need opportunities to mourn, they need time to recover, and sensitive support as they go through the normal reactions of grief such as anger, weeping and depression. Their emotional care is just as important as their need for continuing care at home, or appropriate residential care, and any plans made for them should consider their emotional needs as grieving people. Unfortunately, when people with learning difficulties do react in normal ways to loss, some professionals perceive the reaction only in terms of the primary learning difficulty.

For example, a young man who was usually quiet and placid began to get into very angry tempers at his Day Centre during the months following his father's death. The staff knew that he was bereaved but saw his behaviour only as part of his learning difficulty; they did not recognise that he was reacting normally to his loss; they did not allow that he needed time to recover from his father's death and that he wanted to express his grief in anger, nor that he required support and understanding in the same way as any other grieving person. After having a staff meeting to discuss his 'problem behaviour' they called in a psychologist to put him onto a behaviour modification programme. Their failure to recognise his needs as a grieving person was partly because nobody on the staff understood normal grief; their training had largely been concentrated on looking for abnormalities amongst persons with learning difficulties.

Nobody intends to be deliberately unkind to people with learning difficulties when they are bereaved, but unkindness seems to creep in because of the way that services are organised, or because of short-comings in staff training. One young man, on being told that his father had died, asked: "am I allowed to cry?" His tentative question sums up how vulnerable some people with learning difficulties feel when they are bereaved. It is also a question about the quality of services organised for such people and the attitudes of some people providing them. If social policy does not allow for tears, then what sort of services do we have?

A local support service for bereaved people with learning difficulties might help to prevent some of the sadness and misunderstanding described here. It would not require elaborate organisation. Its members might be interested professionals already working with people with learning difficulties, and representatives of parent groups. One of its functions might be to alert other local professionals to instances of bereavement amongst people with learning difficulties and to help in the planning of sensitive and appropriate

services for them in the months following the bereavement. Another function might be to draw staff's attention to the norms of bereavement, so that people with learning difficulties would have their grief reactions recognised as normal and be given opportunities to grieve.

Three issues should be of concern to all people who have an interest in bereavement problems:

First, **Forward Planning**: when a single carer dies, leaving a severely multiply handicapped person like Miss A, that person should not be removed from her home immediately. Somebody could stay with her for a few days or weeks until she can be carefully introduced to a residential care placement which is appropriate for her. She should feel that she has some choice about her future, a chance to grieve for the dead parent in her own home and a chance to say her last good-byes to that home.

Second, **Honesty**: people with learning difficulties ought to be kept in the picture all the time about a death having occured, whether within their own family or amongst their friends. This might mean making sure that somebody is named as being responsible for breaking bad news and then helping the bereaved person through the following months. Honesty also means giving the person an opportunity to attend the funeral if they wish to, listening to them when they want to talk about what has happened, ensuring that they have mementos of the dead person, letting them know what has happened to the house, their belongings, any pets, clothes and books. In other words, keeping the person with a learning difficulty in the picture the whole time and respecting their need to be a normal grieving person.

Third, **In service training courses** on bereavement could be arranged for all staff working with people who have learning difficulties, in day centres, schools, in residential care and as field social workers. Such

courses would cover normal grief reactions to a death in the family or the death of a close friend, and would alert staff at all levels to what they might expect with regard to supporting bereaved people.

St George's Hospital Medical School, London, has been holding courses for staff working with bereaved people who have learning difficulties; the participants of these courses have found them extremely helpful in giving them insight into bereavement issues. Dr. Sheila Hollins and Dr. Lester Sireling, of St George's Hospital, have also produced a video and books to help staff working with people who have learning difficulties when they are bereaved. □

Maureen Oswin is currently writing a book on bereavement and people with learning difficulties, based on research funded by the JOSEPH ROWNTREE MEMORIAL TRUST. The book will be completed in the spring. From February 1990 she will be available to discuss her findings with voluntary groups or the staff of local authorities and health authorities and can be contacted through the JOSEPH ROWNTREE MEMORIAL TRUST or through the Thomas Coram Research Unit, 41 Brunswick Square, London, WC1 1AZ. Her paper, **Bereavement and Mentally Handicapped People,** published by the King's Fund, December, 1981, is still available from the King's Fund, 126 Albert Street, London NW1 7NF.

The Last Taboo, a video on mental handicap and death, written and directed and produced by Dr Lester Sireling and Dr Sheila Hollins, Section of Psychiatry of Diasbility, St George's Hospital Medical School, Tooting, London, SW17 0RE.

When Dad Died and **When Mum Died,** Shiela Hollins and Lester Sireling, Silent Books, Swavesey, Cambridge, 1989. These two picture books help people with learning difficulties to understand death and feelings of grief.

The case for nationalising death

On 1 April this year the death grant was abolished, having been continuously
eroded in value since its introduction in 1948. Bob Hudson claims that the
government is out of step on managing death and a radical rethink is needed if
hardship and unpleasantness are to be avoided

ABOUT 2,000 people die every day in this
country and the growth in numbers of people
entering the 75 plus age group will force this
figure up even further in the coming decades.

With a current annual turnover of £700m,
funeral parlours may be making a fat profit
out of it all, but who should really take
responsibility for caring for the dying and
paying for the costs of death?

Pressure is now being put on the NHS to
respond more positively to the needs of the
dying. Health Minister Tony Newton argued
that the NHS must take on more
responsibility and build on the pioneering
work of the hospice movement, particularly
in relation to the development of home
support teams for the dying. The National
Association of Health Authorities in its recent
publication *Care for the dying* has urged HAs
to draw up a strategy for care of the dying.

Paradoxically, though, while the state is
being urged to show a fresh interest in
assisting the dying, it is actually withdrawing
from the tradition of helping the bereaved
meet the expense of death. The Beveridge
notion of welfare support from the cradle to
the grave is being further eroded.

The traditional postwar state response to
assisting with the cost of death has been to
provide a universal benefit through the
national insurance scheme — the death grant.
Over the years it has become commonplace

to speak in contemptuous terms of the death
grant, mainly because of the failure to raise
the benefit in line with either inflation or the
actual cost of a funeral. When it was introduced in 1948 it stood at £20, and it was subsequently increased only twice — to £25 in
1957 and to £30 in 1968.

In 1987 the death grant covered 8 per cent of costs

It is something of an irony that this derisory
treatment of the death grant should then be
taken as a justification for its total abolition,
and even for the rewriting of its history. In its
1982 consultative document on the death
grant the government claimed that, from the
outset, the grant had never represented more
than a contribution towards the full cost of
a funeral.

This is blatantly untrue. Using figures
supplied by the Undertakers' Association,
Beveridge (in 1942) estimated the cost of an
adult funeral to be £15 in London and £13 in
industrial centres. He then added a generous
margin for cemetery fees and came up with
the figure of £20 to cover 'the necessary
expenses of a decent funeral'.

The amazing neglect of the death grant to
a position where, in 1987, it was scarcely
covering 8 per cent of a typical funeral bill,
is something for which all political parties
must accept responsibility. But while Labour

and the Alliance have rediscovered a commit-
ment to the universal insurance principle, th
Conservative penchant has always been for
selective targeting of those held to be in
greatest need.

Accordingly, on 1 April the death grant wa
abolished and along with it the entitlements
of many people who have paid almost 40 years
of contributions for a benefit they will nev
receive.

The position now is that a funeral expenses
payment to cover the cost of a modest funeral
is available from the new social fund to tho
in receipt of supplementary benefit, famil,
income supplement or housing benefit.
However, the payment is recoverable from
the estate of the deceased and the savings ru
will be applied to the claimant — anything
above £500 will be deducted from the funeral
payment. As with the scrapping of th
maternity grant, there is no longer a
payment for those falling outside the specified
benefit groups. This is more or less in line with
option three of the 1982 consultati
document, though at that time the govern
ment dropped its plans in the face of
overwhelming opposition.

Of course, private insurance for funerals
common and needs to be taken into account.
Beveridge found that in 1940 the number of
policies in force amounted to a staggering 1
million — over 2.25 for every man, wom

and child in Britain. Many of these policies are still in force.

A survey carried out for the DHSS in the mid 1970s found that 85 per cent of the deceased in social class 5 (unskilled manual workers and their families) were covered by private insurance, but that in most cases the original value had been badly ravaged by inflation to levels of under £100. Families tried to help out, but among the poorer widows and widowers, only one in nine got help from relatives amounting to more than £50. In short, funeral costs were met by drawing heavily on limited savings.

The new reforms clearly have not resolved the old dilemma — the punitive cost of funerals in relation to the cultural significance of a 'decent send off'. A group called the Independent Order of Oddfellows carries out an annual survey into funeral costs. Its 1986 survey discovered one in Portsmouth which amounted to £2,472 (excluding flowers), but a typical cost was around £550.

Concern about these costs is far from new. In 1976, the old prices commission was asked to examine funeral costs because of public concern that they were too high and that the bereaved, in no mood to haggle, were being led into buying unnecessary extras. Unsurprisingly, the funeral trade was found to be 'comfortably profitable'.

These costs have to be considered in relation to the preoccupation of the poor elderly with the cost of dying. As far back as 1843 it was estimated that of the £24m deposited by the working classes in savings banks, 25 per cent was for funerals.

Edwin Chadwick, the great public health proponent of that time, noted: 'Nothing can exceed the working classes' desire for an imposing funeral. They would starve to pay the undertaker.' This is not dissimilar to the recent statement by Age Concern director, David Hobman, that: 'Many pensioners

Camera Press

One funeral in Portsmouth cost £2,472 — flowers were extra.

Maggie Murray/Format

The funeral industry is big business and many pensioners skimp on food and fuel to save to pay for a decent burial.

skimp on food and fuel to save for a decent funeral.'

In their respective centuries, Chadwick and Hobman are pointing out the significance accorded to the funeral rite. People seek in death a level of ostentation denied to them in life, and clearly this can be no occasion for skimping. This is borne out by other studies of working class life. A study of old people in Bethnal Green (Peter Townsend, 1963) for example, found strong approval of an expensive funeral: 'It gave them comfort to think their departure from life would be recognised in this way and not passed over as something uneventful,' the study said.

The 'pauper's funeral' remains a stigma

The converse of this is the fear of a 'pauper's funeral'. The stigma of such a burial stems from Victorian times when to die a pauper was, if anything, even worse than to live as one. Betty Higden, in Dickens' *Our Mutual Friend* was so determined to avoid 'the parish' that she died under a tree with her burial money sewn into her dress. Even today working class communities will club together rather than countenance a pauper's funeral.

Ultimate responsibility for the burial or cremation of those for whom no other arrangements have been made lies with local authorities under section 20 of the 1948 National Assistance Act, but only about one funeral in 500 ends up this way. In relation to the new funeral expenses payment, there is a danger of equating an approach to the social fund with a pauper's burial, and this will discourage the bereaved from making an approach for assistance.

Two main alternatives may be on offer to replace the selectivism of the April 1987 changes — a return to a universal funeral subsidy or, more innovatively, some form of deprivatisation of the funeral service.

The idea of returning to a universal subsidy under the aegis of the national insurance scheme has the support of almost all significant bodies except the last Conservative government. In the lobbying world, in 1982, 21 national organisations united to form the Dignity in Death Alliance and seek an increase in the then death grant to £125.

In some ways this was a fairly modest target, for simply to restore the grant to its real 1948 value would have resulted in a payment

in excess of £200. The latter was the position of the Labour Party in the recent election campaign. The Alliance went one better by proposing to restore the link between the death grant and the cost of a funeral — an estimate of £400. Such an option would not be cheap, and may encourage undertakers to increase their profit margin.

The alternative to subsidising costly funerals is to promote cheaper ones. One possible model is the French system which gives local authorities a monopoly over funerals, though even here there has been a challenge from private enterprise and the occasional spectacle of rival hearses battling for possession of a body.

In Britain, the main challenge has come from a handful of the more radical local authorities. Liverpool, for example, has made plans to run a municipal funeral service which would undercut local undertakers by 25 per cent. Rather predictably, the National Association of Funeral Directors immediately threatened legal action, claiming that Liverpool was acting in excess of its statutory powers. Less radically, Lambeth council has made a deal with a local funeral director, and Lewisham with the Co-op, to provide funerals for less than £400.

The time may not be too far distant when civic funerals will be as readily available as civic weddings. This could lead to a cheaper and vastly different form of funeral which could be more acceptable to many people currently on the threshold of middle age.

In Salford, for example, a newly established funeral planning society has attracted about 200 members. It takes details of personal preferences such as hymns, music, poetry, place of burial or cremation and so forth, so that when the next of kin rings up to inform the society of the death of a member, agreed arrangements can be put in hand immediately. This may well be useful for people like myself who have a partner anxious to be lowered into the ground to the sound of Eric Clapton.

In the meantime, we are saddled with the limited role of the new social fund, involving a punitive approach towards those who have been thrifty and some form of means test for the poor bereaved. Careful monitoring of this new approach will be required. Some hardship seems inevitable. □

Bob Hudson is senior lecturer in social policy at New College, Durham.

Heavenly bodies

Thousands of people who have returned from the 'dead' describe passing into a timeless zone of peace and natural beauty. Is it really possible their soul entered another world, a new spiritual dimension? Chris Stonor investigates a fascinating phenomenon

'Dying has been the happiest experience of my life,' explained a very much alive Pat Burt. 'It has to be the best thing that's ever happened to me.' Pat, an ex-stewardess married to an airline captain, is adept at dying. She has 'died' four times, each time during a medical operation, but has then been resuscitated by doctors.

'The second time I died I fought hard not to come back. I experienced leaving my physical body and then travelling through a tunnel. I felt completely relaxed and unafraid. At the end of the tunnel was a bright light. As I merged with this light I had overwhelming feelings of peace and love—feelings so beautiful they were indescribable. I just wanted to stay there forever. Then I realised something was turning me around against my will and I sensed myself re-enter my physical body.

'When I came round in the hospital bed I cried and cried. I told the doctors, "I don't want to be back here again." I was deeply upset and very depressed for several days.'

It is easy to dismiss Pat as a case for the white coat brigade, but she is just one of tens of thousands of people throughout the world who have had what is now called a 'near death experience' (NDE). Forty per cent of people who clinically 'die' and later come back to life describe a continuation of consciousness after death and of entering a non-physical world.

These people include doctors, psychiatrists and well known personalities (such as Stephanie Beacham and Michael Bentine) whose experiences of what they feel to be an after-life often dramatically change their views on death—and life. As Pat said, 'I'm not frightened of dying any more. Death is simply a transition from one dimension to another, in my view.'

Death is still very much a taboo subject in our society. The prospect of our death is by far the biggest challenge we have to face up to in our lives, but as a society, we are emotionally unprepared for this eventuality. Why? When turning to orthodox science for consolation we are greeted with the belief that our consciousness and mind are one. When you die that's your lot. Death is seen as the ultimate symbol of failure and defeat, to be evaded and denied. Life must be prolonged where possible. As for Western religions and their belief in heaven and hell, we are caught up in a crossfire of views—where ignorance breeds fear and fear feeds ignorance.

The facts of death were the last thing on the mind of Mark Gagne, now twenty-three, when he went into hospital for a routine operation to remove his tonsils at the age of thirteen.

After being given a general anaesthetic, instead of waking up in the hospital bed after a successful operation, his first conscious awareness was of floating near the ceiling, above the operating table, watching the doctors at work.

'I wondered who the person was on the table,' Mark said, 'and then realised it was me. I could see and hear everything going on in the room, even the clock that said 8.05 am. Suddenly, I saw the anaesthetist tapping the dial and heard him say, "I'm losing him, I'm losing him."'

Mark next saw a nurse turn on the heart machine, a doctor massage his chest and then his body go rigid, and jump after

> 'Around forty per cent of people who clinically "die" and later come back to life describe a continuation of consciousness after death and of entering a non-physical world'

Heavenly bodies

being given an electric shock. Yet all the while, as Mark put it, 'I felt unafraid, just completely relaxed and at peace.' He next glanced at the clock at 8.36 am, when he saw the doctor pull the sheet over his physical head and phone through to say, 'Send Gagne's file to the office—I'm afraid I've lost him. You had better notify his family.'

'The next thing I remember,' Mark said, 'was going through a tunnel at great speed and seeing a light at the end. As I moved into this light I felt an incredible feeling of love and then became aware of my aunt, who had died some months before, asking me if I wanted to come with her. I then judged my life—no one else judged me—with complete honesty. I looked at the good things I had done and the bad. I decided that I hadn't learned enough from my life. I decided to come back.'

It was a nurse who heard Mark gasp. She pulled the sheet back and saw his eyelids flickering. Mark later told the doctors of his experience—the descriptions, times and events were all corroborated. One nurse exclaimed, 'How scary.'

From Jesus Christ's resurrection to the East's belief in reincarnation and Karma, religion has always promised eternal life—another conscious 'body' that survives physical death. In one

'I tried to grab the doctors and stop them. I felt happy where I was—but nothing happened. I grabbed one doctor but my hand just went through him'
Vietnam veteran

American study (by Michael Sabom) ninety-three per cent of near death experiencers perceived this 'soul' or separated self to be an invisible, non-physical entity.

Though orthodox science generally scoffs at the very idea of an NDE, it is, paradoxically, the increasing use of sophisticated resuscitation techniques that has led to a higher incidence of reports than ever before.

Yet, it is only now that the experiencers are coming out of the closet. As Margot Grey, a psychologist and author of the bestselling book *Return From Death*, explained, 'People before were afraid of being ridiculed or even being branded mentally unstable. Now there is a feeling that it is getting safer to talk. This is mainly due to the pioneering efforts of doctors like Elisabeth Kübler-Ross and Raymond Moody (author of *Life After Life*), who have questioned the orthodox viewpoint on death; done extensive research into the phenomenon; come up with new findings and had the courage to put their reputations on the line.'

These international findings are unanimous. It doesn't matter what creed, culture or background one originates from. For the majority, the next dimension is a heaven of a place to be in. The psychologist Carl Jung wrote (in *Memories, Dreams and Reflections*, first published in Great Britain in 1963) of the next world, after his own NDE in 1944. 'Once inside, you taste of such completeness.

peace and fulfilment that you don't want to return.'

But before you begin to imagine that the next world is all *that* attractive, be warned. Suicides can have a bad time. As one man explained, who experienced moving into a grey wilderness during a failed attempt: 'I realised I had broken the rules. Life is precious and not to be taken. I would only have had to face the same problems all over again.'

Also, it has to be said that some people experience a negative type of NDE. Fear, panic and a sense of evil are sometimes felt, with a few experiencing a hell-like environment.

Margot Grey told me, 'It is in no way a punishment. I feel these people choose to have this experience as it alerts them to some aspect of their life that needs changing.'

Not surprisingly, many people change after their NDE. For Mark Gagne his transformation was dramatic. From being a school bully, general trouble-maker and lazy pupil, overnight he became a 'do-gooder and swot'. 'My headmaster was so worried about me that I was sent to see a psychiatrist,' laughed Mark. 'Yet for the first time my life made sense. Things just fitted into place.'

He became very perceptive and was known as 'the little wise man'. He later attended a church that follows no set religion. 'Whether you are a Christian, Muslim or Buddhist, you are all part of the same God. Religion just creates barriers between people.'

Spiritual values become increasingly important in some experiencers' lives. They enjoy

and appreciate life more: become more understanding and sympathetic; have more self-respect. Some discover psychic or healing abilities.

Most orthodox doctors pass this evidence off as exceptional or unreliable, while others, like Dr Ian Judson of the Royal Marsden Hospital in London, are less defensive. 'Some cases are very hard to explain,' he told me. 'I feel we should keep an open mind.' But, generally, doctors tell us we only have a body. They say the NDE is an hallucination or delusion, lack of oxygen to the brain, temporal lobe seizure, anaesthesia or just plain fabrication.

The simple truth is that orthodox medicine has done very little research into the NDE. Why? David Lorimer, author of the book *Survival* and Vice-chairman of the British affiliation of the International Association of Near Death Studies (IANDS), remarked, 'The medical profession is afraid to. They know the findings will seriously challenge their beliefs. Changes in brain chemistry are certainly not enough to explain away the complexities of an NDE.' Adding, with a deft jab, 'Also their promotional prospects can be seriously hampered if they are known to be dabbling in psychic research.'

One sceptic, cardiologist Michael Sabom, changed his opinion after conducting his own scientific study. In his book *Recollections of Death*, he concludes that the medical explanations so far proposed for NDEs are insufficient to account for them as a whole.

The spiritual corner packs a harder punch when it comes to

Heavenly bodies

evidence. There are quite a few authenticated cases of blind people who regain their sight on leaving the physical body. They see people in the earthly sphere entering and moving around the room, note the colour of their hair. Once back in their body and blind again, their extensive and detailed descriptions are all corroborated. There are also cases of people meeting a friend or relative whom they didn't know had died.

There are five distinct NDE stages that most soul travellers report: feeling peaceful and calm; leaving the physical body; going through a tunnel; merging into light—reviewing and judging their life; meeting dead relatives and friends—being told they must go back. In this non-physical dimension there is no sense of time. Communication is telepathic. The senses are magnified a hundred-fold. Movement is by a sort of thought projection—think of a place and you're there in seconds. Tremendous insights and knowledge are gained in moments. A feeling of love for fellow man pervades. Awareness of a higher spiritual self is strongly felt.

Only about a third of so-called soul travellers experience this

'I was going through a tunnel at great speed and seeing a light at the end. As I moved into this light I felt an incredible feeling of love, and then became aware of my aunt who had died some months before' Mark Gagne

last phase on temporarily departing the body: 'I found myself in a beautiful country lane. I was strolling down the lane slowly and I felt I had all the time in the world. I could hear the skylarks singing and I thought, "Oh, how lovely".'

'I saw a beautiful landscape—the flowers, trees, the colours were indescribable, not at all like the colours you see here. The peace and joy were overpowering. Somewhere I heard the most wonderful music and there was an organ playing. I felt embraced by such love, it's beyond description.'

'In this place I saw people that I knew had died. There were no words spoken, but it was as if I knew what they were thinking and at the same time I knew *they* knew what I was thinking. I saw my parents approaching me; they appeared as I remembered them. They seemed not at all surprised to see me . . . I communicated with them by some form of telepathy.'

A thirty-three-year-old Vietnam veteran reports that, after a mine explosion in which both his legs and one arm were lost, he followed his body from the battlefield to a helicopter which then took it to a nearby field hospital. He remained with his body all the time. He then watched his own operation. 'I tried to grab the doctors and stop them. I felt happy where I was—but nothing happened. I grabbed one doctor but my hands just went straight through him.'

One aspect of the

final phase is the 'being of light' which some claim they encounter. Some see this light as Christ, others as Buddha. 'Their interpretation of it is coloured by their own cultural background,' says Margot Grey. 'You see what you believe in.'

A fifty-five-year-old Protestant Florida woman explained: 'Just as clear and plain the Lord came and stood and held his hands out for me . . . He stood there and looked down and it was all bright then . . . He was tall with his hands stretched out and he had all white on, like he had a white robe on . . . [His face] was more beautiful than anything you've ever seen . . . His skin was almost glowing and it was absolutely flawless . . . He just looked down at me and smiled.'

In an American census, eighty per cent of experiencers regretted 'not having loved more' at the time of their clinical death and ten per cent realised they had squandered their talents and 'become aware of their enormous potential'.

One woman said, 'My whole life was just going in front of me as I "died" like a very fast computer and I kept thinking about all the different things I had done or perhaps I hadn't done.'

Numerous celebrities have claimed to have had an NDE. Actress Stephanie Beacham of *The Colbys* experienced 'dying' after a routine operation had gone wrong. 'I felt that I was being led away by cloaked figures. But suddenly I saw a close-up of one of the eyes of my daughter Chloe. That told me I wasn't to go. Then everything was like a film being wound backwards, and I became conscious enough to

press the emergency button and nurses came running.'

Has the experience changed her? 'It has affected me in all sorts of ways. And I am forced to conclude that there is life after death, and that I will be going somewhere else.'

Comedian Michael Bentine has 'died' three times. On one occasion he realised that he'd entered another dimension: 'Looking down, I saw that I was attached to a silver chord that stretched downwards for miles. It was quite an amazing experience—beyond all fear or terror. Next I remember seeing a light. Then I experienced sitting in what I took to be a reception room and I remember distinctly waiting for someone, a guide perhaps. Next thing I knew was being drawn back into my body and waking up to see what I took to be an angel. It turned out to be a nurse.

Whatever your views are, near death experiencers are in no doubt. As Pat Burt said, 'I've actually been there and it's a beautiful place.' And, as an almost smug yet sincere afterthought, 'Please never be frightened of dying. It's going to be the nicest thing that's ever happened to you.' □

For further information:
IANDS (UK), PO Box 193,
London SW1.
Cases taken from:
Life After Life *by Dr Raymond Moody (Bantam)*
Recollections of Death *by Dr Michael Sabom (Corgi)*
Return from Death *by Margot Grey (Arkana)*
Reflections on Life after Life *by Dr Raymond Moody (Bantam).*

ADDITIONAL RESOURCES 3.2

(See also Book List)

Whilst recognizing that the best resources in any programme will be the students, staff, and surrounding community, there are now available a wide variety of other resources. These include teaching packs, videos, files, books, radio and T.V. broadcasts, and visitors.
 Note: BY- means available from Being Yourself (see address at end of list).

Check List for Using Resources

1) Do they fit your aims and objectives!
2) Are they suitable, given the abilities of the students
3) Will they need adapting to suit your purpose!
4) Where are they kept, and how are they obtained!

SUPPORTING BEREAVED CHILDREN & FAMILIES	Ed, Dr.Dora Black	Cruse 1993

Practical ways of helping children to express loss, and setting up groups of bereaved children

THE DRAWING OUT FEELINGS' SERIES

	Marge Heegaard	All available from BY and
1) WHEN SOMEONE VERY SPECIAL DIES		Cruse
2) WHEN SOMEONE HAS A VERY SERIOUS ILLNESS		
3)WHEN SOMETHING TERRIBLE HAPPENS		

OXFORD BOOK OF DEATH	Ed. D.J. Enright	Oxford University Press

AM I ALLOWED TO CRY	Maureen Oswin	Souvenir Press

Guidelines for bereaved people who have learning disabilities

DOUGY LETTER	Elisabeth Kübler Ross	MacMillan Education

Written to a dying child

WISE BEFORE THE EVENT	W. Yule & A. Gold	Caloustie Gulbenkian

Helps schools plan in advance how they will deal with a disaster. Foundation

THE WORLDS DISASTERS	Four books on air, environmental, natural and sea disasters	Wayland

EXPLAINING THE UNEXPLAINED (MYSTERIES OF THE PARANORMAL)	Hans Eysenck Carl Sargent	Weidenfeld and Nicholson

FACING THE ISSUES	Barbara Wintersgilt	MacMillan Education

FROM THE CRADLE TO THE GRAVE	Kevin O'Donnell	Edward Arnold

INSIGHTS INTO SOCIETY 'LAST DAYS'	Tape/Slide	Edward Arnold

FORGOTTEN MOURNERS	Book	Jessica Kingsley Publishers

MILESTONES Rites of passage in a multi-faith community	Celia Collinson and Campbell Miller	Edward Arnold
HOW DIFFERENT RELIGIONS VIEW DEATH & THE AFTERLIFE	Christopher Jay Johnson and Marsha G.McGee; Eds.	The Charles Press - USA
WHAT HAPPENS AFTER DEATH (Christian)	David Winter	Lion Publishing 1991
STRAIGHT FROM THE SIBLINGS ANOTHER LOOK AT THE RAINBOW written by and for children who have brothers and sisters with a life threatening illness		Celestial Arts
WHAT ITS LIKE TO BE **ME** written and illustrated by disabled children	Helen Exley	Exley Publications 1989
SELF ESTEEM - A FAMILY AFFAIR	J. I. CLARKE	BY
GROWING UP AGAIN Parenting your children and re-parenting yourself.	J. I. Clarke	BY
SELF - ESTEEM A & B Lower secondary		Daniels BY
CHAIN REACTION Children and divorce	Ofra Ayalon and Adina Flasher	Jessica Kingsley

Case studies are usd to illustrate a range of methods to help children come to terms with separation/divorce and re-marriage of their parents

ALWAYS THERE (Young people in Crisis) 15 min. video featuring Harry Enfield		Samaritans
WHEN YOUR MUM OR DAD HAS CANCER	Ann Couldrick	Sobell Publications
WHAT IS DEATH	Ray Bruce and Jane Wallbank	Edward Arnold

BOOKS WITH A HOLISTIC APPROACH TO EDUCATION

PSYCHOSYNTHESIS AND EDUCATION A Guide to the Joy of Learning	Diana Whitmore	Turnstone
HE HIT ME BACK FIRST Creative Visualisation for Parents and Teachers	Eva D. Fugitt	Jalmar Press USA
WINDOWS TO OUR CHILDREN A Gestalt therapy approach	Violet Oaklander	Real People Press

238

SELF HELP

FEEL THE FEAR DO IT ANYWAY   Dr. Susan Jeffers   Arrow Books
Dr. Susan Jeffers book offers simple but profound techniques and
affermations to work through fear to resolution.

HIV AND AIDS

HEALTHY CHOICE   British Red Cross Youth
VHS video photo copiable fact file and facilitation book
70 Short triggers, good multi-ethnic

HIV, AIDS & Children	Naomi Honigsbaum	National Childrens Bureau

AIDS & YOUNG PEOPLE   Avert, 11 Dene Parade,
                                                                Horsham, W.Sussex

VIDEOS

"THE LAST TABOO" Video on Mental Handicap & Death	Dr. Lester Sterling & Dr. Hollins	St. Georges Hospital Medical School: Section of Psychiatry & Durabilty London SW17 0RE

"THAT MORNING I WENT   Northampton Health
TO SCHOOL"   Authority
This video features a bereavement group for children   Highfield, Cliftonville Rd.,
who have lost by death a parent or sibling   Northampton NN1 5DN

I STILL CAN'T BELIEVE IT.   Lyn Franchino
A Training Video on Basic   & Philip Weetz
communication Skills
for Bereavement Counselling.

'THE FALL OF FREDDIE THE LEAF'   EMI Video
This video follows the life of Freddie from Spring to Autumn   235 Imperial Drive
as he questions the meaning of life and death   Rayners Lane, Harrow
                                                                Middlesex HA2 7HE

'GRIEF'   Neti and Neti Theatre Co.
Using sign language, English and Bengali, this video is a powerful
way of examing loss and bereavment among young people
and its relationship to disruptive behaviour

GAMES

ALL ABOUT ME   Barnados   Being Yourself
Anone competitive board game   73 Liverpool Road,
for therapists to use with children to   Deal,
help them explore their feelings around bereavement.   Kent CT14 7NN

'Being Yourself' is an independent resource centre, offering a wide
range of treaching and therapeutic aids for professionals and parents.
A free catalogue is available.

THE MEMORY STORE

The Memory Store provides a practical way of bringing together important information for children with are
losing contact with their parents. Originally developed for families affected by HIV, it can be used in many other
situations such as adoption, marriage break-up, or other illnesses.

As adults we like to think that we have a philosophy of life which enables us to interpret various experiences. We feel secure in knowing facts and being able to answer questions, but when death intervenes we find ourselves in a situation beyond our control and we realize that there are no definite cut and dried answers. Bert Wood, speaking at a Reading Therapy Sub-Group meeting, movingly described his attempt to 'give sorrow words' after his son's death in a climbing accident. Death is a mystery to us all and reminds us of our own mortality and the fragility of the life we enjoy. Fear of the unknown affects adults as much as children, and we realize that the latter are questioning us on a subject that we would rather avoid, and concerning which we do not have ready answers. In other areas of life we may turn to books to assist our understanding and increase our sense of being in control and we may do the same in this situation. Books about death provide us with pegs on which to base our explanations to children, but they also enable both the children and ourselves to explore a potentially frightening topic in a less threatening way.

It is to be hoped that these books may enable adults and young people to explore and discuss different aspects of grief and perhaps help them to communicate their fears and feelings more openly. One of the reasons we may read novels is to identify with a character and to share in his or her experiences vicariously. In such a way the child's sense of isolation or of being different might be reduced, as he realizes that other children have been through similar experiences, even if these are only in books.

Introduction by Barbara Greenall formerly Librarian at St. Christopher's Hospice.
Booklist by Sarah Wilkie, Hillingdon Library Services.

BEREAVEMENT
Suitable for 11 - 13 years

Rachel Anderson	The Poacher's son	Armada Lions 0006722512

A story set, with harsh realism, in a village community before the First World War. It records the struggle by the Betts family to survive, and to retain their dignity.

Bernard Ashley	Dodgem	Puffin 0140327894

A powerfully written story recounting the difficult relationship between a boy and the father whom he wants to protect. Set against contrasting backgrounds of city streets, institutional life and the gaudy lights of the fairground.

Eve Bunting	A sudden silence	(out of print)

When Jesse's deaf brother is killed by a hit and run driver he must cope not only with his grief but also with his feelings of guilt (that he might have prevented the accident) and the disturbing discovery that he makes about the identity of the driver.

Berlie Doherty	Granny was a buffer girl	Armada Lions 0006727921

On the night before she leaves home Jess and her family talk about their past joys and sorrows. A beautifully told and carefully structured novel with a genuine sense of the continuity of family life. Winner of the Carnegie Medal.

Morris Gleitzman   Two weeks with the queen   Pan
0330313762

Colin's brother has cancer and nobody seems to be doing anything about it - maybe the Queen can help?
When trying to see her, Colin meets Ted, whose friend is dying of AIDS, and through him starts to
understand his own feelings about his brother.

David Hill   See ya, Simon   Viking
0670848662

Simon is in many ways a typical teenage boy - he likes girls, jokes, fantasy games and spending time with
his friends. But Simon has muscular dystrophy; he uses a wheelchair and doesn't have long to live. This
is the story of Simon's last year as told by his best friend Nathan. It is at times funny, at times very
moving, and always rings true.

Geraldine Kaye   Comfort herself   Deutsch
0233976140

Comfort's English mother is killed by a car and she goes to join her father in Ghana. She learns
much of value about Ghanaian and British ways before returning to England.

Patricia MacLachlan   Baby   J. MacRae
1856812294

Baby Sophie is left in the care of a family, with a message from her mother promising to return for her.
Over the next year family and friends care for the child and heal the wounds caused by the death of their
own new-born son. A subtle and memorable read.

Michelle Magorian   Goodnight Mr. Tom   Puffin
0140315411

Willie Beech is a sad, deprived child evacuated to an alien country community during the
second World War. He slowly learns to cope with the changes and conflicting emotions in his
life, including the death of his best friend whose cheerful personality has been a key element in
Willie's development.

Pat Moon   The spying Game   Orchard
1852136243 / 1852138521

When Joe's father is killed in an accident he resents the fact that the man who caused it, whom
he sees as a murderer, is free to continue enjoying life. He becomes obsessed with spying on
him and making his life a misery.

Terry Pratchett   Johnny and the dead   Doubleday
0385403011

A humourous and deceptively thoughtful fantasy, with an off-beat view of life after death. Only
Johnny can see and talk to the dead who inhabit the local cemetery, so he is enlisted by them
to save their resting place from the developers.

Jill Paton Walsh   Gaffer Sampson's luck   Puffin
0140317651

James greatly resents his family's move to East Anglia, and feels acutely the tag of outsider.
However old Gaffer Sampson, ill in bed next door, needs James to help him find his "luck",an
old charm, before it's too late. The search leads James to accepting a dangerous dare from the
village boys, and to forging a warm relationship with the old man. A good choice to read to a
class

Robert Westall   Kingdom by the sea   Mammoth
0749707968

Set in north-east England during the Second World War. When Harry loses his family in a
bombing raid, he runs away rather than be taken in by a fussy aunt. As he travels he meets
various people, like him deeply affected by the war, who help him come to terms with his loss.

Suitable for 13 - 15 years

Sharon Creech	Walk two moons	Piper 0330330004

Sal's grandparents take her on a journey following the route taken by her mother who left home to find herself. As they travel across America she tells them the story of her new friend Phoebe and her mother , who also left home. Talking about Phoebe's feelings helps her come to terms with her own grief.

Rosa Guy	The friends	Puffin 0140366164

Life in New York poses many problems for Phyllisia, a young West Indian girl, who then also has to face difficulties in her home life and with family relationships after the death of her mother.

Janni Howker	Badger on the barge, and other stories	Armada Lions 0006725813

Five short stories with unusual settings, each dealing with relationships between young and old. Two stories in particular deal compassionately with the ability to come to terms with death: "Badger on the barge" shows vividly how members of a family react to and cope with a son's death, and in "Jakey" an independent old man makes his own decisions about life and death.

Linda Hoy	Your friend, Rebecca	Beaver 0099312808

School offers nothing to Rebecca. She has no friends. At home, she and her father separately nurse their grief for her dead mother, barely noticing each other. One day, Rebecca comes across her father crying, which releases feelings of compassion and understanding, leading the story to end with a note of optimism for the future.

Carole Lloyd	The Charlie Barber treatment	Walker 0744514886

A sensitive, unsentimental portrayal of fifteen-year old Simon's reactions to his mother's death. At first he clams up and suppresses his grief, but a new friend, Charlie, helps to release pent-up emotions.

Lois Lowry	A summer to die	(out of print)

Told by Meg, this is the story of an adolescent facing loss for the first time, when her older, much loved and admired sister dies. The maze of emotions is gently explored without exploiting the sympathetic character and close family relationships

Ian Strachan	Boy in the bubble	Mammoth 0749716851

Anne meets Adam, who suffers from SCID (severe combined immunodeficiency) and must spend his life in a sterile bubble. She becomes his "life-taster", a role she sometimes resents, but tensions between them are forgotten when Adam has the chance of a risky but potentially life-saving operation.

Suitable for ages 14 plus

Judy Blume · Tiger eyes · Piccolo
0330269542

One nightmare evening, Darney finds her father fatally wounded and realises that she cannot help him. The shocked family go to stay with relatives, but Darney cannot let go of the past, and her anger and grief heighten her sense of desolation - and threaten to isolate her from her family.

Sandra Chick · I never told her I loved her · Women's Press
0704349124

After the death of her mother, Frankie feels guilty about their frequent fights and finds life with her father tense and difficult.

Cynthia Grant · Phoenix rising, or how to survive your life · Armada Lions
0006737323

When Jessie's older sister Helen dies of cancer, she finds and reads her diary. Learning how Helen came to terms with her impending death helps Jessie come to accept her own grief.

Pete Johnson · We, the haunted · Armada Lions
0006731600

When Caro's boyfriend Paul dies in a boating accident she is inconsolable and in her grief imagines that Paul is still with her. Paul's best friend Dean tells the story of how he helps Caro accept Paul's death.

Alan Frewin Jones · Burning issues · Bodley Head
0370318595

When Spider's grandmother dies she is more upset than she cares to admit, and her family seem to prefer to ignore what has happened - driving her into a less than satisfying relationship with a new boyfriend. She discovers the inner resources to cope with her feelings and start to make her own decisions.

Norma Klein · Going backwards · (out of print)

Charles and his family have problems adjusting when his senile grandmothes moves in with them. After her death, his father starts to act strangely, and not long after also dies. Charles learns after Sam's death that the latter had given his mother an overdose of sleeping tablets, rather than see her suffer.

Sue Mayfield · I carried you on eagles' wings · Hippo
0590559397

A teenage boy, the son of a vicar, has to face up to his mother's illness and, eventually, her death. The title is a quotation from the Bible and the mother's attitude to her own death is primarily a Christian one, which will be of help to some readers but possibly off-putting to others.

Norma Fox Mazer · After the rain · Mammoth
0749703245

It is only in the last few months of her grandfather's life that Rachel grows close to him. During her self-imposed task of accompanying him on the daily walk he is too stubborn to give up, she learns details of his life that help her come to terms with his death.

Jean Ure · One green leaf · Bodley Head
0370307844

Three sixth-formers have to adjust to the illness and eventual death (from cancer) of a close friend.

| Paul and Bonnie Zindel | A star for the latecomer | Red Fox 0099872005 |

Brooke has for so long responded to her mother's hopes and dreams for her, though her own dreams are quite different. When Brooke realises the nature of her mother's illness, it becomes a race against time to achieve her dancing success. At the same time, she retains a clear, firm belief in her own future needs.

Non-fiction

| Jill Krementz | How it feels when a parent dies | Gollancz 0575051833 |

A group of children, ranging in age from seven to sixteen, talk about their experiences and feeling when a parent died.

| Jon Mayled | Death customs | Wayland 085078719X |

A book that outlines the customs of the major world religions in dealing with death.

| L. Rushton | Death customs | Wayland 075021666 |

Very similar to the above - a book in the useful "Understanding religions" series.

DIVORCE, STEP-FAMILIES ETC.

Suitable for 11 - 13 years

| Betsy Byars | The Animal, the Vegetable and John D. Jones | Puffin 0140315632 |

The problems involved in meeting potential siblings for the first time, handled in typical Betsy Byars fashion - perceptive and wryly amusing.

| Caroline B.Cooney | Family reunion | Mammoth 0749705337 |

Is there such a thing as the perfect family? Shelley and Angus think they are doing okay, despite their parents' divorce and their father's remarriage, but Aunt Maggie is inclined to pity them. A light-hearted but thoughtful look at modern American life.

| Paula Danziger | The divorce express | Piccolo 0330296574 |

Fourteen year old Phoebe's parents are divorced, and every weekend she travels to New York to be with her mother. Her friendship with Rosie, who also travels the divorce express, helps her to come to terms with the problems of her split family life.

| Anne Fine | Goggle Eyes | Puffin 0140340718 |

When a classmate is upset about the prospect of her mother remarrying, Kitty tells the story of her mum's relationship with Gerald, an unwanted (by Kitty) boyfriend. A witty and warm account of how Kitty's opinions, and her mother's, change as they get to know "Goggle Eyes" better.

| Catherine Robinson | Seven weeks last summer | Red Fox 0099986000 |

Abby's plans for a long, lazy summer are shattered when she learns that her parents are separating. Devoted to her father, she blames her mother, and relationships between them become very strained. Gradually she learns that there are two sides to the argument and that her father must carry much of the blame.

Jacqueline Wilson   The suitcase kid   Yearling
0385401752

An amusing look at one girl's stand against difficulties of the "double life" she is forced into by her parents' divorce.

Suitable for 13 - 15 years

Josephine Feeney   My family and other   Viking
natural disasters   0670850462

Patrick has to write his life-story for school work, but his parents' marriage is breaking up and his mother refuses to discuss the past. An easy to read book that looks at divorce from a Catholic family's viewpoint.

Non-fiction

Liz Friedrich   Divorce (Understanding   Watts
social issues series)   0863137776

Covers topics such as the changing patterns of marriage and family life, and the legal side of divorce, as well as the emotional effects on those involved.

Jill Krementz   How it feels when parents divorce   (out of print)

nineteen children, aged six to seventeen, discuss honestly what their parents' divorce has meant to them. Very American, but useful in showing that others have been through similar situations, providing hope and some prasctical advice.

A. Mitchell   Divorce (Points of view series)   Wayland
1852108002

One of a very useful series aimed at younger teenagers, looking at divorce from various angles - emotional, practical, legal etc.

GENERAL THEMES OF LOSS

Suitable for 11 - 13 years

Joan Lingard   Tug of war   Penguin
0140343237

Fourteen year old twins, Astra and Hugo, are forced with the rest of their family to leave their home in Latvia when the Russian army advances during the Second World War.

Patricia MacLachlan   Journey   Red Fox
0099107511

Journey refuses to believe that his mother will not come back. Old family photos give him glimpses of the past, and offer clues as to why she went, while the pictures that his grandfather takes help him discover the truth about the family he has now.

Suitable for 13 -15 years

Elizabeth Laird   Kiss the dust   Heinemann
0434947032

An account of the flight of a Kurdish family from Iraq to Iran, and eventually to a new home in Britain, as seen through the eyes of the teenage daughter.

Joan Lingard   Between two worlds   Penguin
014034828X

A sequel to "Tug of war" - the family adapt to their new life in Canada.

Elizabeth Lutzeier   Lost for words   Oxford
0192717073

Aysha and her mother leave Bangladesh to live in England but both of them find it difficult to adjust to life in a strange country.

Joseph McNair   Taking off   Piper
0330322753

Since Lisa's mentally disabled brother was born, her parents have relied on her to amuse and take care of him. Now that he has started at a special school, and her parents taken on long-overdue responsibilities, she feels the gap in her life.

Susan Beth Pfeffer   The year without Michael   (out of print)

On an ordinary summer's day, Jody's brother Michael leaves the house to visit a friend - and is never seen again.

Cynthia Voigt   Homecoming   Armada Lions
0006724590

Dicey and her brothers and sister are travelling with their mother to live with an aunt when their mother disappears, abandoning them in a supermarket car-park. Dicey's strength of character holds the family together in their search for their aunt and, later, their grandmother.

Suitable for ages 14 plus

Claude Gutman   The empty house   Penguin
0140361693

An account by a Jewish teenager, David, of the months following the arrival of the Nazis in Paris. When his parents are taken away by soldiers he is overlooked. With the help of neighbours he escapes eventually to "free" France in the south, but even there safety and happiness are only illusions.

Non-fiction

Derek Heater   Refugees (World issues series)   Wayland
1852104368

Covers refugees in the past (eg. during World War Two) as well as present day problems. Includes some quotes from refugees themselves.

GROWTH AND CHANGE

Suitable for 11 - 13 years

Jay Ashton   Killing the demons   Puffin
0140369929

Samantha is confined to a wheelchair as a result of an accident which also killed her little brother. To escape a difficult reality she loses herself in computer games, where she fights the demons that echo her feelings of guilt. She eventually vanquishes the demons and, in real life, learns to accept that "things happen".

Morris Gleitzman   Blabbermouth   Pan Macmillan
                                                                    0333595017

Rowena cannot speak, but she has plenty to say for herself in this humorous account of her life at a new school and her relationship with her sometimes embarassing father.

Mary Downing Hahn   December stillness   Mammoth
                                                                    0749709758

Kelly decides to base her school project on homelessness on Mr. Weems, a disturbed Vietnam War veteran, but he doesn't want to be part of a project. In attempting to befriend him, Kelly inadvertently causes his death, but in so doing comes to a better understanding of her father, also a war veteran.

Jan Mark   Man in motion   Puffin
                                                                    0140340297

Lloyd is keen on sports and when he moves house it is through his sporting activities that he makes new friends. However one friend's racist views force him to choose where his loyalties lie.

Cynthia Voigt   Izzy Willy Nilly   Armada Lions
                                                                    0006733778

Izzy, a bright and popular American teenager, loses a leg in a car crash and has to adjust to the changes this forces in her life.

Suitable for ages 14 plus

Deborah Hautzig   Second star to the right   Walker Books
                                                                    0744520665

A moving account of fourteen year old Leslie's fight against anorexia nervosa.

FOR SPECIAL NEEDS

Sheila Hollins and   When Mum died   St. George's Mental
Lester Sireling   Health Lib.
                                                                    1874439060

                                    When Dad died   St. George's Mental
                                                                    Health Lib.
                                                                    1874439079

Two short illustrated books to help young people with learning disabilities understand death and bereavement.

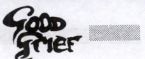

EDUCATOR'S BOOK LIST 3.4

All in the End is Harvest *(an anthology for those who grieve)*	Ed Agnes Whitaker	Darton Longman Todd/Cruse 1984
Am I Allowed to Cry	Maureen Oswin	Souvenir Press 1991
The Bereaved Parent	H Sharnoff Schiff	Souvenir Press 1977
Body, Mind and Death In the Light of Psychic Experience	David Lorimer	Routtedge & Kegan Paul 1984
Care of the Child Facing Death	Lindy Burton	Routledge 1974
Caring for Dying People **of Different Faiths**	Rabbi Julia Neuberger	Austin Cornish 1990
Childhood and Death	Helena Wass & Charles A. Cott	Hemisphere New York 1985
Conciliation and Divorce *A father's letter to his children*	Brian Grant	Barry Rose
The Courage to Grieve	Judy Tatelbaum	Heinemann 1981
The Daniel Diary	Ailsa Fabian	Grafton Books 1988
Death and the Family	Lily Pincus	Faber 1961
Disasters Planning for a Caring Response		H.M.S.O 1991
Divorce Parenting - How **to make it work**	Sol Goldstein	Methuen 1987
The Dying and Bereaved Teenager	Ed. John D. Morgan	Charles Press 1990
Facing Grief, Bereavement **& the Young Adult**	Susan Wallbank	Lutterworth Press 1991
Grief counselling and **Grief Therapy**	William Worden	Tavistock 1983
Families & how to Survive Them	John Cleese Robin Skinner	Methuen 1988
Feel the fear do it anyway	Susan Jeffers	Arrow 1991
Grief in Children	Atle Dyregrov	Jessica Kingsley 1990
A Grief Observed	C.S. Lewis	Faber 1961
Healing Grief	Barbara Ward	Vermilion 1993

Helping Children Cope With Divorce	Rosemary Wells	Sheldon 1989
Helping Children Cope With Separation and Loss	Claudia Jewett	Batsford 1984
How it Feels to be Adopted	Jill Krementz	Gollancz 1984
I only want what's Best For You - A parent's guide to raising well adjusted children	Judith Brown	Kingswood Press 1987
Holistic Living - A Guide to Self-Care	Dr Patrick Pietroni	Dent 1987
Is Death the End ?	Susan E. Tompkins	Christian Education Movement 1979
The Illness and Death of a Child	Mother Frances Dominica	The Church Literature Association 1988
Life after Death	Neville Randall	Corgi Books 1980
Life after Life	Raymond Moody	Bantam Books 1983
Living with Loss	Liz McNeil Taylor	Fontana Paperback 1983
Living with Death and Dying	Elizabeth Kubler Ross	Souvenir 1982
Losing a Parent	Fiona Marshall	Insight 1993
Love, Medicine and Miracles	Bernie Siegal	Century 1988
Loss and Grief in Medicine	Peter Speck	Bailliere & Tindell 1978
The Needs of Children	Mia Kellmer Pringle	Hutchinson 1987
On Children and Death	Elizabeth Kubler Ross	Macmillan 1985
Parents are Forever	Relate (Marriage Guidance)	Relate 1985
Perspectives for Living	Bel Mooney	J. Murray 1992
The Private Worlds of Dying Children	Myra Bluebond-Langer	Princeton University Press 1977
Recovery from Bereavement	C. Murray Parkes	Basic Books N.Y. 1983
A Special Scar (The experiences of people bereaved by suicide)	Alison Wertheimer	London Rutledge 1991
So Will I Comfort You	Jenny Kander	Gracewing 1990

Standpoints - Death	Mog Ball	Oxford University Press
When Bad Things Happen to Good People	Harold S. Kushner	Pan 1982
When Parents Die	Rebbecca Abrams	Letts 1992
Who Dies	Stephen Levine	Gateway 1988

BOOKLETS

What to Do when Someone Dies	Consumer Association Publication - Revised annually
What to Do After Death	Free DHSS leaflet No. D49
The Right to Grieve	A leaflet to help mentally handicap d people who are bereaved. From the King's Fund Ce e
On Divorce	The Children's Society
On Death & on Divorce	National Children's Bureau
Handicap & Bereavement	Friends Book Centre, Euston Road, ondon.
Someone Special Has Died	St. Christopher's Hospice.

JOURNALS

Bereavement Care	Cruse Publication - periodical*
Newsletter	Compassionate Friends - periodical*
Journal on Death/Divorce	National Children's Bureau

*Both organisations have a range of useful leaflets and publications. Send S.A.E.for the list

ARTICLES

Lists on aspects of Loss & Death & Dying available from:	National Children's Bureau National Association for the welfare of children in hospital Relate (previously Marriage Guidance)
Care of Dying Children and Their Families	Guidelines from British Paediatric Assn. King Edward's fund for London and National Assn. of Health Authorities, NAHA, Garth House, 47 Edgbaston Road, Birmingham, B15 2RS.
Reactions to Death:	Teaching and Training 1984 22 (1) p10 - 17. Can the Mentally handicapped grieve ? Some experiences of those who did.

3.5

Useful Addresses

Abortion Law Reform Association (ALRA)
27-35 Mortimer Street
London W1N 7RJ
Tel: 0171 637 7264

Age Concern (Cymru)
4th Floor
1 Cathedral Road
Cardiff CF1 9SD
S. Glamorgan
Tel: (01222) 371566

Age Concern (England)
Astral House
1268 London Road
London SW16 4ER
Tel: 0181 679 8000

Age Concern (Scotland)
113 Rose Street
Edinburgh EH2 3DT
Tel: 0131 220 3345

Age Concern (N. Ireland)
3 Lower Crescent
Belfast BT7 1NR
Tel: (01232) 245729

Association for Children with Life Threatening Terminal Conditions and their Families (ACT)
65 St Michael's Hill
Bristol BS2 8DZ
Tel: 0117 922 1556
ACT aims to inform families and professionals of available services both in the statutory and voluntary sectors through its national database and literature resource.

BACUP (Cancer), for patients and families
3 Bath Place
Rivington Street
London EC2A 3JR
Tel: 0171 696 9000 (Counselling)
Tel: 0171 613 2121 (Cancer Information)
Freephone: 0800 181199

Barnardo's
Tanners Lane
Barkingside
Ilford,
Essex IG6 1QG
Tel: 0181 550 8822

British Agencies for Adoption and Fostering (BAAF)
Skyline House
200 Union Street
London SE1 0LX
Tel: 0171 593 2000

British Association for Counselling (BAC)
1 Regent Place
Rugby
Warwickshire CV21 2PJ
Tel: (01788) 578328/9

British Humanist Association
47 Theobald's Road
London WC1X 8SP
Tel: 0171 430 0908
Advice on non-religious funerals

British Institute of Learning Disabilities
Wolverhampton Road
Kidderminster
Worcestershire DY10 3PP
Tel: (01562) 850251

British Organ Donor Society (BODY)
Balsham
Cambridge
CB1 6DL
Tel: (01223) 893636

British Society for Music Therapy
25 Rosslyn Avenue
East Barnet
Hertfordshire EN4 8DH
Tel/Fax: 0181 368 8879

Cancer Link
17 Britannia Street
London WC1X 9JN
Tel: 0171 833 2451)

Cancer Relief Macmillan Fund
Anchor House
15/19 Britten Street
London SW3 3TZ
Tel: 0171 351 7811

Carers National Association
Ruth Pitter House
20/25 Glasshouse Yard
London EC1A 4JS
Tel: 0171 490 8818
Carers helpline: 0171 490 8898
(Mon-Fri 1-4pm

Centre for Multi-Cultural Education
Institute of Education
London University
20 Bedford Way
London WC12H 0AL
Tel: 0171 612 6721/2

Child to Child Trust
(A Worldwide Health Education Network)
The Coordinator
Institute of Education
20 Bedford Way,
London WC1H 0AL
Tel: 0171 612 6648

Childline
2nd Floor
Royal Mail Building
Studd Street
London N1 0QW
Tel: 0171 239 1000 (Office)
Tel: (0800) 1111 (Children's Line)

Citizens Advice Bureau
(see local telephone directory
for address and telephone number)

Community Health Council
(see local telephone directory
for address and telephone number)

The Compassionate Friends
(Head Office)
53 North Street
Bristol BS3 1EN
Helpline: 0117 953 9639
Admin: 0117 966 5202

Contact a Family
(Support Special Needs)
170 Tottenham Court Road
London W1P 0HA
Tel: 0171 383 3555

Cremation Society of Great Britain
2nd Floor
16/16a Albion Place
Maidstone
Kent ME14 5DZ
Tel: (01622) 688292

Cruse – Bereavement Care
Cruse House
126 Sheen Road
Richmond
Surrey TW9 1UR
Tel: 0181 940 4818/9042

Department of Social Security
(see local telephone directory)

Equal Opportunities Commission (EOC)
Quay Street
Manchester M3 3HN
Tel: 0161 833 9244

Exploring Parenthood
4 Ivory Place
20a Threadgold Street
London W11 4BP
Tel (advice): 0171 221 6681 (10-4pm)

The Foundation for Study of Infant Deaths
14 Halkin Street
London SW1X 7DP
Tel: 0171 235 1721 (Helpline)
Tel: 0171 235 0965 (Enquiries)

Gingerbread
16-17 Clerkenwell Close
London EC1R 0AA
Tel: 0171 336 8183
Advice Line: 0171 336 8184

Grandparents Contacts
Mrs Dallas Warren
Quarry Lodge
1b Haggstones Drive
Oughtibridge
Sheffield S30 3GL
Tel: 0114 286 2883
for those bereaved of their grandchildren.

Graham and Mary Stephens
Tree Tops, Church Street
Wellesbourne
Warwick CV35 9LS
Tel: (01789) 840622
For those whose child died leaving grandchildren.

Health Education Authority
Hamilton House
Mabledon Place
London WC1H 9TX
Tel: 0171 383 3833

Help the Aged
St. James Walk
London EC1R 0BE
Minicom (for deaf users only): (0800) 269626
Advice Line: (0800) 289404
Head Office: 0171 253 0253

Hospice Information
St. Christophers Hospice
51–59 Lawrie Park Road
Sydenham
London SE26 6DZ
Tel: 0181 778 9252

Institute of Family Therapy
43 New Cavendish Street
London W1M 7RG
Tel: 0171 935 1651

Jewish Bereavement Counselling Service
PO Box 6748
London N3 3BX
Tel: 0181 349 0839

Lesbian and Gay Bereavement Project
Vaughan M. Williams Centre
Colindale Hospital
London NW9 5HG
Tel: 0181 200 0511
Tel: 0181 455 8894 (Helpline)

Kings Fund
11-13 Cavendish Square
London W1M 0AN
Tel: 0171 307 2400

The Memorial Advisory Bureau
c/o Michael Dewar
Albemarle Connection
99 Charterhouse Street
Lonfon EC1M 6HR
Tel: 0171 251 5911

Memorials by Artists
Harriet Frazer
Snape Priory
Saxmundham
Suffolk IP17 1SA
Tel: (01728) 688934
For free leaflet or advice – this is a nationwide service.

MIND (National Association for Mental Health)
Granta House
15–19 Broadway
London E15 4BQ
Tel: 0181 519 2122

Miscarriage Association
c/o Clayton Hospital
Northgate
Wakefield
West Yorks WF1 3JS
Tel: (01924) 200799

Multiple Death's Foundation
Queen Charlotte's and Chelsea Hospital
Goldhawk Road
London W6 OXG
Tel: 0181 740 3519/3520

National AIDS Helpline
Tel: (0800) 567123 (Freephone)

**National Association
of Bereavement Services**
20 Norton Folgate
Bishopsgate
London E1 6DB
Helpline tel: (Refferals) 0171 247 1080
Tel/Fax (Admin): 0171 247 0617

National Association of Funeral Directors
618 Warwick Road
Solihull
West Midlands B91 1AA
Tel: 0121 711 1343

**National Association of Hospital
Play Staff**
40 High Street
Landbeach
Camb CB4 4DT

**National Association for the Prevention
of Cruelty to Children (NSPCC)**
National Centre
42 Curtain Road
London EC2A 3NH
Tel: 0171 825 2500
Tel: (0800) 800500
(24hrs Emergency Number)

National Children's Bureau
8 Wakley Street
London EC1V 7QE
Tel: 0171 843 6000

**National Council for One Parent
Families**
255 Kentish Town Road
London NW5 2LX
Tel: 0171 267 1361

Natural Death Centre
20 Heber Road
London NW2 6AA
Tel: 0181 208 2853
*Please enclose six first class stamps when requesting an
information pack.*

National Forum on AIDS and Children
National Childrens Bureau
8 Wakley Street
London EC1V 7QE
Tel: 0171 843 6057

**National HIV Prevention Information
Service**
Health Education Authority
Hamilton House
Mabledon Place
London WC1H 9TX
Tel: 0171 388 9855
National Helpline: (0800) 567123

**National Library for the Handicapped
Child**
Wellington House
Wellington Road
Wokingham
Berks RG40 2AG
Tel (voice and text): (01734) 891101
Fax: (01734) 790989

The National StepFamily Association
Chapel House
18 Hatton Place
London EC1N 8RU
Tel (Office): 0171 372 0846
Helpline Tel: 0171 209 2464

Neti Neti Theatre Co.
George Orwell School
Turle Road
London N4 3LS
Tel: 0171 272 7302

The Open University
Walton Hall
Milton Keynes
MK7 6AA
Tel: (01908) 274066

Parents of Murdered Children Support Group
(see Compassionate Friends)

Pet Bereavement Counselling Service
Aine Wellard
25 Townsend Street
Dublin 2
Tel: 00 3531 677 5097

Rape Crisis Centre
PO Box 69
London WC1X 9NJ
Tel: 0171 916 5466 (Office)
Tel: 0171 837 1600 (24-hour emergency)

Relate Bookshop (formerly Marriage Guidance)
Herbert Gray College
Little Church Street
Rugby CV21 3AP
Tel: (01788) 573241

Research Trust for Metabolic Diseases in Children
Golden Gate Lodge
Weston Road
Crew
Cheshire CW1 1XN
Tel: (01270) 629782

Samaritans (Head Office)
10 The Grove
Slough
Berks SL1 1QP
Tel: (01753) 532713
Tel from 2nd Nov 1995: (0345) 909090

SANDS
(Stillbirth and Neonatal Death Society)
28 Portland Place,
London W1N 4DE
Helpline Tel: 0171 436 5881
Tel (Admin): 0171 436 7940

Schools Outreach
10 High Street
Bromsgrove
Worcs B61 8HQ
Tel: (01527) 574404

Shadow of Suicide
(see Compassionate Friends)

Society for the Protection of Unborn Children
7 Tufton Street
London SW1P 3QN
Tel: 0171 222 5845

Terence Higgins Trust
52–54 Grays Inn Road
London WC1X 8JU
Tel: 0171 831 0330

Twins and Multiple Births Association (TAMBA)
PO Box 30
Little Sutton
South Wirral
L66 1TH
Tel: (01732) 868000 (weekdays 7pm-11pm, weekends 9am-11pm)
For those with twins of multiple births and those having suffered a bereavement within a multiple birth.

Victim Support National Office
Cranmer House
39 Brixton Road
London SW9 6DZ
Tel: 0171 735 9166

Voluntary Euthanasia Society
13 Prince of Wales Terrace
London W8 5PG
Tel: 0171 937 7770

The Woodland Trust
(Plant a Tree Scheme to remember loved ones, also Commemorative Groves)
Autumn Park
Dysart Road
Grantham
Lincolnshire NG31 6LL
Tel: (01476) 74297

ATTRIBUTIONS 3.6

We are pleased to acknowledge the material listed below which can be found within the subject area as shown.

Understanding Loss:

Excerpt from Loss, Grief
and Medicine

Peter Speck
Bailliere Tindall

How Can We Help:

How to Help the Bereaved

Open University
Good Health Guide

Excerpt from Death in the Family

Lily Pincus.
Faber & Faber Ltd.

My Support Group

Adapted from an idea in
'Building Yourself a Rainbow'
Hopson & Scally

Living With Loss:

Loss, Grief and Mourning

Northern Ireland Cruse

How Others Feel

Adapted from an idea by Ray
Amer

Time Line

Adapted from an idea in
Open University Community
Education Childhood Pack

Loss and Health

Adapted from Rahe and
Holmes Social Re-adjustment
Scale, Journal of Human
Stress (4) 1978

Feelings Associated With Loss

Based on an idea of
Lyn Kimm

Coping with Loss

Based on an idea from Life
Skills Training Programme
Hopson and Scally

Creative Activities:

Poor Little Joe

D.Norris. Roan School for
Boys

Hope

D. Grant

His Life and Hers

Frances Maclennan.
"Cadburys 7th Book of
Children's Poetry"
Arrow Books

Sometimes it Happens

Brian Patten
New Angles Book (1)

Anger

Sophie Stevens
Open University Press

The Lesson

Edward Lucie-Smith
Oxford Book of 20th Century
English Verse
Oxford University Press

London

John Betjeman. 'Summoned
by Bells John Murray
(Publishers) Ltd'.

Don't Drink and Drive

Susan Wallbank.
Cruse Counsellor

If God had wanted a Gerbil

Susan Wallbank

To Emily at Four

Susan Wallbank

Grief

Susan Trow

Grief

Nora Leney

Why Me?

Sally Crosher

Death

Sateke Faletau
King Alfred School Chronicle

Lament for Glen

Marjorie Pizer

The Existence of Love

Marjorie Pizer

Grandmother

Robert McGregor "Cadbury's
6th Book of Childrens Poetry"
Arrow Books

From Joyce

Joyce grenfell
Richard Scott Simon Ltd.

Pakistani

Adrian Hussain
'Trade Winds Longmans'

What is Death:

How Long Will You Live

John Hawkins Observer
Sunday Magazine

Frog Story	Adapted from 'Should Children Know' Rudolph M. Schocken Books
On Death and Dying - Excerpt	Elizabeth Kubler Ross Tavistock Publications
Heavenly Bodies	Chris Stonor. Woman's Journal
Ecclesiastes 3 v 1	Good News Bible
Statements on Death	From 'Rites of Passage - Death' Mary Glasgow Publications

Last Rites:

Toraja People of Indonesia	Beginning Religion. Ray Bruce and Jane Wallbank. Edward Arnold.
The Jewish Burial	Margaret Gould
Making Your Own Funeral Service	Jane Warman
A Non-Religious Funeral Service	David J. Williams British Humanist Association
What to do When Someone Dies (Charts)	Consumer Association
Funerals	Bob Hudson The Health Service Journal
Christopher Martin quote	Church Times
Boat People	Social Work Today
Your Own Personal Coat of Arms	Adapted from 'Think Well' School's Council Project
My Favourite Dog	Longman's Greek Anthology Translated J. W. Mackail
The Tired Woman	Quoted before 1850 Authorship Unknown
The Life that I Have	Violet Szabo Carve her name with Pride Hamlyn Publishing Ltd.

CONTRIBUTORS

Paul Bamber is Advisor PSHE, Kent.

Madeline Bland is Senior Teacher, Vyners School.

Marianne Cain was formerly Acting Head Teacher SEN.

Lesley Classick is Head of Department and Year Tutor, Queensmead School.

Angela Flux is HIV/AIDS Co-ordinator, London Borough of Hillingdon.

Barbara Greenall was formerly Librarian, St.Christopher's Hospice.

Louise and Chris Hunter are University Students.

Jamie Houghton was formerly of Greycoat Hospital School.

Lyn Kimm is Senior Teacher, Harlington.

Margaret Leeson and Pupils are from Dover Grammar School.

Mike Roe is an Outreach Worker, Hillingdon Drug Education and Prevention Team.

Sarah Wilkie is Stock Co-ordinator, Education and Youth Department, Hillingdon Library.

Richard Wilson is a Consultant Paediatrician, Kingston Hospital.

Peter Williams is Head of Shavington High School.

Denise Chaplin, Liz Forshaw, Glenys Jackson, Jean Monte and Tanya White are Advisory Teachers, London Borough of Hillingdon.